ADDITIONAL

SPEECHES, ADDRESSES,

AND

OCCASIONAL SERMONS,

BY

THEODORE PARKER,

MINISTER OF THE TWENTY EIGHTH CONGREGATIONAL SOCIETY, IN BOSTON.

IN TWO VOLUMES.

VOL. II.

BOSTON:

TICKNOR AND FIELDS.

M DCCC LXI.

CONTENTS OF VOL. II.

I.

PAGE

Some Thoughts on the Progress of America, and the Influence of her Diverse Institutions. An Address prepared for the Anti-Slavery Convention in Boston, May 31, 1854 1

II.

The New Crime against Humanity. A Sermon preached at the Music Hall, on Sunday, June 4, 1854, with the Lesson for the day of the previous Sunday 71

III.

The Law of God and the Statutes of Men. A Sermon preached at the Music Hall, on Sunday, June 18, 1854 179

IV.

A Sermon of the Dangers which threaten the Rights of Man in America, preached at the Music Hall, on Sunday, July 2, 1854 213

V.

Some Account of my Ministry. Two Sermons preached before the Twenty-Eighth Congregational Society in Boston, on the 14th and 21st November, 1852, on leaving their old and entering a new Place of Worship 295

VI.

A Sermon of the Public Function of Woman, preached at the Music Hall, March 27, 1853 . 370

VII.

A Sermon of Old Age, preached at the Music Hall, on Sunday, January 29, 1854 413

SOME THOUGHTS

ON THE

PROGRESS OF AMERICA,

AND THE

INFLUENCE OF HER DIVERSE INSTITUTIONS.

AN ADDRESS

PREPARED FOR THE

ANTI-SLAVERY CONVENTION IN BOSTON,

MAY 31, 1854.

ADDRESS.

At this day there are two great tribes of men in Christendom, which seem to have a promising future before them — the Sclavonic and the Anglo-Saxon. Both are comparatively new. For the last three hundred years each has been continually advancing in numbers, riches, and territory; in industrial and military power. To judge from present appearances, it seems probable that a hundred years hence there will be only two great national forces in the Christian world — the Sclavonic and the Anglo-Saxon.

The Anglo-Saxon tribe is composite, and the mingling so recent, that we can still easily distinguish the main ingredients of the mixture. There are, first, the Saxons and Angles from North Germany; next, the Scandinavians from Denmark and Sweden; and, finally, the Normans, or Romanized Scandinavians, from France.

This tribe is now divided into two great political

branches, namely, the Anglo-Saxon Briton, and the Anglo-Saxon American; but both are substantially the same people, though with different antecedents and surroundings. The same fundamental characteristics belong to the Briton and the American.

Three hundred years ago, the Anglo-Saxons were scarce three millions in number; they did not own the whole of Great Britain. Now there are thirty or forty millions of men with Anglo-Saxon blood in their veins. They possess the British Islands; Heligoland, Gibraltar, Malta, and the Ionian Isles; St. Helena, South Africa, much of East and West Africa; enormous territories in India, continually increasing; the whole of Australia; almost all of North America, and I know not how many islands scattered about the Atlantic and Pacific seas. Their geographical spread covers at least one sixth part of the habitable globe; their power controls about one fifth of the inhabitants of the earth. It is the richest of all the families of mankind. The Anglo-Saxon leads the commerce and the most important manufactures of the world. He owns seven eighths of the shipping of Christendom, and half that of the human race. He avails himself of the latest discoveries in practical science, and applies them to the creation of "comforts" and luxuries. Iron is his favorite metal; and about two thirds of the annual iron crop of the earth is harvested on Anglo-Saxon soil. Cotton, wheat, and the potato, are his favorite plants.

The political institutions of the Anglo-Saxon secure National Unity of Action for the State, and Individual Variety of Action for each citizen, to a greater degree than other nations have thought possible. In all Christendom, there is scarce any freedom of the Press except on Anglo-Saxon soil. Ours is the only tongue in which Liberty can speak. Anglo-Saxon Britain is the asylum of exiled patriots, or exiled despots. The royal and patrician wrecks of the revolutionary storms of continental Europe, in the last century and in this, were driven to her hospitable shore. Kossuth, Mazzini, Victor Hugo, and Comte, relics of the last revolution, are washed to the same coast. America is the asylum of exiled nations, who flee to her arms, four hundred thousand in a year, and find shelter.

The Sclavonians fight with diplomacy and the sword, the Anglo-Saxon with diplomacy and the dollar. He is the Roman of productive industry, of commerce, as the Romans were Anglo-Saxons of destructive conquest, of war. The Sclavonian nations, from the accident of their geographical position, or from their ethnological peculiarity of nature, invade and conquer lands more civilized than their own. They have the diplomatic skill to control nations of superior intellectual and moral development. The Anglo-Saxon is too clumsy for foreign politics; when he meddles with the affairs of other civilized people, he is often deceived. Russia outwits England continually in the political game now playing for the control of Europe. The Anglo-Saxon, more invasive than the Sclavonian, prefers new and wild lands to old and well-cultivated territories; so he conquers America, and tills its virgin soil: seizes on Africa, — the dry nurse of lions and of savage men, — and founds a new empire in Australia. If he invades Asia, it is in the parts not Christian. His rule is a curse to countries full of old civilization; I take it that England has been a blight to India, and will be to China, if she sets there her conquering foot. The Anglo-Saxon is less pliable than the Romans, a less indulgent master to conquered men; with more plastic power to organize and mould, he has a less comprehensive imagination, limits himself to a smaller number of forms, and so hews off and casts away what suits him not. Austria conquers Lombardy, France Algiers, Russia Poland, to the benefit of the conquered party, it seems. Can any one show that the British rule has been a benefit to India? The Russians make nothing of their American territory. But what civilization blooms out of the savage ground wherever the Saxon plants his foot!

I must say a word of the leading peculiarities of this tribe.

1. There is a strong Love of Individual Freedom. This belongs to the Anglo-Saxons in common with

all the Teutonic family. But with them it seems eminently powerful. Circumstances have favored its development. They care much for freedom, little for equality.

2. Connected with this, is a Love of Law and Order, which continually shows itself on both sides of the ocean. Fast as we gain freedom, we secure it by law and constitution, trusting little to the caprice of magistrates.

3. Then there is a great Federative Power — a tendency to form combinations of persons, or of communities and States — special partnerships on a small scale for mercantile business; on a large scale, like the American Union, or the Hanse towns, for the political business of a nation.

4. The Anglo-Saxons have eminent Practical Power to organize things into a mill, or men into a State, and then to administer the organization. This power is one which contributes greatly to both their commercial and political success. But this tribe is also most eminently material in its aims and means; it loves riches, works for riches, fights for riches. It is not warlike, as some other nations, who love war for its own sake, though a hard fighter when put to it.

5. We are the most Aggressive, Invasive, and Exclusive People on the earth. The history of the Anglo-Saxon, for the last three hundred years, has been one of continual aggression, invasion, and extermination.

I cannot now stop to dwell on these traits of our tribal anthropology, but must yet say a word touching this national exclusiveness and tendency to exterminate.

Austria and Russia never treated a conquered nation so cruelly as England has treated Ireland. Not many years ago, four fifths of the population of the island were Catholics, a tenth Anglican churchmen. All offices were in the hands of the little minority. Two thirds of the Irish House of Commons were nominees of the Protestant gentry; the Catholic members must take the declaration against Transubstantiation. Papists were forbidden to vote in elections of members to the Irish Parliament. They suffered "under a universal, unmitigated, indispensable, exceptionless disqualification." "In the courts of law, they could not gain a place on the bench, nor act as a barrister, attorney, or solicitor, nor be employed even as a hired clerk, nor sit on a grand jury, nor serve as a sheriff, nor hold even the lowest civil office of trust and profit; nor have any privilege in a town corporation; nor be a freeman of such corporation; nor vote at a vestry."* A Catholic could not marry a Protestant: the priest who should celebrate such a marriage was to be hanged. He could not be "a guardian to any child, nor educate his own child, if its mother were a Protestant," or

---

* Bancroft, History of United States, vol. v. p. 66, *et seq.*

the child declared in favor of Protestantism. "No Protestant might instruct a Papist. Papists could not supply their want by academies and schools of their own; for a Catholic to teach, even in a private family, or as usher to a Protestant, was a felony, punishable by imprisonment, exile, or death." "To be educated in any foreign Catholic school was an unalterable and perpetual outlawry." "The child sent abroad for education, no matter of how tender an age, or himself how innocent, could never after sue in law or equity, or be guardian, executor, or administrator, or receive any legacy or deed of gift; he forfeited all his goods and chattels, and forfeited for his life all his lands;" whoever sent him incurred the same penalties.

The Catholic clergy could not be taught at home or abroad: they "were registered and kept, like prisoners at large, within prescribed limits." "All Papists exercising ecclesiastical jurisdiction; all monks, friars, and regular priests, and all priests not actually in parishes, and to be registered, were banished from Ireland under pain of transportation; and, on a return, of being hanged and quartered." "The Catholic priest abjuring his religion, received a pension of thirty, and afterwards of forty pounds." "No non-conforming Catholic could buy land, or receive it by descent, devise, or settlement; or lend money on it as security; or hold an interest in it through a Protestant trustee; or take a lease of ground for more than thirty-one years. If under such a lease he brought his farm to produce more than one third beyond the rent, the first Protestant discoverer might sue for the lease before known Protestants, making the defendant answer all interrogations on oath; so that the Catholic farmer dared not drain his fields, nor inclose them, nor build solid houses on them." "Even if a Catholic owned a horse worth more than five pounds, any Protestant might take it away," on payment of that sum. "To the native Irish, the English oligarchy appeared as men of a different race and creed, who had acquired the island by force of arms, rapine, and chicane, and derived revenues from it by the employment of extortionate underlings or overseers." *

The same disposition to invade and exterminate showed itself on this side of the ocean.

In America, the Frenchman and the Spaniard came in contact with the red man; they converted him to what they called Christianity, and then associated with him on equal terms. The pale-face and the red-skin hunted in company; they fished from the same canoe in the Bay of Fundy and Lake Superior; they lodged in the same tent, slept on the same bear-skin; nay, they knelt together before the same God, who was "no respecter of persons," and had made of one blood all nations of men! The

* Bancroft, *ubi sup.* p. 67, *et seq.*

white man married the Indian's daughter; the red man wooed and won the pale child of the Caucasian. This took place in Canada, and in Mexico, in Peru, and Equador. In Brazil, the negro graduates at the college; he becomes a general in the army. But the Anglo-Saxon disdains to mingle his proud blood in wedlock with the "inferior races of men." He puts away the savage — black, yellow, red. In New England, the Puritan converted the Indians to Christianity, as far as they could accept the theology of John Calvin; but made a careful separation between white and red, " my people and thy people." They must dwell in separate villages, worship in separate houses; they must not intermarry. The general court of Massachusetts once forbid all extra-matrimonial connection of white and red on pain of death! The Anglo-Saxon has carefully sought to exterminate the savages from his territory. The Briton does so in Africa, in Van Dieman's Land, in New Zealand, in New Holland — wherever he meets them. The American does the same in the western world. In New England the Puritan found the wild woods, the wild beasts, and the wild men: he undertook to eradicate them all, and has succeeded best with the wild men. There are more bears than Indians in New England. The United States pursues the same destructive policy. In two hundred years more there will be few Indians left between the Lake of the Woods and the Gulf of Mexico, between the Atlantic and Pacific Oceans.

Yet the Anglo-Saxons are not cruel; they are simply destructive. The Dutch, in New York, perpetrated the most wanton cruelties; the savages themselves shuddered at the white man's atrocity: "Our gods would be offended at such things," said they; "the white man's god must be different!" The cruelties of the French, and, still more, of the Spaniards in Mexico, in the West Indies, and South America, are too terrible to repeat, but too well known to need relating. The Spaniard put men to death with refinements of cruelty, luxuriating in destructiveness. The Anglo-Saxon simply shot down his foe, offered a reward for homicide, so much for a scalp, but tolerated no needless cruelty. If the problem is to destroy a race of men with the least expenditure of destructive force on one side, and the least suffering on the other, the Anglo-Saxon, Briton, or American, is the fittest instrument to be found on the whole globe.

So much for the Anglo-Saxon character in general, as introductory to an examination of America in special. It is well to know the anthropology of the stock before attempting to appreciate the character of the special people. America has the general characteristics of this powerful tribe, but modified by her peculiar geographical and historical position. Our fathers emigrated from their home in a time of great ferment, and brought with them ideas which could not then be organized into institutions at home. This was obviously the case with the theological ideas of the Puritans, who, with their descendants, have given to America most of what is new and peculiar in her institutions. Still more, the early settlers of the North brought with them sentiments not ripened yet, which, in due time, developed themselves into ideas, and then into institutions.

At first necessity, or love of change, drove the wanderers to the wilderness; they had no thought of separating from England. The fugitive pilgrims in the Mayflower, who subscribed the compact, which so many Americans erroneously regard as the "seed-corn of the republican tree, under which millions of her men now stand," called themselves "loyal subjects of our dread sovereign, King James," undertaking to plant a colony "for the glory of God, and advancement of the Christian faith, and honor of our king and country." In due time, as the colonists developed themselves in one, and the English at home in a different direction, there came to be a great diversity of ideas, and an opposition of interests. When mutuality of ideas and of interests, as the indispensable condition of national unity of action, failed, the colony fell off from its parent: the separation was unavoidable. Before many years, we doubt not, Australia will thus separate from the mother country, to the advantage of both parties.

In America, two generations of men have passed

away since the last battle of the Revolution. The hostility of that contest is only a matter of history to the mass of Britons or Americans, not of daily consciousness; and as this disturbing force is withdrawn, the two nations see and feel more distinctly their points of agreement, and become conscious that they are both but one people.

The transfer of the colonists of England to the western world was an event of great importance to mankind; they found a virgin continent, on which to set up and organize their ideas, and develop their faculties. They had no enemies but the wilderness and its savage occupants. I doubt not that, if the emigrant had remained at home, it would have taken a thousand years to attain the same general development now reached by the free States of North America. The settlers carried with them the best ideas and the best institutions of their native land — the arts and sciences of England, the forms of a representative government, the trial by jury, the Common Law, the ideas of Christianity, and the traditions of the human race. In the woods, far from help, they were forced to become self-reliant and thrifty men. It is instructive to see what has come of the experiment. It is but two hundred and forty-six years since the settlement of Jamestown — not two hundred and thirty-four years since the Pilgrims landed at Plymouth; what a development since that time — of numbers, of riches, of material and spiritual power!

In the ninth century, Korb Flokki, a half-mythical person, "let loose his three crows," it is said, seeking land to the west and north of the Orkneys, and went to Iceland. In the tenth century, Gunnbjiorn, and Eirek the Red, discovered Greenland, an "ugly and right hateful country," as Paul Egede calls it. In the eleventh century, Leife, son of Eirek, with Tyrker the Southerner, discovered Vinland, some part of North America, but whether Newfoundland, Nova Scotia, or New England, I shall leave others to determine. It is not yet four hundred years since Columbus first dropped his anchor at San Salvador, and Cabot discovered the continent of America, and cruised along its shores from Hudson's Bay to Florida, seeking for a passage to the East Indies. In 1608 the first permanent British settlement was made in America, at Jamestown; in 1620 the pilgrims began their far-famed experiment at Plymouth. What a change from 1608 to 1854! It is not in my power to determine the number of immigrants before the Revolution. There was a great variety of nationalities — Dutch in New York, Germans in Pennsylvania and Georgia, Swedes and Finns in Delaware, Scotch in New England and North Carolina, Swiss in Georgia; Acadians from Nova Scotia, and Hugenots from France.

America has now a stable form of government. Her pyramid is not yet high. It is only humble powers that she develops, no great creative spirit here as yet enchants men with the wonders of literature and art — but her foundation is wide and deeply laid. It is now easy to see the conditions and the causes of her success. The conditions are, the new continent, a virgin soil to receive the seed of liberty: the causes were, first, the character of the tribe, and next, the liberal institutions founded thereby.

The rapid increase of America in most of the elements of national power, is a remarkable fact in the history of mankind.

Look at the increase of numbers. In 1689, the entire population of the English colonies, exclusive of the Indians, amounted to about 200,000. Twenty-five years later there were 434,000, now 24,000,000.*

---

* *Table of Population in* 1715.

Colonies.	Whites.	Negroes.	Total.
New Hampshire	9,500	150	9,650
Massachusetts	94,000	2,000	96,000
Rhode Island	8,500	500	9,000
Connecticut	46,000	1,500	47,500
New York	27,000	4,000	31,000
New Jersey	21,000	1,500	22,500
Pennsylvania and Delaware	43,300	2,500	45,800
Maryland	40,700	9,500	50,200
Virginia	72,000	23,000	95,000
North Carolina	7,500	3,700	11,200
South Carolina	6,250	10,500	16,750
	375,750	58,850	434,600

The present population of the United States con-

In 1754, another return was made to the Board of Trade, in the following

Table of Population in 1754.

Whites.	Blacks.	Total.
1,192,896	292,738	1,485,634

We will now give the population at seven successive periods, as indicated by the returns of the official census of the United States.

Table of Population from 1790 *to* 1850.

Years.	Whites.	Free Colored.	Slaves.	Total.
1790	3,172,464	59,466	697,897	3,929,827
1800	4,304,489	108,395	893,041	5,305,925
1810	5,862,004	186,446	1,191,364	7,239,814
1820	7,872,711	238,197	1,543,688	9,654,596
1830	10,537,378	319,599	2,009,043	12,866,020
1840	14,189,555	386,348	2,487,355	17,069,453
1850	19,630,738	428,661	3,198,324	23,257,723

The following is the official report of Immigration from 1790 to 1850. Much of it is conjectural and approximate.

Table of Immigration from 1790 *to* 1850.

From 1790 to 1800	120,000
" 1810 to 1820	114,000
" 1820 to 1830	203,979
" 1830 to 1840	778,500
" 1840 to 1850	1,542,840
	2,759,329

The immigrants are thus conjecturally distributed among the nations of the earth. The estimate is a rough one.

Table of Nationality.

Celtic — Irish, (one half)	1,350,000
Teutonic — Germans, Danes, Swedes, etc. (one fourth)	675,000
Miscellaneous — All other nations	734,329

The following statement exhibits the nationality of the immi-

sists of the following ingredients. The numbers are conjectural and approximate.

Table of Nationality.

White Immigrants since 1790, and their white descendants	4,350,934
Africans, and their descendants	3,626,585
White Immigrants previous to 1790, and their white descendants	15,279,804

This does not include the Indians living within the territories and States of the Union. These facts show that a remarkable mingling of families of the Caucasian stock is taking place. The exact statistics would disclose a yet more remarkable mingling of the Caucasian and the Æthiopian races going on. The Africans are rapidly "bleaching" under the in-

---

gration to the United States for the calendar year, 1851, (Dec. 31, 1850 to Dec. 31, 1851) : —

Nationality of Immigrants in 1851.

From Great Britain and Ireland	264,222
" Germany	72,283
" France	20,107
Of these there were Males	245,017
" Females	163,745
" Unknown	66

Table of Immigration for the first four months of 1853.

From the British Islands	15,023
" French Ports	8,768
" German Ports	3,511
" Belgian and Dutch	2,747
" Spanish, Portuguese, and Italian	135

fluence of democratic chemistry. If only one tenth of the "colored population" has Caucasian blood in its veins, then there are 362,698 descendants of this "amalgamation;" but if you estimate these *hybrids* as one in five, which is not at all excessive, we have then 725,397.

The thirty-one States now organized have a surface of 1,485,870 square miles, while the total area of the United States, so far as I have information, on the 17th of May, 1853, was 3,220,000 square miles. In the States, on an average, there are not sixteen persons to the square mile; in the whole territory, not eight to a mile. Massachusetts, the most densely peopled State, has more than one hundred and twenty-six to the mile, while Texas has but eighty-nine men for a hundred miles of land, more than eight hundred acres to each human soul.

In 1840, there were ten States, whose united populations exceeded 4,000,000, which yet had no town with 10,000 inhabitants.*

---

* The following table shows the occupation of 4,798,870 persons in 1840, ascertained by the census: —

Table of Occupation.

Engaged in Mining	15,211
" Agriculture	3,719,951
" Commerce	117,607
" Manufactures . .	791,749
" Navigation (Ocean) .	56,021
" " (Inland Waters)	33,076
" Learned Professions . .	65,255

Look next at the products of industry in the United States.*

---

* I take these results of the census of 1840, as deduced by Professor Tucker, in his admirable book, "Progress of the United States in Population and Wealth in Fifty Years." New York, 1843. 1 vol. 8vo.

Value of Annual Products of Industry, 1840.

	Dollars.
Agriculture	654,387,597
Manufactures	236,836,224
Commerce	79,721,086
Mining	42,358,761
The Forest	16,835,060
The Ocean	11,996,108
Total,	1,063,134,736

In 1850, the iron-crop in the United States amounted to 564,755 tons. The ship-crop was 1,360 vessels, with a measurement of 272,218 tons. The increase of American shipping is worth notice, and is shown in the following

Table of American Tonnage from 1815 *to* 1850.

Years.	Tons.
1815	1,368,127
1820	1,280,165
1825	1,423,110
1830	1,181,986
1835	1,824,939
1840	2,180,763
1845	2,417,001
1850	3,535,454

The tonnage is still on the increase. In 1851, it amounted to 3,772,439, and at this moment must be considerably more than 4,000,000. The first ship built in New England was the "Blessing of the Bay," a "bark of thirty tons," launched in 1634. Not far

The contrast between the Spanish and the Anglo-Saxon settlements in America is amazing. A hun-

---

from the spot where her keel was laid, a ship has recently been built, three hundred and ten feet long, and more than six thousand tons burden.

On the 30th September, 1851, there were, if the accounts are reliable, 12,805 miles of railroad in the United States. At present there are probably about 15,000 miles.

To show the increase of American commerce, consider the following

Table of Imports and Exports from 1800 *to* 1852.

Years.	IMPORTS. Dollars.	EXPORTS. Dollars.
1800	91,252,768	70,971,780
1805	120,000,000	95,566,021
1810	85,400,000	66,757,974
1815	113,041,274	52,557,753
1820	74,450,000	69,691,669
1825	96,340,075	99,535,388
1830	70,876,920	73,849,508
1835	149,895,742	121,693,577
1840	107,141,519	132,085,946
1845	117,254,564	114,646,606
1850	178,138,318	161,898,720
1852	212,613,282	209,641,625

The most important articles of export for five-and-twenty years appear in the following

Table of the chief articles of Export from 1825 *to* 1850.

Years.	Cotton. Dollars.	Breadstuffs and Provisions. Dollars.	Tobacco. Dollars.
1825	36,846,649	11,634,449	6,115,623
1830	29,674,883	12,075,430	5,586,365
1835	64,961,302	12,009,399	8,250,577
1840	63,870,307	19,067,535	9,883,957
1845	51,739,643	16,743,421	7,469,819
1850	71,484,616	26,051,373	9,951,023
1852	87,965,732	25,857,177	10,031,283

The greatest amount of cotton was exported in 1852,–

dred years ago, Spain, the discoverer of America, had undisputed sway over all South America, except Brazil and the Guianas. All Mexico was hers — all Central America, California unbounded on the north, extending indefinitely, Louisiana, Florida, Cuba, Porto Rico, and part of Hayti. She ruled a population of twenty million men. Now Cuba trembles in her faltering hand; all the rest has dropped from the arms of that feeble mother of feeble sons. In 1750 her American colonies extended from Patagonia to Oregon. The La Plata was too far north for her southern limit, the Columbia too far south for her northern bound. The Mississippi and the Amazon were Spanish rivers, and emptied the waters of a continent into the lap of America, the Mexique Gulf, which was also a Spanish sea. But Spain allowed only eight-and-thirty vessels to ply between the mother country and the family of American daughters on both sides of the continent. The empire of Spain, mother country and colonies, extending from Barcelona to Manilla, with more sea-coast than the whole continent of Africa, employed but sixteen thousand sailors in her

---

1,093,230,639 pounds; but the greatest value of cotton was in 1851, amounting to $112,351,317. In 1847, the value of breadstuffs and provisions exported was $68,701,921.

The government revenues for the fiscal year 1852, were $49,728,386,89; there was a balance in the treasury of $10,911,-645.68; making the total means for that year, $60,640,032.57. On the 1st January, 1853, the national debt amounted to $65,-131,692.

commercial marine. Portugal forbid Brazil to cultivate any of the products of the Indies.

Look at this day at Anglo-Saxon, and then at Spanish America. In 1606 there was not an English settlement in America. In 1627 only two, Jamestown and Plymouth. But the Spanish colonies date back to 1493. Compare the history of the basin of the Amazon with the valley of the Mississippi. The Amazon with its affluents commands seventy thousand miles of internal navigation, draining more arable land than all Europe contains, the largest, the most fertile valley in the world. It includes 1,796,000 square miles. Every thing which finds a home on earth will flourish in the basin of the Amazon, between the level of the Atlantic and the top of the Andes. But the tonnage on the Amazon does not probably equal the tonnage on Lake Champlain. Only an Anglo-Saxon steamer ruffles the waters of the Amazon. Parà, at its mouth, more than three hundred years old, contains less than 20,000 inhabitants.

The Mississippi with its tributaries drains 982,000 square miles, and affords 16,694 miles of steam navigation. In 1851 there were 1,190 steamboats on its bosom, measuring 249,054 tons, running at an annual cost of $39,774,194; the value of the merchandise carried on the river in 1852 was estimated at $432,651,240, more than double the whole foreign trade of the United States for that year. New Orleans, at the mouth of the Mississippi, was founded in 1719, and in 1850 contained 119,461 inhabitants: in 1810 it had not 18,000!

The Anglo-Saxon colonists brought with them the vigorous bodies and sturdy intellect of their race; the forms of representative and constitutional government; publicity of political transactions; trial by jury; a fondness for local self-government; an aversion to centralization; the Protestant form of religion; the Bible; the right of private judgment; their national administrative power; and that stalwart self-reliance and thrift which mark the Englishman and American wherever they go. New Spain had priests and soldiers; New England ministers and schoolmasters. In two centuries, behold what consequences come of such causes! No Chilian vessel ever went to Spain!

But America itself is not unitary; there is a Spanish America in the United States. Unity of Idea and Interest by no means prevails here.

America was settled by two very different classes of men, one animated by moral or religious motives, coming to realize an idea; the other animated by only commercial ideas, pushing forth to make a fortune, or to escape from jail. Some men brought religion, others only ambition; the consequence is, two antagonistic ideas, with institutions which correspond, antagonistic institutions.

First there is the Democratic Idea: that all men are endowed by their Creator with certain natural rights; that these rights are alienable only by the possessor thereof; that they are equal in all men; that government is to organize these natural, unalienable, and equal rights into institutions designed for the good of the governed; and therefore government is to be of all the people, by all the people, and for all the people. Here government is development, not exploitation.

Next there is the Oligarchic Idea, just the opposite of this: that there is no such thing as natural, unalienable, and equal rights, but accidental, alienable, and unequal powers: that government is to organize the might of all for the good of the governing party; is to be a government of all, by a part, and for the sake of a part. The governing power may be one man, King Monarch; a few men, King Noble; or the majority, King Many. In all these cases, the motive, the purpose, and the means, are still the same, and government is exploitation of the governed, not the development thereof. So far as the people are developed by the government, it is that they may be thereby exploitered.

Neither the Democratic nor the Oligarchic idea is perfectly developed as yet; but the first preponderates most at the north, the latter at the south — one in the Free, the other in the Slave states.

The settlers did not bring to America the Democratic Idea fully grown. It is the child of time. In all great movements there are three periods — first, that of Sentiment — there is only a feeling of the new thing; next of Idea — the feeling has become a thought; finally of Action — the thought becomes a thing. It is pleasant to trace the growth of the democratic sentiment and idea in the human race, to watch the efforts to make the thought a thing, and found domestic, social, ecclesiastical, and political institutions, corresponding thereto. Perhaps it is easier to trace this here than elsewhere. It has sometimes been claimed that the Puritans came to America to found such institutions. But they had no fondness for a Democracy; the thought did not enter their heads that the Substance of man is superior to the Accidents of men, his nature more than his history. New Englandmen on the 4th of July claim the compact on board the Mayflower, as the foundation of Democracy in America, and of the Declaration of Independence. But the signers of that famous document had no design to found a democracy. Much of the liberality of the settlers at Plymouth seems to have been acquired by their residence in Holland, where they saw the noblest example of religious toleration then in the world.

The democratic idea has had but a slow and gradual growth even in New England. The first form of government was a theocracy, an intense tyranny in the name of God. The next world was for the "Elect" said puritan theology; "let us also have this," said the Elect. The distinction between clerical and laical was nowhere more prominent than in puritan New England. The road to the ballot-box lay under the pulpit; only church-members could vote, and if a man's politics were not marked with the proper stripe it was not easy for him to become a church-member. The "Lords Brethren" were as tyrannical in the new world as the "Lords Bishops" in the old.

There was a distinction between "gentlemen," with the title of *Mr.*, and men, with only the name, *John*, *Peter*, and *Bartholomew*, or the title "*Goodman.*"

Slavery was established in the new world; there were two forms of it: — absolute bondage of the Africans and the Indians; the conditional bondage of white men, called "servants," slaves for a limited period. Before the Revolution the latter were numerous even in the north.

The Puritan had little religious objection to the establishment of slavery. But the Red man would fight, and would not work. It was not possible to make useful slaves of Indians; the experiment was tried; it failed, and the savage was simply destroyed.

In theocratic and colonial times at the north, the democratic idea contended against the church; and gradually weakened and overcame the power of the clergy and of all ecclesiastical corporations. At length all churches stand on the same level. The persecuted Quaker has vindicated his right to free inspiration by the Holy Ghost; the Baptist enjoys the natural right to be baptized after the apostolic fashion; the Unitarian to deny the Holy Trinity; the Universalist to affirm the eternal blessedness of all men; and the philosophical critic to examine the claims of Christianity as of all religions, to sweep the whole ocean of religious consciousness, draw his net to land, gather the good into vessels, and cast the bad away.

The spirit of freedom contended against the claims of ancestral gentility. In the woods of New England it was soon found that a pair of arms was worth more than a "coat of arms," never so old and horrid with griffins. A man who could outwit the Indians, "whip his weight in wild cats," hew down trees, build ships, make wise laws, and organize a river into a mill, or men into towns and states, was a valuable person; and if born at all was well born. "Men of no family" grew up in the new soil, and often overtopped the twigs cut from some famous tree. In the humblest callings of life, I have found men of the most eminent European stocks. But it was rare that men of celebrated families settled in

America: monarchy, nobility, prelacy did not emigrate, it was the People who came over. And in 1780, the Convention of Massachusetts put this in the first Article of the Constitution of the State: "All men are born free and equal, and have certain natural, essential, and unalienable rights." All distinction of gentle and simple, bond and free, perished out of Massachusetts. The same thought is repeated in the constitutions of many northern states.

This spirit of freedom contended against the claims of England. "Local self-government" was the aim of the colonies. Opposition to centralization of authority is very old in America. I hope it will be always young. England was a hard master to her western children; she left them to fight their own battles against the Indians, against the French; and this circumstance made all men soldiers. In King Philip's war every man capable of bearing arms took the field, first or last. The frontier was a school for soldiers. The day after the battle of Lexington, a hundred and fifty men, in a large farming town of New Hampshire, shouldered their muskets and marched for Boston, to look after their brethren.

It was long before there was a clear and distinct expression of the Democratic idea in America. The Old Testament helped it to forms of denunciatory speech. The works of Milton, Sidney, Locke, and the writers on the law of nature and of nations were of great service. Rousseau came at the right time, and aided the good cause. Calvin and Rousseau, strange to say, fought side by side in the battle for freedom. It was a great thing for America and the world, that this idea was so clearly set forth in the Declaration of Independence, announced as a self-evident truth. A young man's hand came out of the wall, and wrote words which still make many tremble as they read.

The battle for human freedom yet goes on; its victory is never complete. But now in the free States of the north the fight is against all traditional forms of evil. The domestic question relates to the equal rights of men and women in the family and out of it; there is a great social question, — "Shall money prevail over man, and the rich and crafty exploiter the poor and the simple?" In the church, men ask — "Shall authority — a book or an institution, each an accident of human history — prevail over reason, conscience, the affections, and the soul — the human substance?" In the State, the minority looks for the eternal principles of Right; and will not heed the bidding of famous men, of conventions, and majorities; appeals to the still, small voice within, which proclaims the Higher Law of God. Even in the north a great contest goes on.

The democratic idea seems likely to triumph in the north, and build up its appropriate institutions — a family without a slave, a family of equals; a community without a lord, a community of coöperators; a church without a bishop, a church of brethren; a State without a king, a State of citizens.

The institutions of the free States are admirably suited to produce a rapid development of the understanding. The State guarantees the opportunity of education to all children. The free schools of the north are her most original institution, quite imperfect as yet. The attempts to promote the public education of the people have already produced most gratifying results.

More than half of the newspaper editors in the United States have received all their academical education in the common school. Many a Methodist and Universalist minister, many a member of Congress, has been graduated at that beneficent institution. The intelligence and riches of the north are due to the common schools. In the free States books are abundant; newspapers in all hands; skilled labor abounds. Body runs to brain, and work to thought. The head saves the hands. Under the benignant influence of public education, the children of the Irish emigrant, poor and despised, grow up to equality with the descendants of the rich; two generations will efface the difference between them. I have seen, of a Sunday afternoon, a thousand young Irish women, coming out of a Catholic church, all well dressed, with ribbons and cheap ornaments, to help elevate their self-respect; and when remembering the condition of these same women in their native land, barefoot, dirty, mendicant, perhaps thievish, glad of a place to serve at two pounds a year, I have begun to see the importance of America to the world; and have felt as John Adams, when he wrote in his diary, "I always consider the settlement of America with reverence and wonder, as the opening of a grand scene and design of Providence, for the illumination of the ignorant, and the emancipation of the slavish part of mankind, all over the earth."

The educational value of American institutions, in the free States, is seldom appreciated. The schools open to all, where all classes of the people freely mingle, and the son of a rude man is brought into contact with the good-manners and self-respectful deportment of children from more fortunate homes;* the churches where everybody is welcome, — if not black; the business which demands intelligence, and educates the great mass of the people; the public lectures, delivered in all the considerable towns of New England, the winter through; the newspapers, abundant, cheap, discussing every thing with as little reserve as the summer wind; the various social meetings of incorporated companies to discuss their affairs; the constitution of the towns, with their meetings, two or three times a year, when officers are chosen, and taxes voted, and all municipal affairs

* In the large towns of the north — even of Massachusetts — the *colored children* are not allowed in the common schools.

abundantly discussed; the public proceedings of the courts of law, so instructive to Jurors and spectators; the local legislatures of the States — each consisting of from two to four hundred members, and in session four or five months of the year; the politics of the nation brought home to every voter in the land, — all these things form an educational power of immense value, for such a development of the lower intellectual faculties, as men esteem most in these days.

But, the Oligarchic Idea is also at work. You meet this in all parts of the land, diligently seeking to organize itself. It takes no new forms, however, which are peculiar to America. It reënacts the old statutes which have oppressed mankind in the eastern world: it attempts to revive the institutions that have cursed other lands in darker days. Now the few tyrannize over the many, and devise machinery to oppress their fellow-mortals; then the majority thus tyrannize over the few, over the minority. There are two forms of Democracy — the Satanic and the Celestial: one is Selfishness, which knows no Higher Law; the other Philanthropy, that bows to the Justice of the Infinite God, with a "Thy will be done." In America we find both — the democratic Devil and the democratic Angel.

The Idea of the North is preponderatingly democratic in the better sense of the word; new justice is organized in the laws; government becomes more and more of all, by all, and for all. You trace the progress of humanity, of liberty, equality, and fraternity in the constitution of the free States from Massachusetts to Wisconsin.

But in the southern States, the Oligarchic Idea prevails to a much greater extent, and becomes more and more apparent, and powerful. The South has adopted the institution of Slavery, elsewhere discarded, and clings to it with strange tenacity. In South Carolina, the possession of slaves is made the condition, *sine quâ non*, of eligibility to certain offices. The constitution provides that a citizen shall not "be eligible to a seat in the House of Representatives, *unless legally seized and possessed, in his own right*, of a settled freehold estate of five hundred acres of land and, *ten negroes*." *

The Puritans of New England made no very strong objection to Slavery. It was established in all the colonies of the North and South. White servitude continued till the Revolution. As late as 1757, white men were kidnapped, "spirited away," as it was called, in Scotland, and sold in the colonies.

Negro slavery began early. Even the gentler Puritans at Plymouth had the Anglo-Saxon antipathy to the colored race. The black man must sit aloof from the whites in the meeting-house, in a "negro pew;" he must "not be joined unto them in burial;" a place was set apart, in the graveyard at Plymouth,

---

* Art. I. § 6.

for colored people, and still remains as "from time immemorial." In 1851, an Abolitionist, before his death, insisted on being buried with the objects of his tender solicitude. The request was complied with.

After the Revolution, the northern States gradually abolished Slavery, though not without violent opposition in some places. In 1788 three colored persons were kidnapped at Boston, and carried to the West Indies; the crime produced a great excitement, and led to executive and legislative action. The same year, the General Presbyterian Assembly of America issued a pastoral letter, recommending "the abolition of Slavery, and the instruction of the negroes in letters and religion." In 1790, Dr. Franklin, president of the "Pennsylvanian Society for the Abolition of Slavery," signed a memorial to Congress, asking that body "to countenance the restoration of liberty to the unhappy men who alone in this land of freedom are degraded into perpetual bondage, and who, amid the general joy of surrounding provinces, are groaning in servile subjection; that you will devise means for removing this inconsistency from the character of the American people; that you will permit mercy and justice towards this distressed race; and that you will step to the very verge of the power vested in you for discouraging every species of traffic in the persons of our fellow men."

The memorial excited a storm of debate. Slavery

was defended as a Measure of political economy, and a Principle of humanity, South Carolina leading in the defence of her favorite institution. Yet many eminent southern men were profoundly convinced of the injustice of Slavery; others saw it was a bad tool to work with.

Since that time the southern idea of Slavery appears to have changed. Formerly, it was granted by the defenders of Slavery that it was wrong; but they maintained: 1, that Americans were not responsible for the wrong, as England had imposed it upon the colonies; 2, that it was profitable to the owners of slaves; and 3, that it was impossible to get rid of it. Now the ground is taken that Slavery is not a wrong to the slave, but that the negro is fit for a slave, and a slave only.

I pass by the arguments of the southern clergy and the northern clergy — whose conduct is yet more contemptible — to cite the language of the prominent secular organs of the south. The Richmond Examiner, one of the most able journals of the South, declares: —

"When we deprive the negro of that exercise of his will which the white calls liberty, we deprive him of nothing; on the contrary, when we give him the guidance and protection of a master, we confer on him a great blessing." *

---

* See above vol. i. p. 394, *et seq.*

"To treat two creatures so utterly different as the white man and the negro man on the same system, is an effort to violate elementary laws." "The aphorisms of the Declaration of Independence" are illogical when applied to the negro. "They involve the assumption that the negro is the white man, only a little different in external appearance and education. But this assumption cannot be supported." "A law rendering perpetual the relation between the negro and his master is no wrong, but a right." "Negroes are not men, in the meaning of the Declaration of Independence."

"'Have n't negroes got souls?' asks some sepulchral voice. 'Have they no souls?' That question we never answer; we know nothing about it. *Non mi ricordo;* they may have souls, for aught we know to the contrary; so may horses and hogs."

"We expect the institution of Slavery to exist, forever." "The production of cotton, rice, sugar, coffee, and tobacco, demand that which Slavery only can supply. And in all portions of this Union where these staples are produced, it will be retained. And when we get Hayti, Mexico, and Jamaica, common sense will doubtless extend it, or rather, reëstablish it there too." *

I will now quote a little from the Mr. De Bow's large work: — †

* Richmond (Va.) Semi-weekly Examiner, January 4, 1853.

† The Industrial Resources, etc., of the Southern and Western

"No amount of education or training can ever render the negro equal in intellect with the white." "'You cannot make a silk purse out of a sow's lug,' is an old and homely adage, but not the less true; so you cannot make any thing from a negro but negroism, which means barbarism and inferiority." "As God made them so they have been, and so they will be; the white man, the negro, and the jackass; each to his kind, and each to his nature; true to the finger of destiny (which is the finger of God), and undeviatingly pursuing the track which that finger as undeviatingly points out."*

"Is the negro made for slavery? God in heaven! what are we, that because we cannot understand the mystery of this Thy will, we should dare rise in rebellion, and call it wrong, unjust, and evil? The kindness of nature fits each creature to fulfil its destiny. The very virtues of the negro fit him for slavery, and his vices cry aloud for the shackles of bondage!" "It is the destiny of the negro, if by himself to be a savage; if by the white, to be a serf." "They may be styled human beings, though of an inherently degraded species. To attempt to relieve them from their natural inferiority is idle in itself, and may be mischievous in its results." †

States: embracing a View of their Commerce, Agriculture, Manufactures, Internal Improvements; Slave and Free Labor, Slavery Institutions, Products, etc., of the South, etc., with an Appendix. By J. D. B. de Bow, etc. In 3 vols. 8vo. New Orleans, 1852.

* De Bow, vol. ii. p. 199. † *Id.* p. 203.

"Equality is no thought nor creation of God. Slavery, under one name or another, will exist as long as man exists; and abolition is a dream whose execution is an impossibility. Intellect is the only divine right. The negro cannot be schooled, nor argued, nor driven into a love of freedom."*

"Alas for their folly! (the abolitionists). But woe! woe! a woe of darkness and of death, a woe of hell and perdition to those who, better knowing, goad folly on to such an extreme. This is, indeed, the sin not to be forgiven; the sin against the Holy Ghost, and against the Spirit of God! The beautiful order of creation breathed down from Almighty Intelligence, is to be moulded and wrought by fanatic intelligence, until dragged down, at last, to negro intelligence!"†

Chancellor Harper, of South Carolina, in an Address delivered before "the Society for the Advancement of Learning" at Charleston, makes some statements a little remarkable: —

"The institution of slavery is a principal cause of civilization." "It is as much the order of nature that men should enslave each other, as that other animals should prey upon each other." "The savage can only be tamed by being enslaved or by having slaves." "The African slave-trade has given and will give the boon of existence to millions and

---

* De Bow, vol. ii. p. 204. † *Id.* p. 197.

millions in our country who would otherwise never have enjoyed it." *

He quotes the Bible to justify Slavery: —

"'They shall be your bondmen for ever.'" "Servitude is the condition of civilization. It was decreed when the command was given, 'Be fruitful and multiply, and replenish the earth and subdue it;' and when it was added 'In the sweat of thy face shalt thou eat bread.' Slavery was "forced on us by necessity, and further forced upon us by the superior authority of the mother country. I, for one, neither deprecate nor resent the gift." "I am by no means sure that the cause of humanity has been served by the change in jurisprudence which has placed their murder on the same footing with that of a freeman." "The relation of master and slave is naturally one of kindness." "It is true that the slave is driven to his labor by stripes; such punishment would be degrading to a freeman, who had the thoughts and aspirations of a freeman. In general, it is not degrading to a slave, nor is it felt to be so."†

It is alleged that "the slave is cut off from the means of intellectual, moral, and religious improvement, and in consequence his moral character becomes depraved, and he addicted to degrading vices." To this the democratic Chancellor of South Carolina replies: —

---

* De Bow, vol. ii. pp. 206–210. † *Id.* pp. 214–217.

"The Creator did not intend that every individual human being should be highly cultivated, morally and intellectually." "It is better that a part should be highly cultivated, and the rest utterly ignorant." "Odium has been cast upon our legislation on account of its forbidding the elements of education to be communicated to slaves. But, in truth, what injury is done them by this? He who works during the day with his hands does not read in intervals of leisure for his amusement, or the improvement of his mind." "Of the many slaves whom I have known capable of reading, I have never known one to read any thing but the Bible, and this task they imposed on themselves as matter of duty." "Their minds generally show a strong religious tendency, . . . and perhaps their religious notions are not much more extravagant than those of a large portion of the free population of our country." "It is certainly the master's interest that they should have proper religious sentiments."

"A knowledge of reading, writing, and the elements of arithmetic, is convenient and important to the free laborer . . . but of what use would they be to the slave?" "Would you do a benefit to the horse or the ox by giving him a cultivated understanding or fine feelings?" *

* De Bow, vol. ii. p. 217, *et seq.*

"The law has not provided for making those marriages [of slaves] indissoluble; nor could it do so." "It may perhaps be said, 'that the chastity of wives is not protected by law from the outrages of violence.'" "Who ever heard of such outrages being offered? . . . One reason, doubtless, may be, that often there is no disposition to resist, . . . there is little temptation to this violence as there is so large a population of this class of females [slave wives] who set little value on chastity." "It is true that in this respect the morals of this class are very loose . . . and that the passions of the men of the superior caste tempt and find gratification in the easy chastity of the females. This is evil . . . but evil is incident to every condition of society."

"The female slave [who yields to these temptations] is not a less useful member of society than before. . . . She has done no great injury to herself or any other human being; her offspring is not a burden but an acquisition to her owner; his support is provided for, and he is brought up to usefulness; if the fruit of intercourse with a free man, his condition is perhaps raised somewhat above that of his mother."

"I do not hesitate to say, that the intercourse which takes place with enslaved females is less debasing in its effects [on man] than when it is carried on with females of their own caste, . . . the attraction is less, . . . the intercourse is generally casual, . . . he is less liable to those extraordinary fascinations."

"He, [the slave husband,] is also liable to be separated from wife or child, . . . but from native character and temperament, the separation is much less severely felt." *

"The love of liberty is a noble passion. But, alas! it is one in which we know that a large portion of the human race can never be gratified." "If some superior power should impose on the laborious poor of this, or any other country, this ['a condition which is a very near approach to that of our slaves'] as their undeniable condition . . . how inappreciable would the boon be thought." "The evils of their situation they [the slaves] but slightly feel, and would hardly feel at all if they were not sedulously instructed into sensibility." "Is it not desirable that the inferior laboring class should be made up of such who will conform to their condition without painful aspirations and vain struggles?" †

"I am aware that, however often assumed, it is likely to be repeated again and again: — How can that institution be tolerable, by which a large class of society is cut off from the hope of improvement and knowledge; to whom blows are not degrading, theft no more than a fault, falsehood and the want of

* De Bow, vol. ii. p. 219, *et seq.* † *Id.* p. 222.

chastity almost venial; and in which a husband or parent looks with comparative indifference on that which to a free man would be the dishonor of a wife or child? But why not, if it produce the greatest aggregate of good? Sin and ignorance are only evils because they lead to misery." *

"The African negro is an inferior variety of the human race, . . . and his distinguishing characteristics are such as peculiarly mark him out for the situation which he occupies among us . . . the most remarkable is their indifference to personal liberty." "Let me ask if this people do not present the very material out of which slaves ought to be made." "I do not mean to say that there may not be found among them some of superior capacity to many white persons. . . . And why should it not be so? we have many domestic animals — infinite varieties, distinguished by various degrees of sagacity, courage, strength, swiftness, and other qualities."

"Slavery has done more to elevate a degraded race in the scale of humanity; to tame the savage, to civilize the barbarous, to soften the ferocious, to enlighten the ignorant, and to spread the blessing of Christianity among the heathen, than all the missionaries that philanthropy and religion have ever put forth." "The tendency of slavery is to elevate the character of the master," "to elevate the female char-

* De Bow, vol. ii. p. 222.

acter." "There does not now exist a people in a tropical climate, or even approaching to it, where slavery does not exist that is in a state of high civilization. Mexico and the South American republics, having gone through the farce of abolishing slavery, are rapidly degenerating." "Cuba is daily and rapidly advancing in industry and civilization; and it is owing exclusively to her slaves. St. Domingo is struck out of the map of civilized existence, and the British West Indies shortly will be so." "Greece is still barbarous, and scantily peopled." "Such is the picture of Italy — nothing has dealt upon it more heavily than the loss of domestic slavery. Is not this evident?" *

A writer in the same work, speaking of the future of the South, refers to the British and French West Indies as follows: —

"The mind of the devout person who contemplates the condition of the *ci-devant* slave-colonies of these two powers, must become impressed with the fact, that Providence must have raised up those two examples of human folly for the express purpose of a lesson to these States, to save which from human errors it has, on more than one occasion, manifestly and directly interposed." "England itself . . . is in some sort the slave of southern blacks."

"The few articles which are most necessary to

---

* De Bow, vol. ii. pp. 222–229.

modern civilization — sugar, coffee, cotton, and tobacco, are products of compulsory black labor." *

Another writer, whom I take to be a clergyman and a Jesuit,† goes so far as to forbid all sympathy for the sufferings of slaves: —

"Sympathy for them could do them no good, because a relief from slavery could not elevate them — could do them no good, but an injury. Hence such sympathy is forbidden;" meaning it is forbidden by God, in such passages as this: "Thine eye shall not pity him" (Deut. xix. 13). He maintains that African slavery is a punishment divinely inflicted on the descendants of Ham for his offence. Ham, he thinks, married a descendant of Cain, and his children inherited the "mark" set upon the first murderer!

Let us now look at some facts connected with slavery in America.

No nation has, on the whole, treated its African slaves so gently as the Americans. This is proved by the rapid increase of the slave population. Com-

* De Bow, vol. iii. pp. 39, 40.

† "John Fletcher of Louisiana," in his "Studies on Slavery in (119) Easy Lessons." Natchez, 1852. 8vo. pp. xiv. and 637. The author luxuriates in the idea of slavery, and gives the public a paradigm of the Hebrew verb עָבַד, *to slave*, in *kal, niphal, pihel, puhol, hiphil, hophal, hithpael;* and a declension of the "*factitious euphonic segholate*" noun, עֶבֶד, *a slave.*

pare America in this respect with some of the British West Indies.*

In seventy-three years, from 1702 to 1775, the increase of the colored population of Jamaica, was 158,614; but in that period there were imported and retained in the island 360,622; so the slave-owners in seventy-three years, must have used up and destroyed about 300,000 human beings. This dreadful exploitation continued a long time. From 1775 to 1794, about 113,000 more were imported; but in 1791 there were only 260,000 colored persons in Jamaica. In sixteen years, the loss was more than 47,000 greater than the entire importation. To say it all in a word: in 1702, Jamaica started with 36,000 slaves; up to 1791, she had imported and retained in bondage 473,000 more; making a total of 509,000 souls, and in 1791, she had only 260,000 to show as the result of her traffic in human souls. There was a waste of 249,000 lives! †

About 750,000 slaves were imported into Jamaica between 1650 and 1808. If that number seems ex-

---

* In 1658 there were in Jamaica	1,400 slaves.
1670 " " "	8,000 "
1673 " " "	9,504 "
1702 " " "	36,000 "
1734 " " "	86,546 "
1775 " " "	194,614 " and free colored persons.

† From '91 to 1808, about 150,000 more were imported, and the slave population in 1808 was only 323,827, showing a waste of more than 86,000 lives in eighteen years! Importation was ille-

cessive, diminish it to 700,000, which is certainly below the fact, then add all the children born in the one hundred and eighty-four years which elapsed before the day of emancipation came. Remember that only 311,000 were there to be emancipated in 1834, and it is plain what a dreadful massacre of human life had been going on in that garden of the western world.*

---

gal, but still carried on after the latter date; at least 80,000 must have been smuggled in, in the next nine years.

In 1817 the number of slaves was	346,150
In 1826 it had fallen to . . .	331,119
In 1833 " . . .	311,692

After the importation ceased, more pains was taken to preserve the Africans; but the table shows how mortality went on with increased velocity.

Years.	Registered Births.	Registered Deaths.
From 1817 to 1820	24,348	25,104
" 1823 to 1826	23,026	25,171
" 1826 to 1829	21,728	25,137

* The same thing took place in all the British West Indies. Look at the following

Table of Slave Population of British Guiana.

Number in 1820	77,376
" 1826	71,382
" 1832	65,517
Loss in twelve years	11,859

Table of Births and Deaths.

Years.	Registered Births.	Registered Deaths.
1817 to 1820	4,868	7,140
1820 to 1823	4,512	7,188
1823 to 1826	4,494	7,634
1826 to 1829	4,684	5,731
1829 to 1832	4,086	7,016

About 1,700,000 slaves have been imported into the British West Indies. Of all this number, and the vast families of children born thereof, in 1834, there were only 780,993 to be emancipated.

Look at the course of things in the United States. In 1714, the number of colored persons was 58,850; in 1850, 3,626,985.*

The United States can show ten Africans now living for every one brought into the country, while the British West Indies, in 1834, could not show one living man for each two brought thither as slaves.†

A Texan newspaper, the Columbian Planter, of

---

* Here is a conjectural and approximate

Table of Importation of African Slaves to the United States.

Before	1714	30,000
From 1715 to 1750		90,000
" 1750 to 1760		35,000
" 1760 to 1770		74,000
" 1770 to 1790		34,000
After 1790		70,000
	Total,	333,500

† The above facts, and the authorities for them, are taken from a valuable and readable book by H. C. Carey, "The Slave-Trade, Domestic and Foreign; why it exists, and how it may be extinguished." Philadelphia, 1853. 1 vol. 12mo. pp. 426. Another work, by M. Charles Comte, contains much information relative to slavery, and its effects in ancient and modern times: "Traité de Législation ou Exposition des Lois Générales suivant lesquelles les Peuples prospérent, deperissent, ou restent stationaires," etc. (3me Edition. Bruxelles. 1837.) Livre v.

In De Bow, vol. ii. p. 340, *et seq.*, is a statement of the importa-

April 5, 1853, deprecates all discussion of slavery, and thus speaks of the slave code of that State; — "We consider it the duty of the County Court to have these local laws compiled and printed in a cheap form, and a copy placed on each plantation in the county. But we cannot, with what we consider the true policy and interest of the South, open the columns of the Planter for their publication."

"We regard the institution of domestic slavery as purely a local subject which should lie at the feet of the Southern Press with deathlike silence; for its great importance will not admit of its discussion."

---

tion of Slaves to Charleston, from 1804 to 1807, whence I construct the following

Table of South Carolina Slave-Trade, 1804–1807.

70	vessels	owned in	England . .	brought	19,649	slaves.
3	"	"	France . .	"	1,078	"
61	"	"	Charleston .	"	7,723	"
59	"	"	Rhode Island .	"	8,238	"
4	"	"	Baltimore . .	"	750	"
3	"	"	other Southern Ports	"	787	"
3	"	"	" Northern Ports	"	650	"
					39,075	

Of these, 3,433 were imported on account of citizens of the slave-holding States, and 35,642 on account of capitalists in countries where slavery was prohibited! Newport, in Rhode Island, was famous for the slave-trade, and its prosperity fell with that business. The cost of paving the only street in the town paved with stone, was defrayed by a tax of ten dollars on each slave brought into the harbor! So late as 1850, Boston vessels were engaged in the African slave-trade. The domestic slave-trade still employs many northern vessels, — 1033 slaves were shipped at Baltimore, for various southern ports in 1851.

I will mention three cases of cruelty which have lately come to my knowledge. A black free man in a city of Kentucky, had a wife who was a slave. One evening her master, who had a grudge against the husband, found him in the kitchen with her, and ordered him out of the house. He went, but left the gate of the back yard open as he passed out. The white man ordered him to return and shut it; the black man grumbled and refused; whereupon the white man shot him dead! The murderer was a "class leader" in the church, and attended a meeting shortly after this transaction. He was asked to "comfort the souls of the meeting, and improve his gift" by some words of exhortation. He declined on the ground that he felt dissatisfied with himself, that he himself "needed to be strengthened, and wished for the prayers of the brethren." They appointed a committee to look into the matter, who reported that he had done nothing wrong. The affair was also brought before a magistrate, who dismissed the case!

Here is another yet more atrocious. A slave-holder in South Carolina had inflicted a brutal and odious mutilation, which cannot be named, on two male slaves, for some offence. Last year, the master attempted to inflict the same barbarity upon a third slave. He ordered another black man to help bind the victim. The slave, struggling against them both, seized a knife, killed the master, and then took his own life.

The neighbors came together, ascertained the facts, and hung up the slave's dead body at the next four corners, as a terror to the colored people of the place! No account of it was published in the newspapers. Slavery "should lie at the feet of the Southern Press with deathlike silence!"

While writing this address I receive intelligence of a slave woman recently whipped to death in Missouri. An incautious German, who had not been long enough in the country to become converted to "American Christianity," and so callous to such things, published an account of the transaction in a German newspaper. The murderers were not punished.

The following advertisement is taken from a newspaper published in Wilmington (North Carolina) in March, 1853. Nothing in Mrs. Stowe's work is so atrocious; for American fiction halts this side of the American fact: —

225 Dollars Reward. — State of North Carolina, New Hanover County. — Whereas, complaint upon oath has this day been made to us, two of the Justices of the Peace for the State and county aforesaid, by Benjamin Hallett, of the said county, that two certain male slaves belonging to him, named Lott, aged about twenty-two years, five feet four or five inches high, and black, formerly belonging to Lott Williams, of Onslow Co.; and Bob, aged about sixteen years, five feet high, and black, have absented themselves from their said master's service, and supposed to be lurking about this county, committing acts of felony and other misdeeds. These are, therefore, in the name of the State aforesaid, to command the said slaves forthwith to return home to

their masters; and we do hereby, by virtue of the Act of the General Assembly in such cases made and provided, intimate and declare, that if the said Lott and Bob do not return home and surrender themselves, any person may kill and destroy the said slaves, by such means as he or they may think of without accusation or impeachment of any crime or offence for so doing, and without incurring any penalty or forfeiture thereby.

Given under our hands and seals, this 28th day of February, 1853.

W. N. PEDEN, J. P. [seal.]
W. C. BETTENCOURT, J. P. [seal.]

225 DOLLARS REWARD. — Two hundred dollars will be given for negro Lott, either dead or alive; and twenty-five dollars for Bob's head, delivered to the subscriber in the town of Wilmington.

BENJAMIN HALLETT.

March 2, 1853.

I will next proceed to show some of the effects of Democracy at the North, and Despotism at the South.

First notice the effect on the Increase of Population. In 1790, the entire population of the territory now occupied by the slave States was 1,961,372, exclusive of Indians; that of the free States was 1,968,455.

In 1850, with an addition of immense territories — Florida, Louisiana, Texas, New Mexico — the population of the Slave States amounted to 9,719,779; the free States and Territories, not including Oregon and California, had 13,348,371 souls. The population of the free States has increased about six hundred per cent., that of the slave only about four hundred per cent.

Let us compare a free and a slave State which lie side by side. In soil and climate, Kentucky is superior to Ohio — only the stream separates them. Slavery is on one side, freedom on the other, and what a difference!

Kentucky contains 37,680 square miles. It is well watered with navigable rivers — the Ohio, Cumberland, Kentucky, Green, and Salt. The soil is admirable, producing abundantly; the climate mild and salubrious. It abounds in minerals — coal, iron, lead. The salt springs were famous even with the French and Indians. Rice, cotton, and the sugar-cane grow in Kentucky.

Ohio contains 39,964 square miles of land, no better watered, with a soil not superior, less favored with mineral riches, yet also abounding in iron and coal; the climate is sterner, the water power less copious.

In 1790, Kentucky had 73,077 inhabitants, Ohio not a white man. In 1800, Kentucky had 220,959; Ohio only 45,365. But in 1850, Kentucky had only 982,405, while Ohio had grown to 1,980,427 souls. To-day, Kentucky has not 775,000 freemen, while Ohio has more than 2,000,000.

In 1810, Louisville, the capital of Kentucky, numbered 4,012 persons; Cincinnati, the chief town of Ohio, contained 9,644. Now Louisville has less than

50,000, and Cincinnati more than 150,000; while Cleveland and Columbus, in the same State, have risen from nothing to cities each containing 20,000 inhabitants.

Look next at the effect of these different institutions on the Productive Industry of the different sections of the land. In the North, labor is respected. In 1845, there were in Boston 19,037 private families; there were 15,744 who kept no servant, and only 1,069 who had more than one. Is Boston poor? In 1854, the property of her citizens, taxable on the spot, is more than $225,000,000.

In 1847, the real property in Boston was valued at $97,764,500, $45,271,120 more than the value of all the real estate of South Carolina, with her 24,500 square miles of land. South Carolina "owns" 384,984 slaves; at $400 a head, they would come to $153,993,600. The actual property of the inhabitants of Boston, in 1854, is sufficient to buy all those slaves, and then leave a balance sufficient to pay the market value of all the houses and land in that proud State.

In 1839, the census value of the annual agricultural products of the entire South was $312,380,151; that of the free States $342,007,446. Yet the South had an advantage by nature, and 249,780 more persons engaged in agriculture.

The manufactures of the South for that year were worth $42,178,184; of the North, $197,658,040.

The aggregate earnings of all the South were $403,429,718, of the North $658,705,108. The entire earnings of the two Carolinas, Georgia, Alabama, Mississippi, and Louisiana, amounted to $189,321,719; those of New York to $193,806,433.

Omitting the territories and California from the estimate, in 1850, the fifteen slave States contained 190,297,188 acres of land in farms; the fifteen Northern States only 97,087,778 acres. But the Northern farms were worth $283,023,483, while the Southern were valued at only $253,583,234. The South has 93,000,000 acres the most land, and it is worth $30,000,000 the least.

The South has invested $95,918,842 in manufacturing establishments which give an annual return of $167,906,350: while the North has $431,290,351 in manufactures with a yearly earning of $845,430,428.

In 1853, the South had 438,297 tons of shipping; at $40 a ton it was worth $17,331,880. The North had 3,831,047 tons worth $153,241,880.

On the first of September, 1852, the South had 2,144 miles of railroad; the North 9,661 miles. The cost of 1,140 miles of railroad in Massachusetts with its equipment was $56,559,982.

In 1850, the aggregate value of all the property real and personal of the fifteen slave States was $2,755,411,554; that of fifteen free States — omitting California — was $3,186,683,924. But in the southern estimate the value of the working men is included; appraising the 3,200,412 at $400 apiece, they come to $1,280,164,800: deduct this from the gross sum, and there remains $1,475,246,754 as the worth of all the material property of all the persons in the fifteen slave States; while the inhabitants of the free States have material property amounting to $3,186,683,924.

The different effects of democracy and despotism appear in the higher forms of industry — the Inventions which perform the work of human hands. From 1790 to 1849, there were 16,514 patents granted for inventions made in the free States, and only 2,202 in the slave States. I omit patents granted to citizens of the District of Columbia, and to foreigners. In 1851, 64 patents were granted to citizens of the slave States; 656 to those of the free States. Besides, many of the Southern patents are granted to men born and bred at the North.

It is not too much to say, that the machinery of Pennsylvania, New York, and Massachusetts, driven by water and steam, earns every year more than all the three million slaves of the entire South. Even Chancellor Harper confesses that "free labor is cheaper than the labor of slaves." The South kidnaps men, breeds them as cattle, brands them as cattle, beats them as cattle, sells them as cattle — does not know "whether they have a soul or not;" declares them cursed by God, not fit for human sympathy, incapable of development, indifferent to liberty, to chastity, without natural affection; breaks up their marriages, forbids them to be taught reading and writing — behold the practical results!

Look at the effect of these two institutions, the democratic and the despotic, on the Intellectual Education of the people, in the North and South.

In 1839, there were in the slave States, at schools and colleges, 301,172 pupils; in the free States, 2,212,444 pupils at school and college. New York sends, to school and college, more than twice as many young persons as all the slave States.

At that time there were in Connecticut 163,843 free persons over twenty years of age; of these only 526 were unable to read and write. In South Carolina, there were 111,663 free persons over twenty, and of these 20,615 were reported as unable to write or read. The ignorant men of Connecticut were almost all foreigners, those of South Carolina natives of that soil. A sixth part of the voters of South Carolina are unable to read the ballot they cast.

According to the census of 1850, in the year 1849, the South paid $2,717,771 for public Schools; the North $6,834,388. The South had 976,966 children at School; the North 3,106,961.

The South had 2,867,567 native whites over twenty years of age; of these 532,605 were unable even to read — more than eighteen per cent. In the North there were 6,649,001 native whites over twenty, and only 278,575 thus illiterate — not four and one fourth per cent.

In 1850, there were in the United States 2,800 newspapers and other periodicals, from the daily to the quarterly, issuing annually about 422,700,000 copies, to about 5,000,000 subscribers. Of these journals, 716 were in the slave States — including those printed in the capital of America — and 2,084 in the free States. The circulation of southern periodicals, however, is limited: their average is not more than one half or two thirds that of the northern journals.

Almost all who are eminent in science, literature, or art, — naturalists, historians, poets, preachers — are northern men. The southern pulpit produces nothing remarkable but Evidences of the Divinity of Slavery.

The respective Military Power of the democratic and despotic institutions was abundantly tested in the revolutionary war. From 1775 to 1783, the free population of the slave States was 1,307,549; there were also 657,527 slaves. New England contained 673,215 free persons, and 3,886 slaves. During the nine years of that war, the slave States furnished the continental army with 58,421 regular soldiers; New England alone furnished 118,380 regulars. The slave States had also 12,719 militia-men, and New England 46,048 militia-men.

After the battle of Bunker Hill, when the States in Congress were called on to furnish soldiers, South

Carolina, in consequence of her "peculiar institutions," asked that hers might remain at home. In 1779 (March 29th) a committee of Congress reported that "the State of South Carolina is unable to make any effectual effort, with militia, by reason of the great proportion of the citizens necessary to remain at home to prevent insurrection among the negroes, and prevent the desertion of them to the enemy." From 1775 to 1783, South Carolina contained 166,018 free persons, Connecticut only 158,760. During the nine years of the war, South Carolina sent 5,508 soldiers to the army, and Connecticut 39,831. While the six slave States could raise only 58,421 soldiers, and 12,779 militia-men; Massachusetts alone contributed 67,937 soldiers to the continental army, and 15,155 militia-men — in all 83,092!

The Demoralizing Influence of American Despotism is fearfully obvious in the conduct of the General Government. It debases the legislative and the executive power; the Supreme Court is its venal prostitute. You remember the Inaugural of Mr. Pierce: —

"I believe that involuntary servitude is recognized by the Constitution. I believe that it stands like any other admitted right. I hold that the laws of 1850 [the Fugitive Slave Act] commonly called the 'compromise measures,' are strictly constitutional, and to be unhesitatingly carried out." "The laws to enforce these [rights to property in the body and soul of men,] should be respected and obeyed, not with a reluctance encouraged by abstract opinions as to their propriety in a different state of society, but cheerfully, and according to the decisions of the tribunal to which their exposition belongs."

The effect of Slavery on the Morality of the North is painful to reflect upon. Northern merchants engage in the internal slave-trade; in the foreign slave-trade; they own plantations at the South; they lend money to the South, and take slaves as security. The Northern church is red with the guilt of bondage; most of its eminent preachers are deadly enemies to the freedom of the African. How many clerical defenders has the Fugitive Slave Act found in the North? The court house furnished kidnappers at Philadelphia, New York, and Boston; the Church justified them in the name of God. I know of no Church which has ever showed itself more cowardly than the American. Since 1849, the Bible Society dares not distribute the Scriptures to slaves. The American Tract Society adapts its publications to the Southern market, by expunging every word hostile to the patriarchal institution. Mr. Gurney says, "If this love had always prevailed among professing Christians, where would have been the sword of the crusader? *Where the African slave-trade? Where the odious system which permits to man a property in his fellow man, and converts rational beings into mar-*

ketable chattels?" The American Tract Society alters the text, and instead of what I have italicized, it prints: "Where the tortures of the Inquisition? Where every system of oppression and wrong by which he who has the power revels in luxury and ease at the expense of his fellow men!"

In 1850 and 1851, the most prominent preachers in the North came out in public and justified the kidnapping of men in Philadelphia, New York, and Boston. It is true some noble ministers lifted up their voice against it; but the theological leaders went for man-stealing, and knew no Higher Law.

Commercial and political journals denounced every minister who applied the golden rule of the Gospel to the poor fugitives from Slavery. Several clergymen were driven from their parishes in Massachusetts, because they preached against kidnapping. Metropolitan newspapers invited merchants to refuse to trade with towns where the Fugitive Slave Bill was unpopular: lawyers and doctors opposed to Slavery must not be employed.

Anti-slavery sentiments are carefully excluded from school-books: the writers want a Southern market. The principal men in the Northern colleges appear to be on the side of oppression. The political and commercial Press of the North is mainly on the side of the slave-holder. While preparing this paper, I find in a northern newspaper — the Boston Courier of April 26, 1853 — an advertisement as follows: —

"A RARE CHANCE FOR CAPITALISTS!

"FOR SALE.

"The Pulaski House, at Savannah, and Furniture, and a number of PRIME NEGROES, accustomed to hotel business," etc.

The advertisement is dated "Savannah, 19*th April*."

On that day, 1851, Boston landed at Savannah a man whom she had kidnapped in her own streets: on that day, in 1775, a few miles from Boston, a handful of farmers and mechanics first drew the sword of America against the oppressions of her parent, "in the sacred cause of God and their country." Nemesis is never asleep! If men are to be advertised for sale in a Boston newspaper, it is well that the advertisement should date from the Battle of Lexington, or the Declaration of Independence.

Last year the State of Illinois passed "An Act to prevent the immigration of free negroes" into that State. A man who brings a free negro or mulatto into the State is to be fined not less than $100, nor more than $500, and to be imprisoned not more than a year. Every negro thus coming, shall be fined fifty dollars, and, if unable to pay, shall be sold to any person "who will pay said fine and costs, for the shortest time." "Every person who shall have one fourth negro blood shall be deemed a mulatto." Delaware has just passed a similar law, though with penalties less severe.

In the commercial journals of the free and the slave States, the most scandalous abuse has been poured out upon Mrs. Stowe for her Uncle Tom's Cabin, and its Key. "Priestess of Darkness" is one of the pleasant epithets applied to her. The Duchess of Sutherland receives, also, a large share of abuse from the same quarter. When the kidnapper is honored; when "prime negroes" are advertised for sale; when clergymen recommend man-stealing in the name of Christ and of God, it is very proper that ladies of genius and philanthropy should be held up as objects of scorn and contempt! Men who know no Law higher than the Fugitive Slave Bill, must work after their kind.

It is a strange spectacle which America just now offers. Exiles flee hither, four hundred thousand in a year, and are welcome; while Americans born take their lives in their hand, and fly to Canada, to Nova Scotia, for an asylum. Unsuccessful "rebels," who have committed "treason" at home, find a shelter in America, a welcome, and the protection of the democratic government; while 3,300,000 men, guilty of no crime, are kept in a bondage worse than Siberian. The "chief judicial officer" of South Carolina thinks of all "distinguishing characteristics" of the negroes "the most remarkable is their indifference to personal liberty." But democratic Calhoun, with Clay, Webster, and all the leaders of the South, must unite to make the Fugitive Slave Bill, and hinder those men who are indifferent to personal liberty from running away! After all the tumult, fifteen hundred fugitives got safely out of the slave soil of the United States in the year 1853. Alas, they must escape to the territories of a monarch! Of all the ground covered by the Declaration of Independence, not an inch is free soil, except the five thousand miles which Britain regained by the Ashburton treaty. Every foot of monarchic British soil can change a slave to a free man; while in all the three million square miles of democratic America there is not an inch of land where he can claim the natural and unalienable right to life, liberty, and the pursuit of happiness. English is the only tongue for liberty; it is also the only speech in which kidnapping is justified by the clergy in the name of God. The despots of the European continent point with delight to the American democrats enslaving one another, and declaring there is no Higher Law.

There can be no lasting peace between the two conflicting ideas I have named above. One wants a Democracy, the other a Despotism; each is incursive, aggressive, exterminating. Which shall yield? The answer is plain: Slavery is to perish out of America; Democracy is to triumph. Every census makes the result of the two ideas more apparent. The North increases in numbers, in riches, in the intellectual development of the great mass of its people — out of all proportion to the South. Slavery is a bad tool to work with. In the South, there is little skilled labor, little variety of industry; rude farm labor, rearing corn, coffee, tobacco, sugar, cotton, that is all. At Boston, at New York, on the Kennebec, and the Penobscot, northern men build ships of oak from Virginia, and hard pine from Georgia; they get the pitch and tar from Carolina, the hemp from Kentucky — that State which has no shipping. Labor is cheap on the fair land of the Carolinas, the best in the world for red wheat; labor is dear in Pennsylvania, but she undersells the Carolinas in the wheat market. Tennessee has rich mines of iron ore — the fine bloomer iron; slave labor is cheap, coal abundant. Work is dear in Pennsylvania; but there free labor makes better iron at cheaper rates. The South is full of water power; within six miles of the President's house there is force enough to turn all the mills of British Manchester; it runs by as idle as a cloud. The southerner draws water in a northern bucket, drinks from a northern cup; with a northern fork and spoon he eats from a northern dish, set on a northern table. He wears northern shoes made from southern hides; northern coats, hats, shirts; he keeps time with a northern watch; his wife wears northern jewels, plays on a northern pianoforte; he sleeps in a northern bed; reads (if read he can) a northern book; and writes (if writing be not a figure of speech) on northern paper, with a pen from the North. The laws of Mississippi must be printed in a northern town! The southerner has no market near at hand, no variety of labor, little that is educational in toil; industry is dishonorable. It is the curse of Slavery which makes it so!

Three forces now work against this institution: Political Economy, showing that it does not pay; the Public Opinion of England, France, Germany, of all Christendom, heaping shame on the "model republic" — "the first and most enlightened nation in the world;" the still small voice of Conscience in all men. The Political Economist scoffs at the absolute Right; the Partisan Politician mocks at the Higher Law; the Pharisee in the pulpit makes mouths at the invisible Spirit, which silently touches the hearts of women and of men. But he who knows the world because he knows Man, and man's God, understands very well that though Justice has feet of wool, her hands are of iron. These three forces — it is plain what they will do with American Slavery.

This institution of Slavery has brought us into most deadly peril. A story is told of some Italian youths, of famous family in the Middle Ages. Borgia and his comrades sat riotously feasting, long past midnight, hot with young blood, giddy with passion, crazed with fiery wine. In their intemperate laughter they hear the hoarse voice of monks in the street, coming round the corner, chanting the Miserere as service for the dying, Have mercy upon me, oh God, according to thy loving-kindness! "What is that?" cries one. "O," answers another, "it is only some poor soul going to hell, and the priests are trying to cheat the devil of his due! Push round the wine." Again comes the chant, For I acknowledge my transgression, and my sin is ever before me! "How near it is; under the windows," says a reveller, turning pale, "What if it should be meant for one of us; let me look." He opens the window, the torches flash in from the dark street, and the chant pours on them, Purge me with hyssop, and I shall be clean: wash me, and I shall be whiter than snow! They all spring to their feet. "Whom is it for," they cry out. Deliver me from blood-guiltiness oh God, thou God of my salvation; and my tongue shall sing aloud of thy righteousness, is the answer. They throw open the door — the mother of Borgia rushes in; "You are all dead men," she cries, "I poisoned the wine myself. Confess and make your peace with God, here are his ministers." The white-robed priests fill up the room chanting, The sacrifices of God are a broken spirit; a broken and a contrite heart, oh God, thou wilt not despise! "But here is an antidote for my son," cries the mother of Borgia, "Take it!" He dashes the cup on the ground — and the gay company lies there, pale-blue, poisoned, and dead! Shall that be the fate of America? Yes; if she cast the cup of healing to the ground! Other admonitions must come, yet more terrible, before we learn for whom the Miserere is now wailing forth.

If America were to keep this shameful pest in the land, then ruin is sure to follow, — ruin of all the dear-bought institutions of our fathers. The slaves double in about twenty-five years; so in A. D. 1930, there would be 27,000,000 of slaves! What a thought! The question is not merely, shall we have Slavery and Freedom, but Slavery OR Freedom. The two cannot long continue side by side.

When this hindrance is taken away, there is a noble career open before this young giant. There is a new continent, now for the first time married to the civilized world. Various races of men mingle their blood — Indians, Africans, Caucasians; various tribes — Celtic Irish, Welsh, Scotch, Anglo-Saxon, Norwegian, Swedish, Danish, Dutch, German, Polish, Swiss, French, Spanish; all these are here. Each will contribute its best to the general stock. Democratic institutions, and democratic education will give an intellectual development to the mass of men such as the world never saw. There is no fear of war; the army and the navy do not number thirty thousand men. The energies of the nation will be directed to their natural work — subduing material Nature, and developing human Nature into its higher forms. Now we are excessively material in our tastes — one day, if this great obstacle be overcome, America will be eminent also for science, letters, art, and for the noblest virtues which adorn mankind. No nation had ever so fair an opportunity — shall we be false to our origin, and the heart's high hope? Humanity says, "No!"

THE NEW CRIME AGAINST HUMANITY.

A

SERMON

PREACHED AT

THE MUSIC HALL, IN BOSTON,

ON

SUNDAY, JUNE 4, 1854.

WITH THE LESSON FOR THE DAY OF THE PREVIOUS SUNDAY.

INTRODUCTORY.

On Sunday, May 28, after the usual introductory services, Mr. Parker pronounced the following

LESSON FOR THE DAY.

I see by your faces, as well as by your number, what is expected of me to-day. A person has just sent me a request, asking me, "Cannot you extemporize a sermon for this day?" It is easier to do it than not. But I shall not extemporize a Sermon for to-day — I shall extemporize the Scripture. I therefore pass over the Bible words which I designed to read from the Old Testament and the New, and will take the Morning Lesson from the circumstances of the past week. The time has not come for me to preach a sermon on the great wrong now enacting in this city. The deed is not yet fully done: any counsel that I have to offer is better given elsewhere than here, at another time than now. Neither you nor I are quite calm enough to-day to look the matter fairly in the face, and see entirely what it means. Before the events of the past week took place, I had proposed to preach this morning, on the subject of War, taking my theme from the present commotions in Europe, which also will reach us, and have already. That will presently be the theme of my morning's sermon. Next Sunday, I shall preach on THE PERILS INTO WHICH AMERICA IS BROUGHT AT THIS DAY BY THE NEW CRIME AGAINST HUMANITY. That is the theme for next Sunday: the other is for to-day. But before I proceed to that, I have some words to say in place of the Scripture lesson, and instead of a selection from the Old Testament prophets.

Since last we came together, there has been a man stolen in this city of our fathers. It is not the first; it may not be the last. He is now in the great slave-pen in the city of Boston. He is there against the law of the Commonwealth, which, if I am rightly informed, in such cases prohibits the use of State edifices as United States jails. I may be mistaken. Any forcible attempt to take him from that barracoon of Boston, would be wholly without use. For, beside the holiday soldiers who belong to the city of Boston, and are ready to shoot down their brothers in a just or an unjust cause, any day when the city government gives them its command and its liquor, I understand that there are one hundred and eighty-four United States marines lodged in the Court House, every man of them furnished with a musket and a bayonet, with his side arms, and twenty-four ball cartridges. They are stationed, also, in a very strong building, and where five men, in a passage way about the width of this pulpit, can defend it against five-and-twenty, or a hundred. To "keep the peace," the Mayor, who, the other day, "regretted the arrest" of our brother, Anthony Burns, and declared that his sympathies were wholly with the alleged fugitive — and of course wholly against the claimant and the Marshal — in order to keep the peace of the city, the Mayor must become corporal of the guard for kidnappers from Virginia. He must keep the peace of our city, and defend these guests of Boston over the graves, the unmonumented graves, of John Hancock and Samuel Adams.

A man has been killed by violence. Some say he was killed by his own coadjutors: I can easily believe it; there is evidence enough that they were greatly frightened. They were not United States soldiers, but volunteers from the streets of Boston, who, for their pay, went into the Court House to assist in kidnapping a brother man. They were so cowardly that they could not use the simple cutlasses they had in their hands, but smote right and left, like ignorant and frightened ruffians as they are. They may have slain their brother or not — I cannot tell. It is said by some that they killed him. Another story is, that he was killed by a hostile hand from without. Some say by a bullet, some by an axe, and others still by a knife. As yet, nobody knows the facts. But a man has been killed. He was a volunteer in this service. He liked the business of enslaving a man, and has gone to render an account to God for his gratuitous wickedness. Twelve men have been arrested, and are now in jail to await their examination for wilful murder!

Here, then, is one man butchered, and twelve men brought in peril of their lives. Why is this? Whose fault is it?

Some eight years ago, a Boston merchant, by his mercenaries kidnapped a man "between Faneuil Hall and old Quincy," and carried him off to eternal slavery. Boston mechanics, the next day, held up the half-eagles which they received as pay for stealing a man. The matter was brought before the Grand Jury for the County of Suffolk, and abundant evidence was presented, as I understand, but they found "no bill." A wealthy merchant, in the name of trade, had stolen a black man, who, on board a ship, had come to this city, had been seized by the mercenaries of this merchant, kept by them for a while, and then, when he escaped, kidnapped a second time in the city of Boston. Boston did not punish the deed!

The Fugitive Slave Bill was presented to us, and Boston rose up to welcome it! The greatest man in all the North came here, and in this city told Massachusetts she must obey the Fugitive Slave Bill with alacrity — that we must all conquer our prejudices in favor of justice and the unalienable rights of man. Boston did conquer her prejudices in favor of justice and the unalienable rights of man.

Do you not remember the "Union Meeting" which was held in Faneuil Hall, when a "political soldier of fortune," sometimes called the "Democratic Prince of the Devils," howled at the idea that there was a Law of God higher than the Fugitive Slave Bill? He sneered, and asked, "Will you have the 'Higher Law of God' to rule over you?" and the multitude which occupied the floor, and the multitude that crowded the galleries, howled down the Higher Law of God! They treated the Higher Law to a laugh and a howl! That was Tuesday night. It was the Tuesday before Thanksgiving day. On that Thanksgiving day, I told the congregation that the men who howled down the Higher Law of Almighty God, had got Almighty God to settle with; that they had sown the wind, and would reap the whirlwind. At that Meeting, Mr. Choate told the people — "REMEMBER! REMEMBER! *Remember!*" Then nobody knew what to "remember." Now you know. That is the state of that case.

Then you "remember" the kidnappers came here to seize Thomas Sims. Thomas Sims was seized. Nine days he was on trial for more than his life, and never saw a judge — never saw a jury. He was sent back into bondage from the city of Boston. You remember the chains that were put around the Court House; you remember the judges of Massachusetts stooping, crouching, creeping, crawling, under the chain of Slavery, in order to get to their own courts. All these things you "remember." Boston was non-resistant. She gave her "back to the smiters" — from the South; she "withheld not her cheek" — from the scorn of South Carolina, and welcomed the "spitting" of kidnappers from Georgia and Virginia. To-day we have our pay for such conduct. You have not forgotten the "fifteen hundred gentlemen of property and standing," who volunteered to conduct Mr. Sims to Slavery, — Marshal Tukey's "gentlemen." They "remember" it. They are sorry enough now. Let us forgive — we need not forget. "REMEMBER! REMEMBER! *Remember!*"

The Nebraska Bill has just now been passed. Who passed it? The fifteen hundred "gentlemen of property and standing" in Boston, who, in 1851, volunteered to carry Thomas Sims into Slavery by force of arms. They passed the Nebraska Bill. If Boston had punished the kidnapping of 1845, there would have been no Fugitive Slave Bill in 1850. If Massachusetts, in 1850, had declared the bill should not be executed, the kidnapper would never have shown his face in the streets of Boston. If, failing in this, Boston had said, in 1851, "Thomas Sims shall not be carried off," and forcibly or peacefully, by the majesty of the great mass of men, had resisted it, no kidnapper would have come here again. There would have been no Nebraska Bill. But to every demand of the Slave power, Massachusetts has said "Yes, yes! — we grant it all!" "Agitation must cease!" "Save the Union!"

Southern Slavery is an institution which is in earnest. Northern Freedom is an institution that is not in earnest. It was in earnest in '76 and '83. It has not been much in earnest since. The Compromises are but provisional! Slavery is the only finality! Now, since the Nebraska Bill is passed, an attempt is made to add insult to insult, injury to injury. Last week, at New York, a brother of Rev. Dr. Pennington, an established clergyman, of large reputation, great character, acknowledged learning, who has his diploma from the University of Heidelberg, in Germany, — a more honorable source than that from which any clergyman in Massachusetts has received one, — his brother and two nephews were kidnapped in New York, and without any trial, without any defence, were hurried off into bondage. Then at Boston, you know what was done in the last four days. Behold the consequences of the doctrine that there is no Higher Law. Look at Boston, to-day. There are no chains round your Court House — there are only ropes round it this time. A hundred and eighty-four United States soldiers are there. They are, I am told, mostly foreigners — the scum of the earth — none but such enter into armies as common soldiers, in a country like ours. I say it with pity — they are not to blame for having been born where they were and what they are. I pity the scum as well as I pity the mass of men. The soldiers are there, I say, and their trade is to kill. Why is this so?

You remember the meeting at Faneuil Hall, last Friday, when even the words of my friend, Wendell Phillips, the most eloquent words that get spoken in America, in this century, hardly restrained the multitude from going, and by violence storming the Court House. What stirred them up? It was the spirit of our fathers — the spirit of justice and liberty in your heart, and in my heart, and in the heart of us all. Sometimes it gets the better of a man's prudence, especially on occasions like this; and so excited was that assembly of four or five thousand men, that even the words of eloquent Wendell Phillips could hardly restrain them from going at once rashly to the Court House, and tearing it to the ground.

Boston is the most peaceful of cities. Why? Because we have commonly had a peace which was worth keeping. No city respects laws so much. Because the laws have been made by the people, for the people, and are laws which respect justice. Here is a law which the people will not keep. It is a law of our Southern masters; a law not fit to keep.

Why is Boston in this confusion to-day? The Fugitive Slave Bill Commissioner has just now been sowing the wind, that we may may reap the whirlwind. The old Fugitive Slave Bill Commissioner stands back; he has gone to look after his "personal popularity." But when Commissioner Curtis does not dare appear in this matter, another man comes forward, and for the first time seeks to kidnap his man also in the city of Boston. Judge Loring is a man whom I have respected and honored. His private life is mainly blameless, so far as I know. He has been, I think, uniformly beloved. His character has entitled him to the esteem of his fellow-citizens. I have known him somewhat. I never heard a mean word from him — many good words. He was once the law-partner of Horace Mann, and learned humanity of a great teacher. I have respected him a good deal. He is a respectable man — in the Boston sense of that word, and in a much higher sense; at least, I have thought so. He is a kind-hearted, charitable man; a good neighbor; a fast friend — when politics do not interfere; charitable with his purse; an excellent husband; a kind father; a good relative. And I should as soon have expected that venerable man who sits before me, born before your Revolution [Samuel May], — I should as soon have expected him to go and kidnap Robert Morris, or any of the other colored men I see around me, as I should have expected Judge Loring to do this thing. But he has sown the wind, and we are reaping the whirlwind. I need not say what I now think of him. He is to act to-morrow, and may yet act like a man. Let us wait and see. Perhaps there is manhood in him yet. But, my friends, all this confusion is his work. He knew he was stealing a Man born with the same unalienable right to "life, liberty, and the pursuit of happiness," as himself. He knew the slave-holders had no more right to Anthony Burns than to his own daughter. He knew the consequences of stealing a man. He knew that there are men in Boston who have not yet conquered their prejudices — men who respect the Higher Law of God. He knew there would be a meeting at Faneuil Hall — gatherings in the streets. He knew there would be violence.

Edward Greeley Loring, Judge of Probate for the County of Suffolk, in the State of Massachusetts, Fugitive Slave Bill Commissioner of the United States, before these citizens of Boston, on Ascension Sunday, assembled to worship God, I charge you with the death of that man who was killed on last Friday night. He was your fellow-servant in kidnapping. He dies at your hand. You fired the shot which makes his wife a widow, his child an orphan. I charge you with the peril of twelve men, arrested for murder, and on trial for their lives. I charge you with filling the Court House with one hundred and eighty-four hired ruffians of the United States, and alarming not only this city for her liberties that are in peril, but stirring up the whole Commonwealth of Massachusetts with indignation, which no man knows how to stop — which no man can stop. You have done it all!

This is my Lesson for the Day.

SERMON.*

"Then one of the twelve, called Judas Iscariot, went unto the chief priests, and said unto them, What will ye give me, and I will deliver him unto you. And they covenanted with him for thirty pieces of silver. And from that time he sought opportunity to betray him. — MATT. 26 : 14–16.

"Then Judas, which had betrayed him, when he saw that he was condemned, repented himself, and brought again the thirty pieces of silver to the chief priests and elders, saying, I have sinned in that I have betrayed the innocent blood. And they said, What is that to us? See thou to that." — MATT. 27 : 3–4.

WITHIN the last few days, we have seen some of the results of despotism in America, which might in-

* The Sermon which follows was printed in the "Boston Commonwealth," on Monday, from the Phonographic Report of Messrs. Slack and Yerrinton. They copied out their notes at my house, and I revised them. We did not complete our labors till half past three o'clock Monday morning. It may easily be imagined that some errors appeared in the print — for the perishable body weigheth down the mind, and though the spirit be willing, the flesh is too weak to work four-and-twenty hours continuously. Yet the errors were surprisingly few. In this edition of the Sermon, some passages have been added which were omitted in the Report, and some also which though written, were not delivered on Sunday.

BOSTON, June 10, 1854.

deed easily astonish a stranger; but a citizen of Boston has no right to be surprised. The condition of this town from May 24th to June 2d is the natural and unavoidable result of well-known causes, publicly and deliberately put in action. It is only the first-fruit of causes which in time will litter the ground with similar harvests, and with others even worse. Let us pretend no amazement that the seed sown has borne fruit after its kind. Let us see what warning or what guidance we can gather from these events, their cause and consequence. So, this morning, I ask your attention to a SERMON OF THE NEW CRIME AGAINST HUMANITY COMMITTED IN THE MIDST OF US, of the LAST KIDNAPPING which has taken place in Boston.

I know well the responsibility of the place I occupy this morning. To-morrow's sun shall carry my words to all America. They will be read on both sides of the continent. They will cross the ocean. It may astonish the minds of men in Europe to hear of the iniquity committed in the midst of us. Let us be calm and cool, and look the thing fairly in the face.

Of course, you will understand, from my connection with what has taken place in part, that I must speak of some things with a good deal of reserve, and others pass by entirely. However, I have only too much to say. I have had but short time for preparation, the deed is so recent. Perhaps I shall trespass a little on your patience this morning, that hand overrunning my customary hour some twenty or thirty minutes. If any of you find their patience exhausted, and standing too wearisome, they can retire; and if without noise, none will be disturbed, and none offended.

On Wednesday night, the 24th of May, a young man, without property, without friends, I will continue to call his name Anthony Burns, was returning home from his usual lawful and peaceful work in the clothing shop of Deacon Pitts, in Brattle street. He was assaulted by six ruffians, who charged him with having broken into a jeweller's shop. They seized him, forced him to the Court House, thrust him into an upper chamber therein, where he was surrounded by men, armed, it is said, with bludgeons and revolvers. There he was charged with being a Fugitive Slave. A man from Virginia claiming to be his owner, and another man, likewise from Virginia, confronted the poor victim, and extorted from him a confession, as they allege, that he was the claimant's Fugitive Slave: if, indeed, the confession was not purely an invention of his foes, who had made the false charge of burglary; for they who begin with a lie are not to be trusted after that lie has been told. He was kept all night, guarded by ruffians hired for the purpose of kidnapping a man. No friend was permitted to see him; but his deadliest foes, who clutched at what every one of us holds tenfold dearer than life itself, were allowed access. They came and went freely, making their inquisition, extorting or inventing admissions to be used for Mr. Burns's ruin.

At nine o'clock, the next morning, Thursday, (May 25th,) the earliest hour at which the courts of Massachusetts ever open, he was brought to the court room and arraigned before Edward Greeley Loring, Judge of Probate, one of the Fugitive Slave Bill Commissioners of the City of Boston, and immediately put on trial. "Intimidated" by the mob about him, and stupefied with terror and fear, he makes no defence. "As a lamb before his shearers is dumb, so he opened not his mouth." How could he dare make a defence, treated as he had been the night before?—confronted as he was by men clutching at his liberty?—in a court room packed with ruffians, where the Slaveholders' counsel brought pistols in their breasts? He had been in duress all night, with inquisitors about him. His claimant was there, with documents manufactured in Alexandria; with a witness brought from Richmond; with two lawyers of Boston to aid them.

What a scene it was for a Massachusetts Court! A merchant from Richmond, so Mr. Brent called himself; another from Alexandria, who was a sheriff and member of the Virginia Legislature—for such Col. Suttle has been—they were there to steal a man! They had him already in jail; they went out and came in as they liked, and shut from his presence everybody who was not one of the minions hired to aid them in their crime.

Further, they had two lawyers of Boston giving them the benefit of their education and their knowledge of the law; and in addition to that, the senior lawyer, Seth J. Thomas, brought considerable experience, acquired on similar occasions, — for he has been the kidnappers' counsel from the beginning. The other lawyer was a young man of good culture and amiable deportment, I think with no previous stain on his reputation. This is his first offence. I trust it will be also his last — that he will not bring shame on his own and his mother's head. I know not how the kidnappers enticed the young man to do so base a deed; nor what motive turned him to a course so foul as this. He is a young man, sorely penitent for this early treason against humanity. Generous emotions are commonly powerful in the bosoms of the young. A young man with only cruel calculation in his heart is a rare and loathsome spectacle. Let us hope better things of this lawyer; that a generous nature only sleeps in him. It is his first offence. I hope he will bring forth "fruits meet for repentance." Judge of him as charitably as you can. Of Mr. Thomas I have only this to add: — that he is chiefly known in the Courts as the associate of Mr. Curtis in attempts like this; the regular attorney of the stealers of men, and apparently delighted with his work. He began this career by endeavoring to seize William and Ellen Craft. He is a member of the Democratic party who has not yet received his reward.

On the side of the kidnapper, there were also the District Marshal, the District Attorney, the Fugitive Slave Bill Commissioner, and sixty-five men whom I counted as the Marshal's "guard." When the company was ordered to disperse, and the guard to remain, I tarried late, and counted them. I reckoned sixty-five in the court room, and five more outside. I may have been mistaken in the count.

On the other side there was a poor, friendless negro, sitting between two bullies, his wrists chained together by stout handcuffs of steel, — a prisoner without a crime, chained; on trial for more than life, and yet there was no charge against him save that his mother had been a Slave!

Mr. Burns had no counsel. The kidnapper's lawyers presented their documents from Alexandria, claiming him as a Slave of Col. Suttle, who had escaped from "service." They brought a Virginia merchant to identify the prisoner. He was swiftly sworn and testified with speed. The claimant's lawyers declared that Mr. Burns had acknowledged already that he was Col. Suttle's Slave, and was willing to go back. So they demanded a "certificate;" and at first it seemed likely to be granted at once. Why should a Fugitive Slave Bill Commissioner delay? Why does he want evidence? Injustice is swift of foot. You know what was done in New York, the very same week: — three men were seized, carried before a Commissioner, and, without even a mock trial, without any defence, hurried to bondage, pitiless and forever! Only an accident, it seems, saved Boston from that outrage.

But there came forward in the court room two young lawyers, Richard H. Dana and Charles M. Ellis, noble and honorable men, the pride of the mothers that bore them, and the joy of the fathers who have trained them up to piety and reverence for the law of God. Voluntarily, gratuitously, they offered their services as counsel for Mr. Burns. But it was said by the kidnappers that he did "not want counsel;" that he "would make no defence;" that he was "willing to go back." Messrs. Dana and Ellis did not wish to speak with him, or seemed to plead that he might be their client. I spoke with him. His fear gave him a sad presentiment of his fate. He feared that he should be forced into Slavery. How could he think otherwise? Arrested on a lying charge; kept in secret under severe and strict duress; guarded by armed men; confronted by his claimant; seeing no friends about him, how could he do otherwise than despair? If he went back at all, it was natural that he should "wish to go back easily," fearing that if he resisted his claimant in Boston, he "must suffer for it in Alexandria." His "conqueror," he thought, would take "vengeance" on him when he got him home, if he resisted his claim. That is the best evidence which I have seen, that the man had ever been a Slave: he knew the taste and the strength of the Slave-driver's whip. That was not brought forward in "evidence." If I had been the kidnapper's counsel, I should have said, "The man is doubtless a Slave: he is afraid to go back!" When I was in the court room, as I was about to ask poor Burns if he would have counsel, one of the "guard" said to me, "You will never get him to say he wants a defence." Another more humanely said, "I hope he will; at any rate, it will do no harm to try." I asked him, and he said, "Do as you think best."

But still the counsel felt a delicacy in engaging under such circumstances. For they thought that if, after all, he was to be sent to bondage, and when in the hands of the Slave-master should be tortured the more for the defence they had made for him in Boston Court House, it would surely be better to let the Marshal take his victim as soon as he liked, and allow the Fugitive Slave Bill Commissioner to earn his "thirty pieces of silver" without delay. They begged for time, however, that the intimidated man might make up his mind, and determine whether he would have a defence or not.

There is no end to human atrocity. The kidnapper's lawyers objected to the delay, and wished the "trial" to proceed at once "forthwith." They said that the claimant, Col. Suttle was here, having come all the way from Alexandria to Boston, at great cost; that the case was clear; that Burns made no defence; and they asked for an instant decision. The Democratic lawyer [THOMAS] thought it was not worth while to delay; there was only the liberty of a man at stake — a poor man, with no reputation, no friends, nothing but the "natural, essential, and unalienable rights," wherewith he was "endowed by his Creator" — nothing but that: — let the Virginia Colonel have his Slave! That is Administration Democracy in Massachusetts. There are two Democracies — the Celestial and the Satanic. One, — it is the Democracy of the Beatitudes of the New Testament and of Jesus Christ; that says, "My brother, you are as good as I: come up higher, and let me take you by the hand; and we will help each other." Such Democracy is the worship of the great God. The other, — it says, "I am as good as you, and if you don't let me triumph over you I will smite you to the ground." That is the Democracy of Caleb Cushing, the Democracy of the Administration, and of a great many political men, Democrat and Whig, and neither Whig nor Democrat.

Commissioner Loring asked Mr. Burns if he wanted time to think of the matter, and counsel to aid in his defence. I shall never forget how he looked round that court room, at the Marshal, at the kidnapper's lawyers, at the Commissioner, the claimant and his witness! Save the counsel whom he had never seen before, there was scarce a friendly face that his eye rested on. At length he said timidly and catching for breath, "Yes." Mr. Loring put off the case until Saturday. The Fugitive Slave Bill Commissioner was to lecture at Cambridge on Friday. He is a Professor at Harvard College, and he could not conveniently hold court on that day. He is a Judge of Probate, and looks after widows and orphans; he must be in the Probate Office on Monday. Saturday was the most convenient day for the Commissioner. So in a matter which was to determine whether the prisoner should be a free man or only a thing which might be sold and beaten as a beast, the "court" allowed him forty-eight hours delay! It really gave him time to breathe a little. Let us be grateful to the Commissioner! He gave more favor than any Fugitive Slave Bill Commissioners have done before, I believe.

You know the rest: He was on trial ten days. He was never in a Court; all this time he has not seen a jury; he has not even seen a judge; the process is "summary," not "summary in time," as Mr. Loring declares: but it is "without due form of law." The Democratic *chargé des affaires* at Turin says, "the negro is the connecting link between the human and brute creation."* Why do you want a Court to make a negro a Slave in Boston? Surely, a Commissioner is enough in such a case. Let him proceed as swiftly as he will:—the kidnapper's lawyers said—"forthwith;" not in a hurry, but "immediately."

You remember what followed. You have seen the streets crowded with armed men. You have read the newspapers, the handbills, and the posters. You remember the Faneuil Hall meeting, when all the influence of the platform scarce kept the multitude from tearing the Court House that night to the ground. You remember the attack on the Court House—a man killed and twelve citizens in jail, charged with crimes of an atrocious character. You recollect the conventions—Free Soil and Anti-Slavery. You call to mind the aspect of Court Square last Monday. Boston never saw such an Anniversary week. There were meetings of theological societies, philanthropic societies, reformatory societies, literary societies: and Boston was in a state of siege—the Court House full of United States soldiers—marines from the Navy Yard, troops from the Forts, from New York, from Portsmouth, from Rhode Island. The courts sat with muskets at their backs, or swords at their bosoms; drunken soldiers charged

---

* See above, Vol. I. p. 394.

bayonet on the witnesses, on counsel, and on strangers, who had rights where the soldier had none. The scene last Friday you will never forget — business suspended, the shops shut, the streets blocked up, all the "citizen-soldiery" under arms. Ball cartridges were made for the city government on Thursday afternoon in Dock Square, to be fired into your bosoms and mine; United States soldiers loaded their pieces in Court Square, to be discharged into the crowd of Boston citizens whenever a drunken officer should give command; a six pound cannon, furnished with forty rounds of canister shot, was planted in Court Square, manned by United States soldiers, foreigners before they enlisted. The town looked Austrian. And at high change, over the spot where, on the fifth of March, 1770, fell the first victim in the Boston Massacre, — where the negro blood of Christopher Attucks stained the ground, — over that spot Boston authorities carried a citizen of Massachusetts to Alexandria as a Slave; "and order reigns in Boston" — or Warsaw, call it which you will.

So much for a brief statement of facts.

Pause with me a moment, and look at the General Causes of the fact. Here are two great forces in the nation. One is SLAVERY, FREEDOM is the other. The two are hostile — deadly foes, irreconcilable. They will go on fighting till one kills the other outright. From 1775 to 1788, Freedom generally prevailed over Slavery. It was the period of Revolution, when the nation fell back on its religious feelings, and thence developed the great political ideas of America. But even then Slavery was in the midst of us. It came into the Constitution, and from the adoption of the Federal Constitution to the present time, it has advanced, and Freedom declined. It has gone over the Alleghanies, over the Rio del Norte, over the Cordilleras; it extends from the forty-ninth parallel to the thirty-second, from the Atlantic to the Pacific; it has gone into ten new States, into all the Territories except Oregon.

Since the annexation of Texas, in 1845, Slavery has been the obvious master, Freedom the obvious servant. Fidelity to Slavery is the *sine qua non* for office holders. Slavery is the "peculiar institution" of the industrial Democracy of America. Slavery is terribly in earnest, as Freedom has never been since the Revolution. It controls all the politics of the country. It strangles all our "great men." There is not a great Democrat, nor a great Whig, who dares openly oppose Slavery. All the commercial towns are on its side. There is not an anti-slavery governor of any State in the Union. The Supreme Courts of the States are all pro-slavery, save in Vermont. The leading newspapers are nearly all on the side of wrong — almost all the commercial, almost all the political newspapers. I know but few exceptions — of course

I do not speak of those devoted to Philanthropy — The Democratic Evening Post, truly Democratic, of New York, and the New York Tribune, which is truly Democratic, though it hoists another banner. Many of the theological journals — Protestant as well as Catholic — are cruelly devoted to Slavery. But proudly above all the religious journals of the land rises the "Independent," and bears a noble witness to the humane spirit of Christianity. These are eminent exceptions, which would do honor to any nation.

The friends of Freedom appeal religiously to the souls and consciences of men: Piety and Justice demand that all be free; the appeal immediately touches a few. They address also the Reason and the Understanding of men: Freedom is the great idea of politics; it is self-evident that "all men are created equal." That argument touches a few more. But the religious, who reverence God's Higher Law, and the intellectual, who see the great ideas of politics, they are few. Slavery addresses the vulgar interests of vulgar men. To the Slave-holder it gives political power, pecuniary power; and here is an argument which the dullest can understand, and the meanest appreciate. Able and cunning men feel this, and avail themselves of Slavery to secure money and political power. These are the objects of most intense desire in America. They are our highest things — marks of our "great men." Office is transient nobility; money is permanent, heritable nobility. Accordingly, Slavery is the leading idea of America — the "great American institution." I think history furnishes no instance of one section of a country submitting so meanly to another as we have done in America. The South is weak in numbers and in money — the North strong in both. The South has few schools, no commerce, few newspapers, no large mass of intelligent men, wherein the North abounds. But the most eminent Southern men are devoted to politics, while the Northern turn to trade: and so the South commands the North. I am only translating facts into ideas, and bringing the condition of America to the consciousness of America. Some men knew these things before, but the mass of men know them not.

So much for the General Causes.

Now look at some of the Special Causes. I shall limit myself chiefly to those which Massachusetts has had a share in putting into activity.

In 1826, on the ninth of March, Mr. Edward Everett made a speech in Congress. He was the Representative of Middlesex County. Once he was a minister of the church where John Hancock used to worship, and as clergyman officially resided in the house which John Hancock gave to that church. Next, he was a Professor in Harvard College, where the Adamses — the three Adamses, Samuel, John, and John Quincy were educated, and where John Hancock had graduated. He represented Lexington, and Concord, and Bunker Hill, and in his speech he said: —

"Neither am I one of those citizens of the North who would think it immoral and irreligious to join in putting down a servile insurrection at the South. I am no soldier, Sir. My habits and education are very unmilitary; but there is no cause in which I would sooner buckle a knapsack to my back, and put a musket to my shoulder, than that." "Domestic Slavery . . . is not, in my judgment, to be set down as an immoral or irreligious institution." "Its duties are presupposed by religion." "The New Testament says, 'Slaves, obey your masters.'"

The Daily Advertiser defended Mr. Everett, declaring that it was perfectly right in him to justify the continuance of the relation between the master and his slaves, and added, — I am now quoting from the Daily Advertiser of March 28, 1826: — "We hold that it is not time, and never will be, that we should be aroused to any efforts for their redemption." That was the answer which the "respectability of Boston" gave to Mr. Everett's speech. True, some Journals protested against the iniquitous statement; even the Christian Register was indignant. But Middlesex County sent him again. Lexington, and Concord, and Bunker Hill, returned their apostate representative a second, a third, a fourth, and a fifth time. And when he was weary of that honor, the State of Massachusetts made him her Governor, and he carried to the State House the same proclivities to despotism which he had evinced in his maiden speech.

In 1835, the Anti-Slavery men and women were mobbed in Boston by an assembly of "respectable gentlemen;" the Mayor did not stop the tumult, the destruction of property, and the peril to life! There were no soldiers in the streets, then; nobody, I think, was punished.

The next winter, the General Assemblies of several Southern States sent resolutions to the Massachusetts General Court, whereof this is one from South Carolina:—

"The formation of abolition societies, and the acts and doings of certain fanatics, calling themselves abolitionists, in the non-slaveholding States of this confederacy, are in direct violation of the obligations of the compact of the Union."

South Carolina requested the Government "promptly and effectually to suppress all those associations," and would consider "the abolition of Slavery in the District of Columbia as a violation of the rights of citizens, and a usurpation to be at once resisted." Georgia asked Massachusetts "to crush the traitorous designs of the abolitionists." Virginia required the non-slaveholding States "to adopt penal enactments, or such other measures as will effectually suppress all associations within their respective limits, purporting to be, or having the character of, abolition societies;" and that they "will make it highly penal to print, publish, or distribute newspapers, pamphlets, or other publications, calculated or having a tendency, to incite the Slaves of the Southern States to insurrection and revolt." How do you think Massachusetts answered? In solemn resolutions the Committee of the Massachusetts Legislature declared that "the agitation of the question of domestic Slavery had already interrupted the friendly relations between the several States of the Union;" expressed its "entire disapprobation of the doctrines and speeches of such as agitate the question," and advised them "to abstain from all such discussion as might tend to disturb and agitate the public mind." That was the voice of a Committee appointed by the Massachusetts Legislature. True, it was not accepted by the House of Representatives, but the Report was only too significant. What followed?

In 1844, one of the most eminent lawyers of this State was sent by Massachusetts to the city of Charleston, to proceed legally and secure the release of Massachusetts' colored citizens from the jails of Charleston, where they were held without charge of crime, and contrary to the Constitution of the United States. Mr. Hoar was mobbed out of Charleston by a body of respectable citizens, the High Sheriff aiding in driving him out.

Mr. Hoar made his report to the Governor of Massachusetts, and said: —

"Has the Constitution of the United States the least practical validity or binding force in South Carolina, excepting when she thinks its operation favorable to her? She prohibits the trial of an action in the tribunals established under the Constitution for determining such cases, in which a citizen of Massachusetts complains that a citizen of South Carolina has done him an injury; saying that she has herself already tried that cause, and decided against the plaintiff."

The evil complained of continues unabated to this day. South Carolina imprisons all the free colored citizens of the North who visit her ports in our ships.

In 1845, Texas was admitted, and annexed as a Slave State, with the promise that she might bring in four other Slave States.

In 1847 and '48, came the Mexican War, with the annexation of an immense territory as Slave soil. Many of the leading men of Massachusetts favored the annexation of Texas. New England might have stopped it; Massachusetts might have stopped it; Boston might have stopped it. But Mr. Webster said "she could not be aroused." The politicians of Massachusetts favored the Mexican war. It was a war for Slavery. Boston favored it. The newspapers came out in its defence. The Governor called out the soldiers, and they came. From the New England pulpit we heard but a thin and feeble voice against the war.

But there were men who doubted that wrong was right, and said, "Beware of this wickedness!" The sober people of the country disliked the war: they said, "No! let us have no such wicked work as this!" Governor Briggs, though before so deservedly popular, could never again get elected by the people. He had violated their conscience by issuing his proclamation calling for volunteers.

In 1850 came the Fugitive Slave Bill. You all remember Mr. Webster's Speech on the Seventh of March. Before that time he had opposed all the great steps of the Slave Power — the Missouri Compromise, the annexation of Texas, the Mexican War, the increase of Slave territory. He had voted, I think, against the admission of every Slave State. He was opposed to the extension of American Slavery, "at all times, now and for ever." He claimed the Wilmot Proviso as his "thunder." He "could stand on the Buffalo platform" in 1848. But in 1850, he proffered his support to the Fugitive Slave Bill, "with all its provisions, to the fullest extent." He volunteered the promise that Massachusetts would "obey," and that "with alacrity." You remember his speech at the Revere House — discussion "must be suppressed, in Congress and out;" Massachusetts must "conquer her prejudices" in favor of the unalienable rights of man, which she had fought the Revolution to secure. You have not forgotten his speeches at Albany, at Syracuse, at Buffalo; nor his denial of the Higher Law of God at Capron Springs in Virginia — "The North Mountain is very high; the Blue Ridge higher still; the Alleghanies higher than either; yet this 'Higher Law' ranges an eagle's flight above the highest peak of the Alleghanies." What was the answer from the crowd? "Laughter." The multitude laughed at the Higher Law. There is no Law above the North Mountain, above the Blue Ridge, above the peaks of the Alleghany — is there? The Fugitive Slave Bill reaches up where there is no God!

Men of property and standing all over New England supported the apostasy of Mr. Webster. You remember the letters from Maine, from New Hampshire, and the one from Newburyport. I am sure you have not forgotten the letter of the nine hundred and eighty-seven prominent men in and about Boston, telling him that he had "convinced the understanding and touched the conscience of a nation." Good men, whom I have long known, and tenderly loved, put their names to that letter. Did they think the "Union in danger?" Not one of them. A man of great understanding beguiled them.

You remember the tone of the newspapers, Whig and Democratic. With alacrity they went for kidnapping to the fullest extent. They clasped hands in order to seize the black man. When the time came, Mr. Eliot gave the vote of Boston for the Fugitive Slave Bill. When he returned to his home, some of the most prominent men of the city went and thanked him for his vote. They liked it. I believe no "eminent man" of Boston spoke against it. They "strained their consciences," as Mr. Walley has just said, "to aid in the passage of the Fugitive Slave Act." Boston fired a hundred guns on the Common, at noon-day, in honor of that event.

I know there was opposition — earnest and fierce opposition; but it did not come from the citizens of "eminent gravity," whom Boston and Massachusetts are accustomed stupidly to follow. You know what hatred was felt in Boston against all men who taught that the natural law of God was superior to the Fugitive Slave Bill, and Conscience above the Constitution.

You have not forgotten the "Union meeting" in Faneuil Hall. I never saw so much meanness and so little manhood on that platform. The Democratic Herods and the Whig Pilates were made friends that day that they might kidnap the black man. You recollect the howl of derision against the Higher Law of God, which came from that ignoble stage, and was echoed by that ignoble crowd above it and below — speakers fit for fitting theme.

When the Fugitive Slave Bill was proposed, prominent men said "It cannot pass: the North will reject it at once; and even if it were passed, it would be repealed the next day. We will petition for its repeal." After it was passed, they said: "It cannot be executed, and never will be." But when asked to petition for its repeal, the same men refused — "No, it would irritate the South." I received the petitions which our fellow-citizens sent from more than three hundred towns in Massachusetts. I took the smallest of them all, and sent it to the Representative of Boston, Mr. Eliot, with a letter, asking him to present it to the House. He presented it — to me! It was not "laid on the table;" he put it in the post-office. I sent it back to Washington, to some Southern or Western member, and he presented it in Congress.

The next Congress reaffirmed the Fugitive Slave Bill.

> "Twice they routed all their foes,
> And twice they slew the slain."

The new Representative from Boston, Mr. Appleton, gave the vote of Boston for it. He was never censured for that act. He was approved, and re-elected.

You remember the conduct of the Boston newspapers. Almost all of them went for the Fugitive Slave Bill. They made Atheism the first principle in American politics — "There is no Higher Law." The instinct of commerce is adverse to the natural rights of labor: so the chief leaders in commerce wish to have the workingman but poorly paid; the larger gain falls into their hands; their laborer is a mill, they must run him as cheap as they can. So the great cities of the North were hostile to the Slave — hostile to freedom. The wealthy capitalists did not know that in denying the Higher Law of God they were destroying the rock on which alone their money could rest secure. The mass of men in cities, servants of the few, knew not that in chaining the black man they were also putting fetters on their own feet. Justice is the common interest of all men! Alas, that so few know what God writes in letters of fire on the World's high walls!

You have not forgotten the general tone of the pulpit, — "Conscience and the Constitution," at Andover. Mr. Stuart says, Keep the laws of men, come what may come of the Higher Law of God. One minister of Boston said, "I would drive the Fugitive from my own door." The most eminent Doctor of Divinity in the Unitarian ranks declared he would send his own Mother into Slavery. He says he said brother! Give him the benefit of the ethical distinction: he would send back his own brother! What had Andover and New Haven to say, in their collegiate churches? What the churches of Commerce in New York, Boston, Philadelphia, Albany, Buffalo? They all went for kidnapping. "Down with God and up with iniquity." That was the short of the lower law religion which littered the land. The ecclesiastical teachers did more to strengthen infidelity then, than all the "infidels" that ever taught. What else could you expect from lower law divines? All at once this blessed Bible seemed to have become a treatise in favor of man-stealing. Kidnapping arguments were strewn all the way through from Genesis to Revelation. These were the reverend gentlemen who call me "infidel," or "atheist!" Nothing has so weakened the Church in America as this conduct of these "leading ministers" at that time. I mean ministers of churches that are rich in money, which lead the fashion and the opinion of the day. What defences of kidnapping have I heard from clerical lips! "No matter what the law is — it must be executed. The men who made the Fugitive Slave Bill, and those who seek to execute it are 'Christian men,' 'very conscientious!'" Turn back and read the newspapers of 1850 and 1851. Nay, read them not — they are too bad to read!

When the Fugitive Slave Bill was before Congress, some of the Northern politicians said to the people, "Let it pass; it will 'save the Union,' and we will repeal it at the next session of Congress." After it had passed they said, "Do not try to repeal it; that would irritate the South, and 'dissolve the Union;' it will never be executed; it is too bad to be." But when the kidnapper came to Boston, and demanded William and Ellen Craft, the same advisers said, "Of course the *niggers* must be sent back; the law must be enforced because it is law!"

At length the time came to execute the act. Morton was busy in New York, Kane in Philadelphia, Curtis, the Boston Commissioner, was also on his feet. William and Ellen Craft fled off from the stripes of America to the lion of England. Shadrach — he will be remembered as long as Daniel — sang his psalm of deliverance in Canada. Taking him out of the Kidnappers' Court was high treason. It was "levying war." Thomas Sims will not soon be forgotten in Boston. Mayor Bigelow, Commissioner Curtis, and Marshal Tukey, they will also be remembered; they will all three be borne down to posterity, riding on the scourged and bleeding shoulders of Thomas Sims. The government of Boston could do nothing for the Fugitive but kidnap him. The officers of the County nothing; they were only cockade and vanity. The Supreme Court could do nothing; the Judges crouched, and crawled, and went under the chain. The Free Soil Governor could do nothing; the Free Soil Legislature nothing. The Court House was in chains. Faneuil Hall was shut. The victim was on trial. A thousand able-bodied men sat in Tremont Temple all day in a Free Soil Convention, and — went home at night! Most of the newspapers in the city were for kidnapping. The greater part of the clergy were for returning the Fugitive:—"Send back our brother." Some of the towns held meetings, and passed resolutions against the rendition of the Fugitive—Lynn, New Bedford, Worcester. And, in consequence, the leading commercial papers of Boston threatened to cut off all trade with New Bedford; they would not buy its oil: would have no dealings with Lynn, they would not tread her shoes under their feet: they would starve out Worcester. In Boston, wealthy traders entertained the kidnappers from the South. Merchants and Railroad Directors withdrew their advertising from newspapers which opposed the stealing of men. More than one minister in New England was driven from his pulpit for declaring the Golden Rule superior to the Fugitive Slave Bill!

When Judge Woodbury decided not to grant the writ of *habeas corpus*, and thus at one spurt of his pen cut off Mr. Sims's last chance for liberty and life, the Court House rang with plaudits, and the clapping of hands of "gentlemen" who had assembled there! Fifteen hundred "gentlemen, of property and standing," volunteered to escort the poor Fugitive out of the State, and convey him to bondage forever. It was not necessary. When he stepped from Long Wharf on board John H. Pearson's brig, —the owner is sorry for it now, and has repented, and promises to bring forth fruits meet for repentance; let that be remembered to his honor,—when Thomas Sims stepped on board the "Acorn," these were his words, "And this is Massachusetts liberty!" There was that great stone finger pointing from Bunker Hill towards Heaven; and this was "Massachusetts liberty!" "Order reigned in Warsaw." But it was some comfort that he could not be sent away till soldiers were billeted in Faneuil Hall; then, only in the darkest hour of the night!

Boston sent back the first man she ever stole since the Declaration of Independence. Thomas Sims reached Savannah on the nineteenth of April, seventy-six years after the first battle of the Revolution, fought on the soil of Lexington. He was sent back on Saturday, and the next Sunday the "leading ministers" of this city — I call them leading, though they lead nobody — gave God thanks. They forgot Jesus. They took Iscariot for their exemplar. "The Fugitive Slave Bill must be kept," they said, "come what will come to Justice, Liberty, and Love; come what may come of God."

I know there were noble ministers, noble men in pulpits, whose hearts bled in them, and who spoke brave warning words of liberty, some were in the country, some in town. I know one minister, an "orthodox man," who in five months helped ninety-and-five fugitives flee from American stripes to the freedom of Canada! I dare not yet tell his name! Humble churches in the country towns — Methodist, Baptist, Unitarian — of all denominations save that of Commerce — dropped their two mites of money into the alms-box for the Slave, and gave him their prayers and their preaching too. But the "famous churches" went for "law" and stealing men.

Slavery had long been master at Washington: the "Union meeting" proved that it was master at Boston; proved it by words. The capture and sending back of Thomas Sims proved it by deeds. No prominent Whig openly opposed the Fugitive Slave Bill or its execution. No prominent Democrat opposed it. Not a prominent clergyman in Boston spoke against it. I mean a clergyman of a "rich and fashionable church"—for in these days the wealth and social standing of the church make the minister "prominent." Intellectual Power, Eloquence, Piety,—they do not make a "prominent minister" in these days.* Not ten of the rich men of Massachusetts gave the weight of their influence against it. Slavery is master; Massachusetts is one of the inferior counties of Virginia; Boston is only a suburb of Alexandria. Many of our lawyers, ministers, merchants, politicians, were negro-drivers for the South. They proved it by idea before; then by deed. Yet there were men in Boston who hated Slavery—alas! they had little influence.

Let me not pass by the Baltimore Conventions,

* Dr. Charles Lowell, with the humane piety which has beautified his long and faithful ministry, at that time opposed the fugitive slave bill with manly earnestness.

and the two platforms. The Fugitive Slave Bill was the central and topmost plank in them both. Each confessed Slavery to be master; it seemed that there was no North; Slave soil all the way from the South of Florida to the North of Maine. All over the land Slavery ruled.

You cannot forget Mr. Pierce's Inaugural Address, nor the comments of the Boston press thereon. He says the Fugitive Slave Bill is to be "unhesitatingly carried into effect;" "not with reluctance," but "cheerfully and willingly." The newspapers of Boston welcomed the sentiment; and now Mr. Pierce's organ, the Washington Union, says it is very proper this Bill should be enforced at Boston, for "Boston was among the first to approve of this emphatic declaration." So let the promise be executed here till we have enough of it!

You know the contempt which has been shown towards everybody who opposed Slavery here in Massachusetts. Horace Mann — there is not a man in the State more hated than he by the "prominent politicians," — or more loved by the People — because he opposed Slavery with all his might; and it is a great might. Robert Rantoul, though a politician and a party man, fought against Slavery; and when he died, though he was an eminent lawyer, the members of the Suffolk Bar, his brother lawyers, took no notice of him. They wore no crape for Robert Rantoul! He had opposed Slavery; let him die unnoticed, unhonored, unknown. Massachusetts sent to the Senate a man whose chief constitutional impulse is the instinct of decorum — Mr. Everett, who had been ready to buckle on his knapsack, and shoulder his musket, to put down an insurrection of Slaves; a Cambridge professor of Greek, he studied the original tongue of the Bible to learn that the Scripture says "slaves," where the English Bible says only "servants." Fit Senator.

Then came the Nebraska Bill. It was at once a Measure and a Principle. As a measure, it extends the old curse of Slavery over half a million square miles of virgin soil, and thus hinders the growth of the Territory in population, riches, education, in moral and religious character. It makes a South Carolina of what might else be a Connecticut, and establishes Paganism in the place of Christ's piety. As a Principle, it is worse still — it makes Slavery national and inseparable from the national soil; for the principle which is covertly indorsed by the Nebraska Bill might establish Slavery in Massachusetts — and ere long the attempt will be made.

In the House of Representatives, forty-four Northern men voted for the enslavement of Nebraska. They are all Democrats — it is an administration measure. Mr. Everett, the Senator from Boston, "did not know exactly what to do." The thing was discussed in Committee, of which he was a member; but when it came up in public, it "took him by surprise." He wrote, I am told, to eleven prominent Whig gentlemen of Massachusetts, and asked their advice as to what he should do. With singular unanimity, every man of them said, Oppose it with all your might! But he did not. Nay, his vote has not been recorded against it yet. I am told his vote was in favor of prohibiting aliens from voting in that territory; his name against the main question has never been recorded yet. Nay, he did not dare to present the remonstrance which three thousand and fifty of his fellow clergymen manfully sent to their clerical brother, and asked him to lay before the Senate. Did any one suppose that he would dare do it? None who knew his antecedents.

There was an Anti-Nebraska meeting in Boston, at Faneuil Hall. It was Siberian in its coldness — it was a meeting of icebergs. The platform was Arctic. There seemed to be no heart in the speeches. It must have been an encouragement to the men at Washington who advocated the Bill. I suppose they understood it so. I am sure I should. The mass of the people in Massachusetts who think at all, are indignant; but so far as I can learn, the men who control the politics of Boston, or who have controlled them until the last week, feel no considerable interest in the matter. In New York, men of great property and high standing came together and protested against this iniquity. New York has been, for once, and in one particular, morally in advance of Boston. The platform there was not Arctic, not even Siberian. Such a meeting could not have been held here.

Now, put all these things together, and you see the causes which bore the fruits of last week; — in general, the triumph of Slavery over Freedom, and in special, the indifference of Massachusetts, and particularly of Boston, to the efforts which are made for Freedom; her zeal to promote Slavery and honor its defenders. Men talk of dividing the Union. I never proposed that. Before last week I should not have known where to begin. I should have had to draw the line somewhere North of Boston.

Last week Massachusetts got part of her pay for obeying the Fugitive Slave Bill with alacrity; for suppressing discussion; for conquering her prejudices; pay for putting cowardly, mean men in the place of brave, honorable men; pay for allowing the laws of Massachusetts to be trodden underfoot, and her Court House of Northern granite to be surrounded by Southern chains. Thomas Sims was scourged on the 19th of April, when he was carried back to Savannah. Boston did not feel it then. She felt it last week — felt it sorely. In September, 1850, we heard the hundred guns fired on Boston Common, in honor of the Fugitive Slave Bill — fired by men of "eminent gravity." Last Friday you saw the cannon! One day you will see it again grown into many cannons. That one was only a devil's grace before a devil's meat! No Higher Law, is there? Wait a little longer, and you shall find there is a "lower law," a good deal lower than we have yet come to! Sow the wind, shall we? When the whirlwind comes up therefrom, it has a course of its own, and God only can control the law of such storms as those. We have not yet seen the full consequences of sowing atheism with a broad hand among the people of this continent. We have not yet seen the end. These are only the small early apples that first fall to the earth. There is a whole tree full of them. When some autumnal storm shakes the boughs, they will cover the ground — sour and bitter in our mouths, and then poison.

Yet this triumph of Slavery does not truly represent the wishes of the Northern people. Not a single Pro-Slavery measure has ever been popular with the mass of men in New England or Massachusetts. The people disliked the annexation of Texas in that unjust manner: they thought the Mexican War was wicked. They were opposed to the extension of Slavery; they hated the Fugitive Slave Bill, and rejoiced at the rescue of Shadrach. The kidnapping of Thomas Sims roused a fierce indignation. Only one town in all New England has ever returned a Fugitive — all the rest hide the outcasts, while Boston bewrays him that wandereth. The Nebraska act is detested by the people.

A few editors have done a manly duty in opposing all these manifold iniquities. A few ministers have been faithful to the spirit of this Bible, and to their own conscience, heedless of law and constitution. Manly preachers of all denominations — save the commercial — protested against kidnapping, against enacting wickedness by statute. From humble pulpits their voices rang out in Boston and elsewhere. But what were they among so many? There were Theological Journals which stoutly resisted the wickedness of the prominent men, and rebuked the mammon-worship of the churches of commerce. The Independent at New York, the Congregationalist at Boston, not to mention humbler papers, did most manly service — now with eloquence, now with art, then with satyric scorn, — always with manly religion. Even in the cities, there were editors of secular prints who opposed the wicked law and its execution.

No man in New England, within the last few years, has supported Slavery without at the same time losing the confidence of the best portion of the people — sober, serious, religious men, who believe there is a law of God writ in the nature of things. Even Mr. Webster quailed before the Conscience of the North: the Supreme Court of Massachusetts no longer enjoys the confidence of the people; the most "prominent clergymen" of New England — pastors I mean of the richest churches — are not looked up to with the same respect as before.

The popularity of "Uncle Tom's Cabin" showed how deeply the feelings of the world were touched by this great outrage. No one of the encroachments of Slavery could have been sustained by a direct popular vote. I think seven out of every ten of all the New England men would have voted against the Fugitive Slave Bill; nine out of ten against kidnapping. But alas! we did not say so — we allowed wicked men to rule over us. Now behold the consequences! Men who will not love God must fear the devil.

Boston is the test and touchstone of political principles and measures. Faneuil Hall is "the Cradle of Liberty," and therein have been rocked the great ideas of America — rocked by noble hands.

Well, if Boston had said, "No Texan annexation in that wicked way!" we might have had Texas on fair conditions. If Boston had opposed the Mexican War, all New England would have done the same — almost all the North. We might have had all the soil we have got, without fighting a battle, or taking or losing a life; at far less cost; and have demoralized nobody. If, when the Fugitive Slave Bill was before Congress, Boston had spoken against that iniquity, all the people would have risen, and there would have been no Fugitive Slave Act. If, after that Bill was passed, she had said "No kidnapping," there would have been none. Then there would have been no Nebraska Bill, no repeal of the Missouri Compromise, no attempt to seize Cuba and Saint Domingo. If the fifteen hundred gentlemen of "property and standing" in Boston, who volunteered to return Mr. Sims to bondage, or the nine hundred and eighty-seven who thanked Mr. Webster for the Fugitive Slave Bill, had come forward on the side of Justice, they might have made every Commissioner swear solemnly that he would not execute that Act. Thus the "true Sons of Liberty," on the seventeenth of December, 1765, induced Commissioner Oliver to swear solemnly, at noon-day, in "presence of a great crowd," and in front of the Liberty Tree, that he would not issue a single stamp! Had that been done, there would have been no man arrested. There are only eight Commissioners, and public opinion would have kept them all down. We should have had no kidnappers here.

Boston did not do so; Massachusetts did no such thing. She did just the opposite. In 1828, the Legislature of Georgia passed resolutions relative to the Tariff, declaring that the General Government had no right to protect domestic manufactures, and had been guilty of a "flagrant usurpation;" she will insist on her construction of the Constitution, and "will submit to no other." Georgia carried her point. The Tariff of 1828 went to the ground! South Carolina imprisons our colored citizens: we bear it with a patient shrug,—and pay the cost:

Massachusetts is non-resistant; New England is a Quaker, — when a blustering little State undertakes to ride over us. Georgia offers a reward of five thousand dollars for the head of a non-resistant in Boston, — and Boston takes special pains to return Ellen Craft to a citizen of Georgia, who wished to sell her as a harlot for the brothels of New Orleans! Northern clergymen defended the character of her "owner" — a man of "unquestionable piety." You know what denunciations were uttered in this city against the men and women who sheltered her! Boston could not allow the poor woman to remain. Did the churches of Commerce "put up a prayer" for her? "Send back my own mother!" Not a Northern minister lost his pulpit or his professional respectability by that form of practical atheism. Not one! At the South not a minister dares preach against Slavery; at the North — think of the preaching of so many "eminent divines!"*

---

* My friend, the Rev. Dr. Edward Beecher, thinks I have been unjust to the ministers, — judging from the Sermon as reported in the Commonwealth. So he published the following article in that paper on Friday, June 9. I gladly insert it below. It comes from a powerful and noble man. I wish he had made out a stronger case against me.

"THEODORE PARKER AND THE MINISTRY.

"*Mr. Editor:* — In his Sermon, last Sabbath, Mr. Parker seems to charge the clergy of the country with a general, if not universal delinquency in the cause of freedom, with respect to the Fugitive Slave Law. He says, 'You all remember the tone of *the pulpit.*'

My friends, we deserve all we have suffered. We are the scorn and contempt of the South. They are

---

As if on that subject *the pulpit* had been an unit. He adds, 'What had Andover and New Haven to say in their collegiate churches? What the churches (of commerce) of New York, of Boston, of Philadelphia, of Albany, of Buffalo? They all went for kidnapping. "Down with God and up with kidnapping." That was the short of the lower law religion that littered the land. The ecclesiastical teachers did more to strengthen infidelity than all the infidels that ever taught.' He does not say that these charges are true of a part only of the ministry. His language would convey to any reader ignorant of the fact, the opposite impression. He says that when Thomas Sims was sent back, 'the clergy were for returning the Fugitive. "Send back our brother."' 'The next Sunday the leading ministers of the city — I call them *leading* — though they lead nobody — gave God thanks.'

"Speaking of the Slave Bill and its execution, he says, 'Not a prominent clergyman spoke against it.'

"And when he speaks of the Nebraska Bill, he scarcely mentions the petition of the three thousand and fifty ministers. And then, not as if he desired to give them due praise, he merely mentions it incidentally, in dealing with Mr. Everett — 'He did not dare to present the remonstrance which three thousand and fifty of his fellow clergymen sent to their clerical brother, and asked him to lay before the Senate.' And again, 'The cowardice of Mr. Everett has excited the clergy of New England — of all the North; they are stung with the reproach of the people, and ashamed of their past neglect.' Just as if they had not been self-moved by their own honorable impulses. The bearing of all these passages, considered in the general drift of the Sermon, is undeniably to implicate the clergy as a whole, in the delinquencies charged.

"Now, if Mr. Parker were to be represented, on both continents, as an advocate of kidnapping, and of the Fugitive Slave Law, he would probably regard it as unjust. But he does not seem to be sufficiently alive to the idea, that it is unjust to convey the idea that this is true of clergymen who have from the first opposed

our masters, and treat us as Slaves. It is ourselves who made the yoke. We offer our back to the

---

these measures as earnestly and decidedly as he himself. He seems to be fully convinced that to rob even one slave of his liberty is a crime. He does not seem as deeply to feel that it is a crime to rob even our ministers of that reputation which in his own case he prizes so highly. Even if the cases of fidelity were few, for that very reason they should receive from a lover of the cause the more careful and particular notice and praise. In cases like these, if ever, discriminations and truthful statements of facts are a sacred duty. Let those be censured who deserve censure, and let those be commended who deserve praise.

" Allow me, then, to state some of the facts of the case chiefly concerning the Orthodox Congregational pastors and churches, leaving to other denominations, if they see fit, to state similar facts, more at large, in their own case. From my own knowledge, I am assured that it would not be difficult to multiply them, especially if a full account were to be given of all the unpublished sermons of the times.

" It is not true, as Mr. P.'s statements imply, that Mr. Parker was the only one who preached and wrote and prayed against the Fugitive Slave Law.

" The Congregationalist, then edited by Rev. H. M. Dexter, Rev. Mr. Storrs, and myself, devoted all its energies to a conflict with the Fugitive Slave Bill, and a vindication of the claim of the higher law. Some of its articles were considered of such importance as to be honored with special attention and censure, by Mr. Choate, at the Boston Union Saving meeting. Our articles, if collected, would make a large volume.

" The law was also most earnestly opposed from the pulpit, by many ministers, Mr. Stone, Mr. Dexter, and myself among the number. The same thing was true of a large number of the clergymen of New England and the Middle States. I have before me published Sermons or other Addresses to this effect from Storrs and Spear, of Brooklyn, N. Y.; Beecher, of Newark, N. J.; Thompson and Cheever, of New York; Bacon, of New Haven, Conn.; Colver, of Boston; Walcott, now of Providence;

Slave-driver's whip. A Western man travels all through Kentucky — he was in Boston three days

---

Leavitt, then of Newton, Mass.; Withington, of Newbury, Mass.; Whitcomb, of Stoneham, Mass.; Thayer of Ashland, Mass.; Arvine, of West Boylston, Mass., and others. Nothing can be more able and eloquent than their defence of God's law, as opposed to the infamous Slave Bill. Others also were published which I have not on file, and I know of several very able discourses against the law which were not published. If a true report could be made of all the Sermons then preached, and of the influence then exerted in other ways by the ministry of the North, there is reason to believe that a very large majority would be found to have set themselves decidedly against the law, and to have advocated its entire disobedience.

"The fact is that undue importance has been given to those of the ministry who favored obedience to that law, and they have been made to overshadow its more numerous opponents.

"In relation to Andover the facts are these: — Professor Stuart, who for some years had ceased to act as Professor in the Seminary, published his views, greatly to the regret of a large portion of his brethren. That the body of the Professors of the Institution did not sympathize in these views, is evident from the fact that when a paper approving the compromise was circulated there, Professors Park, Phelps, and Edwards refused to sign. Only one acting Professor did sign, much to his own subsequent regret. This does not justify the sweeping affirmation.

"'Andover went for kidnapping.' Mr. Parker ought to be more careful, and less free in the use of such wholesale charges. Moreover, the positions of Professor Stuart were thoroughly exposed by members of his own denomination.

"The Rev. Rufus Clark, now of East Boston, published in the columns of the Atlas, a thorough refutation of his pamphlet, in a series of very able articles, which were subsequently republished in a pamphlet form.

"Rev. George Perkins of Connecticut, performed a similar service in that State. Rev. Mr. Dexter, of Boston, exposed himself

ago — and hears only this rumor: "the Yankees are cowards; they dare not resist us. We will drive

---

to an excited retort from Professor Stuart, for his keen and able exposure of his course on the Compromises.

"That there was a sad failure on the part of too many of the clergy of Boston and other commercial cities, cannot be denied; nor do I desire to avert from them merited censure. But ought the labors of such men as the clerical editors and contributors of the Independent to be passed by in silence, in speaking of the prominent clergy of the city of New York?

"As to the other cities named, if there were but one exception in each, it ought to have been prominently named and honored. I do not doubt that there were more.

"As to the country churches and pastors of New England, I have already stated my opinion that the vast majority were opposed to the Fugitive Slave Law. It is not just to regard the Nebraska protest as a virtual confession and reparation of past neglect, but rather as a development of the real feeling of the clergy of New England. Charity thinketh no evil, and there is no gain at this time in depreciating the merits of any earnest opponents of the aggressions of slavery.

"As Mr. Parker expects to be read in all parts of this nation and on both sides of the Atlantic, I will not doubt that his strongly avowed appreciation of what is just and honorable in action, will induce him to revise and correct his statement of facts, and instead of such sweeping and indiscriminate censure, to give honor where honor is due.

"EDWARD BEECHER."

I have repeatedly and in the most public manner done honor to the ministers who have opposed this great iniquity, and did not suppose that any one would misunderstand the expressions which Dr. Beecher considers as "sweeping." When he reads in the Bible that "*Jerusalem and all Judea went out*," I suppose he thinks that some persons staid at home. But I am sorry he could not make out a stronger case for his side. I know nothing of what was said *privately*, or of sermons which never get spoken of out of the little parish where they are written. He mentions *sixteen Or-*

them just where we like. We will force the Nebraska Bill down their throats, and then force Saint

thodox ministers who published matter in opposition to the Fugitive Slave Bill. It is not a very large number for all the churches in New Jersey, New York, Connecticut, Rhode Island, and Massachusetts to furnish. I can mention more.

These are the facts in respect to Andover: Professor Stuart, the most distinguished clergyman in all New England, wrote an elaborate defence of the Fugitive Slave Bill, and of Mr. Webster's conduct in defending it. He was induced to do this by Mr. Webster himself. The work is well known — "Conscience and the Constitution," — and it is weak and doting as it is wicked. Professor Stuart, and two other Andover Professors — Rev. Ralph Emerson, D. D., and Rev. Leonard Woods, D. D. — signed the letter to Mr. Webster expressing their "deep obligations for what this speech has done and is doing;" thanking him "for recalling us to our duties under the Constitution, and for the broad, national, and patriotic views" it inculcates, and desiring to "express to you our entire concurrence in the sentiments of your speech." It seems three other Professors — Messrs. Park, Phelps, and Edwards, — did not sign it, and one of the signers — Dr. Woods or Dr. Emerson — did it much to his own subsequent regret. But did he make his regret public? did Andover in public say any thing against the conduct of the signers?

At the Annual Conference of Unitarian Ministers in May, 1851, long and public defences of kidnapping were made by "the most eminent men in the denomination." One Doctor of Divinity vindicated the attempt of his parishioners to kidnap mine, whom I took to my house for shelter. Dr. Dewey's promise to send back his own mother or brother got the heartiest commendation from more than one "prominent minister." Dr. Dewey was compared with "faithful Abraham;" his declaration was "imputed to him for righteousness." Many of the country ministers were of a different opinion. Some of them declared his conduct "atrocious." Of course there were noble men in the Unitarian denomination, who were faithful to the great principles of Christianity. I have

Domingo and Cuba after it." That is public opinion in Kentucky. My brothers, it is very well deserved.

---

often spoken in their praise, and need not now mention their names; too well known to require honor from me.

But I am sorry to say that I can retract nothing from what I have said in general respecting the conduct of the clergy of all denominations at that time. At a large public meeting in Boston, a Vigilance Committee was appointed to look after the Fugitives and furnish them aid. The Committee sent a Circular to every church in Massachusetts, asking for the Fugitives donations of money and clothes; and received replies from *eighty-seven churches*, which gave us $1,484.56!

Here is my letter in reply to Dr. Beecher, from the Commonwealth of June 10, 1854: —

Dr. Edward Beecher and Theodore Parker.

Rev. Edward Beecher, D. D.: — My dear Sir, I have just read your letter in the Commonwealth of this morning, in which you maintain that the statements in my last sermon respecting the delinquency of the Northern clergy were too sweeping, and that I did injustice to the ministers who stoutly resisted the Fugitive Slave Bill and its execution. Perhaps the language of the sermon would seem to warrant your opinion. But I have so many times, and in so public a manner, expressed my respect and veneration for those noble men who have been found faithful in times of peril, that I cannot think I am in general obnoxious to the charge you make against me.

In respect to the special sermon of last Sunday, I beg leave to inform you that the *whole* was neither printed nor preached; the entire sermon is now in press, and when you see it, I think you will find that I do no injustice to the men you speak of. As I spoke, Sunday, I did not suppose any one would misunderstand my words, or think I wished to be regarded as the only one found faithful. Certainly I have many times done honor to the gentlemen you mention, and to the journals you refer to — with others you do not name. And allow me to say, the conduct of yourself and all your family has not only been a strong personal encourage-

The North hated the Missouri Compromise. Daniel Webster fought against it with all his manly might; and then it was very manly and very mighty. When he collects his speeches, in 1850, for electioneering purposes — a political pamphlet in six octavos — he leaves out all his speeches and writings against the Missouri Compromise! His friend, Mr. Everett, writes his memoir, and there is nothing about Mr. Webster's opposition to the extension of Slavery; about the Missouri Compromise not one single word.

My friends, the South treat us as we deserve. They make compromises, and then break them. They say we are cowards. Are they mistaken? They put our seamen in jail for no crime, but their complexion. We allow it. Then they come to New England, and in Boston steal our fellow-citizens —

---

ment to me, but a theme of public congratulation which I have often brought forward in lectures, and sermons, and speeches. I am a little surprised that you should suppose that by the *churches of commerce* in New York, Boston, etc., I mean *all the churches* of these towns. I still think that from 1850 to 1852, the general voice of the New England churches, so far as it was heard through the press, was in favor of the Fugitive Slave Bill and its execution. This was especially true of the rich and fashionable churches in the great commercial towns. Surely you cannot forget the numerous clerical eulogies on the late Mr. Webster, which sought to justify all his political conduct. I do not think you have made out a very strong case for Andover.

I am sorry to have given pain to a man whose life is so noble and his character so high; but believe me,

Respectfully and truly yours,

THEODORE PARKER.

no! our fellow subjects, our fellow Slaves. We call out the soldiers to help them! Go into a bear's den, and steal a young cub, and if you take only one, all the full-grown bears in the den will come after you and follow till you die, or they die, or their strength fails and they must give up the pursuit.

> " O, Justice! thou art fled to brutish beasts,
> And men have lost their reason!"

The Nebraska Bill has hardly got back to the Senate again, when a Virginian comes here to see how much Boston will bear. He brings letters to "eminent citizens of Boston," lodges at the Revere House, and bravely shows himself to the public in the streets. He walks upon the Common, and looks at the eclipse — the eclipse of the sun I mean; not the eclipse of Boston; that he needs no glass to look at, as there is none smoked dark enough to hinder it from dazzling his eyes. He gets two Boston lawyers to help him kidnap a man. He finds a Commissioner, a Probate Officer of Massachusetts, ready to violate the tenure of his own trust, prepared for the work; a Marshal anxious to prove his Democracy by stealing a man; he finds newspapers ready to sustain him: the Governor lets him go unmolested; the Mayor lends him all the police of the city; and then, illegally and without any authority, against the protestations of the Aldermen, calls out all the soldiers among a hundred and sixty thousand people, in order to send one innocent negro into bondage, and gives them orders, it is said, to shoot down any citizen who shall attempt to pass their lines! The soldiers, half drunk, present their horse-pistols at the heads of women — their thumb on the hammer! They stab horses, and with their sabres slash the heads of men!

When Mr. Burns was first seized by the kidnappers, nearly all the daily newspapers took sides against the Fugitive. The city was full of ministers all the week; two Anti-Slavery conventions were held, one of them two thousand men strong; the Worcester "Freedom Club" came down here to visit us: they all went home, and "order reigns in Warsaw." In South Carolina, there is a public opinion stronger than the law. Let Massachusetts send an honored citizen to Charleston, to remonstrate against an iniquitous statute, and most respectable citizens drive him away. Colored citizens of Massachusetts rot in the jails of Charleston. Northern merchants pay the costs. Boston merchants remonstrated years ago, and the Boston Senator did not dare to offer their paper in Congress! Yes, a Boston Senator did not dare present the remonstrances of Boston merchants! The South despises us. Do you wonder at the treatment we receive? I wonder not at all.

Now, let me say another word — it must be a

brief one, — of this particular case. When Mr Burns was kidnapped, a public meeting was called in Faneuil Hall. Who went there? Not one of the men who are accustomed to control public opinion in Boston. If ten of them had appeared on that platform, Mr. Phillips and myself would not have troubled the audience with our speech. We would have yielded the place — to citizens of "eminent gravity" giving their counsel, and there would have been no man carried out of Boston. I could mention ten men, known to every man here, who, if they had been there, would have so made such public opinion, that the Fugitive Slave Bill Commissioner never would have found "evidence" or "law" enough to send Anthony Burns back to Alexandria. There was not one of them there. They did not wish to be there. They cared nothing for Freedom!

In general, the blame of this wickedness rests on the City of Boston, much of it on Massachusetts, on New England, and on all the North. But here I must single out some of the individuals who are personally responsible for this outrage.

I begin with the Commissioner. He was the prime mover.

Now, as a general thing, the Commissioners who kidnap men in America have had a proclivity to wickedness. It has been structural, constitutional. Man-stealing was in their bones. It was an osteological necessity. A phrenologist, examining their heads, would have said: "Beware of this man. He is 'fit for treason, stratagems, and spoils.'"

It seems natural that Mr. Kane should steal men in Philadelphia. His name is warrant to bear out the deed. In Boston, the former kidnapper lost no "personal popularity" by the act. His conduct seems alike befitting the disposition he was born with, and the culture he has attained to; and so appears equally natural and characteristic. But I thought Mr. Loring of a different disposition. His is a pleasant face to look at, dignified, kindly — a little weak, yet not without sweetness and a certain elevation. I have seen him sometimes in the Probate Office, and it seemed to me a face fit to watch over the widow and the fatherless. When a bad man does a wicked thing, it astonishes nobody. When one otherwise noble and generous is overtaken in a fault, we "weep to record, and blush to give it in," and in the spirit of meekness seek to restore such an one. But when a good man deliberately, voluntarily, does such a deed as this, words cannot express the fiery indignation which it ought to stir up in every man's bosom. It destroys confidence in humanity.

The wickedness began with the Commissioner. He issued the writ. It was to end with him, — he is sheriff, judge, jury. He is paid twice as much for condemning as for acquitting the innocent.

He was not obliged to be a Commissioner. He

was not forced into that bad eminence. He went there voluntarily fifteen years ago, as United States Commissioner to take affidavits and acknowledgments. Slave-catching was no part of his duty. The soldiers of Nicholas execute their master's tyranny, because they are forced into it. The only option with them is to shoot with a musket, or be scourged to death with the knout. If Mr. Loring did not like kidnapping, he need not have kept his office. But he liked it. He wrote three articles, "cold and cruel," in the Daily Advertiser, defending the Fugitive Slave Bill.

But if he kept the office he is not officially obliged to do the work. The District Attorney is not suspected of being so heavily fraught with conscience that he cannot trim his craft to sail with any political wind which offers to carry him to port; but even Mr. Hallett refused to kidnap Ellen Craft. He did not like the business. It was not a part of Mr. Loring's official obligation. A man lets himself to a sea-captain as a mariner to go a general voyage. He is not obliged to go privateering or pirating whenever the captain hoists the black flag. He can leave at the next port. A laborer lets himself to a farmer to do general farm work. By and by his employer says, "I intend to steal sheep." The man is not obliged by his contract to go and steal sheep because his employer will. That would be an illegal act, no doubt. But suppose the general government had made a law, authorizing every farmer to steal all the black sheep he can lay his hands on; nay, commanding the felony. Is this servant, who is hired to do general farm work, obliged, in his official capacity, to go and steal black sheep? I do not look at it so. I do not think any man does. A lawyer turns off many a client. A constable refuses many a civil job. He does not like the business. The Commissioner took this business because he liked to take it. I do not say he was not "conscientious." I know nothing of that. I only speak of the act. Herod was "conscientious," for aught I know, and Iscariot and Benedict Arnold and Aaron Burr. I do not touch that question. To their own master they stand or fall. The torturers of the Spanish Inquisition may have been "conscientious."

It was entirely voluntary for Mr. Loring to take this case. There was no official obligation, no professional honor, that required him to do it. He had a "great precedent," even, in Mr. Hallett, to decline it.

In 1843, Massachusetts enacted a law prohibiting any State officer from acting as Slave-catcher, for fear of abuse of our own law. Since that, Mr. Loring has become Judge of Probate. There was a chance for a good man to show his respect for the law of the State which gives him office.

Now see how the case was conducted. I am no lawyer, and shall not undertake to judge the technical subtleties of the case. But look at the chief things which require no technical skill to judge.

The Commissioner spoke very kindly, and even paternally, when he consulted Burns. I confess the tear started to my eye when he looked so fatherly toward the man, like a Judge of Probate, and asked him — Would you like a little time to prepare to make a defence? And when Mr. Burns replied, "Yes," he honorably gave him some time, forty-eight hours, to decide whether he would make a defence on Saturday, May 27. He also honorably gave Mr. Burns and his counsel a little time to make ready for trial. He gave them from Saturday until Monday! True it was only twenty-four hours; Sunday intervened, and lawyers, like other laymen, and ministers, are supposed to be at meeting on Sunday. That twenty-four hours — it was not very much time to allow for the defence of a man whose liberty was in peril! If Mr. Burns had been arraigned for murder, he would have had several months to prepare for his trial, the purse and the arm of Massachusetts to summon witnesses for his defence. But as he was charged with no crime, only with being the involuntary Slave of one of our Southern masters — as the Fugitive Slave Act was not designed to "establish justice" but its opposite, or to "insure the blessings of liberty" but the curse of bondage — he may have only twenty-four hours to make ready for his defence: his counsel and a minister may visit him — others are excluded!

If Mr. Burns had been arraigned for stealing a horse, for slander, or any thing else, not twenty-four hours, or days, but twenty-four weeks would have been granted him to make ready for trial. A common lawsuit, for a thousand dollars, in the Supreme Court of Suffolk, is not ordinarily tried within a year, and if any questions of law are to be settled, not disposed of within two years. Here, however, a man was on trial for more than life, and but twenty-four hours were granted him! I accept that thankfully, and tender Mr. Loring my gratitude for that! It is more than I looked for from any Fugitive Slave Bill Commissioner, except him. I never thought him capable of executing this wickedness. Honor him for this with due honor — no more, no less.

When the hearing began, the kidnapper's counsel urged that the testimony taken at first, when Mr. Burns was brought up, was in the case. The Commissioner held to this monstrous position; and it was only after the urgent opposition of the prisoner's counsel that he consented it should be put in *de novo*.

But after the kidnapping lawyers put in their evidence, the counsel for Mr. Burns asked time for conference and consultation, as the most important questions of law and fact came up; they were weary with long service and exhausting labor — and they begged the Commissioner to adjourn for an hour or two. It was already almost three o'clock. When hard pressed, he granted them thirty minutes to get up their law and their evidence, take refreshment, and come back to court. At length he extended it to forty minutes! Much of that time was lost to one of the counsel by the troops, who detained him at the door. But the next day, after Mr. Burns's counsel had brought in evidence to show that he was in Boston on the first of March — which nobody expected, for Brent alleges that he saw him in Virginia on the nineteenth of March, and that he escaped thence on the twenty-fourth, — then, after a conference with the Marshal, he grants the kidnapper's lawyers an hour and a quarter to meet this new and unexpected evidence. Of course he knew that in granting them this, he really gave them all night to get up their evidence, prepare their defence, and come into Court the next morning, and rebut what had been said. Is that fair? Consider what a matter there was at stake — a man's liberty for ever and ever on earth! Consider that Mr. Loring was judge and jury; — that it was a "court" without appeal; that no other court could pass upon his verdict, and reverse it, if afterwards it was shown to be suspicious or proved to be wrong. He grants Mr. Burns thirty minutes, and the other side at once, an hour and a quarter, virtually all night! That is not all. His decision was limited to one point, namely: the identity of the prisoner. If Mr. Burns answered the description of the Fugitive given in the record, the Commissioner took it for granted, first, that he was a Slave, — there was no proof: second, that he had escaped into another State, — that was not charged in the record, nor proved by testimony; third, that he owed service and labor to Col. Suttle, not to the lessee, who had a limited fee in his services, nor to the mortgagee, who had the conditional fee of his person; but to Col. Suttle, the reversioner, the original claimant of his body.

Now the statute leaves the party claimant his choice between two processes; one under its sixth section, the other under the tenth.

The sixth section obliges the claimant to prove three points, 1. That the person claimed *owes* service; 2. That he has *escaped;* and 3. That the party before the court is the *identical one* alleged to be a Slave.

The tenth section makes the claimant's certificate conclusive as to the first two points, and only leaves the identity to be proved.

In this case, the claimant, by offering proof of service and escape, made his election to proceed under the sixth section.

Here he failed; failed to prove service; failed to prove escape. Then the Commissioner allowed him to swing round and take refuge in the tenth section, leaving identity only to be proved; and this he proved by the prisoner's confession made under duress and in terror, if at all; wholly denied by him; and proved only by the testimony of a witness of whom we know nothing, but that he was contradicted by several witnesses as to the only point to which he affirmed capable of being tested.

So, then, the Commissioner reduced the question precisely to this: Is the prisoner at the bar the same Anthony Burns whom Brent saw in Virginia on the nineteenth day of March last, and who the claimant swears in his complaint escaped from Virginia on the twenty-fourth of March?

One man, calling himself "William Brent, a merchant of Richmond," testified as to the question of identity — "This is Burns." He was asked, When did you see him in Virginia? and he answered, On the nineteenth of March last. But nobody in court knew Mr. Brent, and Mr. Loring himself confessed that he stood "under circumstances that would bias the fairest mind." He had come all the way from Richmond to Boston to make out the case. Doubtless he expected his reward — perhaps in money, perhaps in honor; for it is an honor in Virginia to support the institutions of that State. But, on the other side, many witnesses testified that Burns was here in Boston on the first of March, and worked several days at the Mattapan Iron-Works, at South Boston. Several men, well known in Boston — persons of unimpeached integrity, — testified to the fact. No evidence rebutted their testimony. Nothing was urged to impugn their veracity. The Commissioner says their "integrity is admitted," and "no imputation of bias could be attached" to them. So, to decide between these two, Mr. Loring takes the admissions of the Fugitive, alleged to have been made under duress, in the presence of his "master," made in jail; when he was surrounded by armed ruffians; when he was "intimidated" by fear, — admissions which Mr. Burns denied to the last, even after the decision. This was the proof of identity!

The record called Burns a man with "dark complexion." The prisoner is a "full blooded negro." His complexion is black almost as my coat. The record spoke of Burns as having a scar on his right hand. The right hand of this man had been broken; it was so badly injured that when it was opened, he could only shut it by grasping it with his left. The bone stuck out prominent. The kidnapper's witness testified that Burns was in Virginia on the nineteenth of March. Several witnesses — I know not how many, — testified that he was in Boston nineteen days before!

Mr. Brent stated nothing to show that he had ever had any particular knowledge of Mr. Burns, or particularly observed his person. Some of the witnesses for the prisoner did not testify merely from general observation of his form or features, but they stated that they had noted especially the scar on his cheek, and his broken hand, and they knew him to be the man. Besides, this testimony is of multiplied force, not being that of so many to one fact; that of each stands by itself. There was a cloud of witnesses to prove that Mr. Burns was in Boston from the first of March. If their evidence could be invalidated, it was not attacked in court. Their fairness was admitted.

Not many years ago, a woman was on trial in Boston for the murder of her own child. At first she plead guilty, and, weeping stated the motives which led to the unnatural crime. But the court interfered, induced her to retract the plea, and to make a defence. And in spite of her voluntary admissions made in court, she was acquitted — for there was not evidence to warrant a legal conviction.

Mr. Loring seemed to regard Slavery as a *crimen exceptum;* and when a man is charged with it he is presupposed to be guilty, and must be denied the usual means of defence. So out of the victim's own mouth he extorts the proof that this is the man named in the record.

A man not known to anybody in court brings a paper from Alexandria claiming Anthony Burns as his Slave; the paper was drawn up five hundred miles off; in the absence of Mr. Burns; by his enemies, who sought for his liberty and more than his life. He brought one witness to testify to the identity of the man, who says that, in his fear, Burns said, I am the man. But seven witnesses, whose veracity was not impeached in the court, testify that the prisoner *was in Boston* in the early part of March; and therefore it appears that he is not the Burns who *was in Virginia* on the nineteenth of March, and thence escaped on the twenty-fourth. To decide between the two testimonies — that of one Virginian under circumstances that would bias the fairest mind, and seven Bostonians free from all bias — the Commissioner takes the words put into the mouth of Mr. Burns.

Now, the Fugitive Slave Bill provides that the testimony of the Fugitive shall not be received as evidence in the case. Mr. Loring avoids that difficulty. He does not call it "testimony" or "evidence." He calls it "admissions;" accepts it to prove the "identity," and decides the case against him. But who proves that Mr. Burns made the admissions? There are two witnesses: 1. A man hired to kidnap him, one of the marshal's "guard," a spy, a hired informer, set to watch the prisoner and make inquisition. Of what value was his testimony? 2. Mr. Brent, who had come five hundred miles to assist in catching a runaway Slave, and claimed Mr. Burns as the Slave. This was the only valuable witness to prove the admission. So the admission is proved by the admission of Mr. Brent, and the testimony of Mr. Brent is proved by the admission! Excellent Fugitive Slave Bill "evidence!" Brent confirms Brent! There is, I think, a well-known axiom of the common law, that "admissions shall go in entire"—all that the prisoner said. Now, Mr. Loring rules in just what serves the interest of the claimant, and rules out every thing that serves Mr. Burns's interest. And is that Massachusetts Justice?

Remember, too, that Commissioner Loring is the whole court—a "judge," not known to the Constitution; a "jury" only known in the inquisition! There is no appeal from his decision. The witness came from Virginia to swear away the freedom of a citizen of Massachusetts, charged with no crime. When the Marshal, and the men hired to kidnap, are about the poor black man, it is said he makes an admission that he is the Fugitive; and on that "evidence" Mr. Loring decides that he is to go into bondage for ever. It was conduct worthy of the Inquisition of Spain!* Let doubts weigh for the prisoner, is a rule as old as legal attempts at justice. Here, they weigh against him. The case is full of doubts—doubts on every side. He rides over them all. He takes the special words he wants, and therewith strikes down the prisoner's claim to Liberty.

---

* Tacitus thinks it a piece of good fortune that Agricola died before such "admissions" were made evidence to ruin a man, as in Domitian's time *quum Suspiria nostra subscriberentur!*—Agricola, c. xlv.

Suppose, in the present instance, the fugitive had been described as a man of light complexion, blue eyes, and golden hair: then, suppose some white man, you or I, answered the description, and some ruffian swore to the identity. By that form of law, any man, any woman, in the city of Boston, might have been taken and carried off into bondage straightway, irredeemable bondage, bondage forever.

Commissioner Loring had no better ground for taking away the liberty of Anthony Burns than in the case I have just supposed.

Suppose Col. Suttle had claimed the Mayor and Aldermen of Boston as his Slaves; had brought a "record" from Alexandria reciting their names, and setting forth the fact of their owing service, and their escape from it; had them kidnapped and brought before Mr. Loring. According to his own ruling, the only question he has to determine is this: "the identity of the persons." A witness testifies that the Mayor and Aldermen of Boston are the parties named in the record as owing service and having escaped therefrom. The Commissioner says, "the facts to be proved by the claimant are three.

"1. That the parties charged owed him service in Virginia.

"2. That they escaped from that service.

"These facts he has proved by the record which the statute, (Sec. 10,) declares 'shall be held, and taken to be full and conclusive evidence of the fact of escape, and that the service or labor of the person escaping is due to the party in such record mentioned.'

"Thus these two facts are removed entirely and absolutely from my jurisdiction, and I am entirely and absolutely precluded from applying evidence to them; if, therefore, there is in the case evidence capable of such application, I cannot make it.

"3. The third fact is the identity of the parties before me, with the parties mentioned in the record.

"This identity is the only question I have a right to consider. To this, and to this alone, I am to apply the evidence.

"And then, on the whole testimony, my mind is satisfied beyond a reasonable doubt of the identity of the respondents with the parties named in the record.

"On the law and facts of the case, I consider the claimant entitled to the certificate from me which he claims."

The Mayor and Aldermen go into bondage forever. The liberty of all this audience might be thus sworn away by a Commissioner and another kidnapper.

But the "ruling" is not the worst thing in the case. The Commissioner had prejudged it all. He had prejudged it entirely before he had even begun this mock trial; before he heard the defence; before the prisoner had any counsel to make a defence.

Here is my proof. On Friday, (May 26,) Wendell Phillips went to Cambridge to see Mr. Loring. He is a Professor of Law in Harvard College, teaching law and justice to the young men who go up thither to learn law and justice! Mr. Phillips went there to get permission to visit Mr. Burns, and see if he would make a defence and have counsel. Mr. Loring advised Mr. Phillips to make no defence. He said: "Mr. Phillips, I think the case is so clear that you would not be justified in placing any obstructions in the way of the man's going back, as he probably will."

So, as the matter was decided beforehand, it was to be only a mock trial, and might just as well have been dispensed with. It keeps up some hollow semblance to the form of the Fugitive Slave Bill; but it was all prejudged before Mr. Burns had selected his counsel or determined to have any. Place no "obstructions in the way of the man's going back, *as he probably will!*"

Nor is that all. Before any defence had been made, on Saturday night, Mr. Loring drew up a bill of sale of Anthony Burns. Here it is, in his own handwriting:—

"Know all men in these Presents — That I, Charles F. Suttle, of Alexandria, in Virginia, in consideration of twelve hundred dollars, to me paid, do hereby release and discharge, quitclaim and convey to Antony Byrnes, his liberty; and I hereby manumit and release him from all claims and services to me forever, hereby giving him his liberty to all intents and effects forever.

"In testimony whereof, I have hereto set my hand and seal, this twenty-seventh day of May, in the year of our Lord eighteen hundred and fifty-four."

What should you say of a Judge of the Supreme Court of Massachusetts who should undertake to negotiate a note of hand which was a matter of litigation before him in court? What if the Chief-Justice, before he had heard a word of the case of the last man tried for murder — before the prisoner had any counsel, — had told some humane man taking an interest in the matter, "You would not be justified in placing any obstructions in the way of the man's being hanged as he probably will?" Add this, also: here Commissioner Loring is Justice to draw the writ, Judge, Jury, all in one! Do the annals of judicial tyranny show a clearer case of Judgment without a hearing?

This is not yet the end of the wickedness. Last Wednesday night the kidnapper's court adjourned till Friday morning at nine o'clock. Then the "decision" was to be made. But the kidnapper and his assistants, the Marshal, etc., knew it on Thursday night. How long before, I know not. The men who hired Mr. Loring to steal a man, with the Fugitive Slave Bill for his instrument, they knew the decision at least fourteen hours before it was announced in court — I think twenty hours before.

First, he judged the case before he heard it; second, he judged it against evidence when he heard it; third, he clandestinely communicated the decision to one of the parties half a day before he declared it openly in Court. Could Kane or Curtis do worse? I do not find that they have ever done so bad. Does Boston teem with Epsoms and Dudleys, the vermin of the law? Does New England spawn Jeffreyses and Scroggses, whom we supposed impossible — fictitious characters too bad to be?

Look at the Marshal's conduct. Of his previous character I say nothing. But his agents arrested Mr. Burns on a false charge; threatened violence if he should cry out; they kept him in secret. Nobody came nigh unto him.

The trial was unfairly conducted on the Marshal's part. The public was excluded from the Court House. His servants lined the stairways, insulting the people. Southerners were freely admitted, but Northern gentlemen kept out. Rude, coarse, and insolent fellows found no check. Clergymen and lawyers were turned back, and Southern students of law let in. Two gentlemen were refused admission; but when one declared he was from Virginia, the other from South Carolina, they were both admitted on the instant. The whole Court House seemed to be the property of the Slave power.

He crowded the Court House with soldiers. Some of them were drunk, and charged bayonet upon the counsel and witnesses for Burns, and thrust them away. He employed base men for his guard. I never saw such a motley crew as this kidnapper's gang collected together, save in the darkest places of London and Paris, whither I went to see how low humanity might go down, and yet bear the semblance of man. He raked the kennels of Boston. He dispossessed the stews, bawding the Courts with unwonted infamy. He gathered the spoils of brothels; prodigals not penitent, who upon harlots had wasted their substance in riotous living; pimps, gamblers, the *succubus* of Slavery; men which the gorged jails had cast out into the streets scarred with infamy; fighters, drunkards, public brawlers; convicts that had served out their time, waiting for a second conviction; men whom the subtlety of counsel, or the charity of the gallows had left unhanged. "No eye hath seen such scarecrows." The youngest of the Police Judges found ten of his constituents there. Jailor Andrews, it is said, recognized forty of his customers among them. It is said that Albert J. Tirrell was invited to move in that leprous gang and declined![*] "The wicked walk on every side when the vilest men are exalted!" The publican who fed those locusts of Southern tyranny, said that out of the sixty-five, there was but one respectable man, and he kept aloof from all the rest. I have seen courts of justice in England, Holland, Belgium, Germany, France, Italy, and Switzerland, and I have seen just such men. But they were always in the dock, not the servants of the Court. The Marshal was right; "the statute is so cruel and wicked that it should not be executed by good men." He chose fit tools for fitting work. I do not think Herod sent the guardian of orphans to massacre the innocents of Bethlehem. I doubt that Pontius Pilate employed a Judge of Probate to crucify Jesus between two thieves!

There was an unfairness about the offer to sell Mr. Burns. I do not know whose fault that was. His claimant pretended that he would sell; but when the money was tendered, his agents delayed, equivocated, wore out the time, till it was Sunday; and the deed could not legally be done. It was the man, and not the money they wanted. He offered to sell the man for twelve hundred dollars. The price was

---

* While these sheets are passing through the press I learn that three of the Marshal's guard have been arrested for crimes of violence committed *within twenty-four hours after the rendition. Set a thief to serve a thief.*

exorbitant, he would not bring eight hundred at Alexandria.*

---

* "MR. ATTORNEY HALLETT'S INTERFERENCE WITH THE PURCHASE OF THE FUGITIVE.

"Boston, Saturday, June 3, 1854.

"*To the Editors of the Atlas:* — You have called my attention to an article in your paper this morning, signed L., and to a contradiction of its statement in the Journal of this evening, by authority of the United States District Attorney. I know nothing of the origin of either of these articles, but will, at your request, give you a narrative of my own connection with the recent negotiation for the freedom of 'Byrnes,' believing that such a narrative will be altogether pertinent to the fact which you seek to establish, namely, the interference of the United States District Attorney in the negotiation above referred to.

"On Saturday afternoon last, the Rev. Mr. Grimes called upon me and said that the owner of Byrnes had offered to sell him for twelve hundred dollars, and that he (Grimes) was anxious to raise the money at once. He desired my advice and assistance in the matter, and requested me to draw up a suitable subscription paper for that purpose, which I did in these words: —

"'Boston, May 27, 1854.

"We, the undersigned, agree to pay to Anthony Byrnes, or order, the sum set against our respective names, for the purpose of enabling him to obtain his freedom from the United States Government, in the hands of whose officers he is now held as a Slave.

"'This paper will be presented by the Rev. L. A. Grimes, pastor of the 12th Baptist Church.'

"Upon this paper Mr. Grimes obtained signatures for six hundred and sixty-five dollars, and with the aid of Col. Suttle's counsel, Messrs. Parker and Thomas, who interested themselves in this matter, four hundred dollars more was got in a check, conditionally, and held by Mr. Parker. It was agreed by me that I should be near at hand on Saturday night, to assist and advance the money, which was accordingly done, and my check for eight hun-

There was another trick. At one time it was thought the evidence would compel the reluctant

---

dred dollars, early in the night, was placed in the hands of the United States Marshal for this purpose. About eleven o'clock, all parties being represented, we met at Mr. Commissioner Loring's office. This gentleman, with commendable alacrity, prepared necessary papers.

"At this juncture the actual money was insisted on, which threatened for a time the completion of the negotiation; but anticipating this contingency, which, under all circumstances, was not an unreasonable demand, we adjourned to the Marshal's office, and I prepared myself with the needful tender. The United States Attorney, Mr. Hallett, was in attendance, and the respective parties immediately discussed the mode of procedure. The hour of twelve was rapidly approaching, after which no action could be taken. Mr. Grimes was prepared to receive Byrnes, and anxious to take him as he might peacefully. The matter lingered, and official action ceased.

"I am not disposed to charge any one with designedly defeating the desired end on that occasion. The business was new, the questions raised novel. But when we had proceeded thus far, and were ready in good faith to make good the sum requisite on Monday, in view also of the friendly understanding had after midnight with all parties in interest, we had a right to expect Byrnes's liberation on Monday. When that day came, the owner refused to treat. Learning from rumor only, that four thousand dollars had been named as the sum then asked for, I on Monday addressed Col. Suttle, then in Court, a respectful note, reminding him of the position of things on Saturday night, and urging that Mr. Grimes had the right to expect the original agreement to be carried out, but further asking him, if any additional sum was required: to which he replied, that the 'case is before the Court, and must await its decision.'

"Tuesday morning, I had an interview with Col. Suttle in the U. S. Marshal's office. He seemed disposed to listen to me, and met the subject in a manly way. He said he wished to take the boy back, after which he would sell him. He wanted to see the result

Commissioner to free his victim. Then it was proposed that he should be seized in the Court, and

---

of the trial, at any rate. I stated to him that we considered his claim to Byrnes clear enough, and that he would be delivered over to him, urging particularly upon him that the boy's liberation was not sought for except with his free consent, and his claim being fully satisfied. I urged upon him no consideration of the fear of a rescue, or possible unfavorable result of the trial to him, but offered distinctly, if he chose, to have the trial proceed, and whatever might be the result, still to satisfy his claim.

" I stated to him that the negotiation was not sustained by any society or association whatsoever, but that it was done by some of our most respectable citizens, who were desirous not to obstruct the operation of the law, but in a peaceable and honorable manner sought an adjustment of this unpleasant case; assuring him that this feeling was general among the people. I read to him a letter, addressed to me by a highly esteemed citizen, urging me to renew my efforts to accomplish this, and placing at my disposal any amount of money that I might think proper for the purpose.

" Col. Suttle replied that he appreciated our motives, and that he felt disposed to meet us. He then stated what he would do. I accepted his proposal at once; it was not entirely satisfactory to me, but yet, in view of his position, as he declared to me, I was content. At my request, he was about to commit our agreement to writing, when Mr. B. F. Hallett entered the office, and they two engaged in conversation apart from me. Presently Col. Suttle returned to me, and said: 'I must withdraw what I have done with you.' We both immediately approached Mr. Hallett, who said, pointing to the spot where Mr. Batchelder fell, in sight of which we stood, 'That blood must be avenged.' I made some pertinent reply, rebuking so extraordinary a speech, and left the room.

" On Friday, soon after the decision had been rendered, finding Col. Suttle had gone on board the Cutter at an early hour, I waited upon his counsel, Messrs. Thomas and Parker, at the Court House, and there renewed my proposition. Both these gentlemen promptly interested themselves in my purpose, which was to tender the claimant full satisfaction, and receive the surrender of

either summarily declared a Slave by some other Commissioner, or else carried off with no further mock trial. I think it would have been done; but

---

Byrnes from him, either there, in State street, or on board the Cutter, at his own option. It was arranged between us that Mr. Parker should go at once on board the Cutter, and make an arrangement, if possible, with the Colonel.

"I provided ample funds, and returned immediately to the Court House, when I found that there would be difficulty in getting on board the Cutter. Application was made by me to the Marshal, he interposed no objection, and I offered to place Mr. Parker alongside the vessel. Presently Mr. Parker took me aside and said these words: 'Col. Suttle has pledged himself to Mr. Hallett that he will not sell his boy until he gets him home.' Thus the matter ended.

"In considering, Mr. Editor, whose interference was potent in thus defeating the courteous endeavors of citizens of Boston, peacefully and with due respect to the laws of the land, to put to rest the painful scenes of the past week, it must be borne in mind that the United States Marshal, who, throughout this unfortunate negotiation, has conducted himself towards us with great consideration, consented, individually, to hold the funds, as a party not in interest, thus early acquiescing in the success of our plan; the owner himself was willing to release his claim; his counsel, Messrs. Thomas and Parker, volunteered their aid in raising the money, urged it and interested themselves in its speedy accomplishment — even in the latest moment when it could be effected, with commendable alacrity, they offered their assistance; the United States Commissioner himself consented to be at his post until midnight of Saturday, to give his official service for the object — I repeat, in view of all these considerations, the conclusion must come home irresistibly to every candid mind, that there was one personage, who, officially or individually, in this connection, either did do, or left undone, something whereby his interference became essential to a less painful termination of this case.

"Respectfully,

"HAMILTON WILLIS."

Commissioner Loring was ready to do the work demanded of him, and earn his twofold pay.

The conduct of the Governor requires some explanation. The law of Massachusetts was cloven down by the sword of the Marshal; no officer could be found to serve the writ of personal replevin, designed by the Massachusetts Legislature to meet exactly such cases, and bring Mr. Burns before a Massachusetts court. The Governor could not be induced to attend to it: Monday he was at the meeting of the Bible Society; Thursday at the meeting of the Sunday Schools. If the United States Marshal had invaded the sovereignty of South Carolina, where do you think her Governor would have been?

The conduct of the Mayor of Boston deserves to be remembered. He had the police of the city in Court Square, aiding the kidnapper. It was not their fault. They served against their will. Captain Hayes, of the Police, that day magnanimously resigned his charge.* The Mayor called out the sol-

---

* Here is the note of Mr. Hayes to the City Authorities; one day his children will deem it a noble trophy.

"Boston, June 2, 1854.

"*To His Honor the Mayor and the Aldermen of the City of Boston:*

"Through all the excitement attendant upon the arrest and trial of the Fugitive, by the U. S. Government, I have not rediers at great cost, to some one. He did this on his own responsibility. Five Aldermen have publicly protested against the breach of honor and justice. After the wicked deed was over, he attended a meeting of Sunday School children in Faneuil Hall. When he was introduced to the audience, "Out of the mouth of babes and sucklings" came a hiss! At night, the "citizen soldiery" had a festival. The Mayor was at the supper, and toasted the military — eating and drinking and making merry. What did they care, or he, that an innocent citizen of Boston was sent into bondage forever, and by their hands! The agony of Mr. Burns only flavored their cup. So the butcher's dog can enjoy himself in the shambles, while the slaughter of the innocent goes on around him, "battening on garbage!"

Thus, on the Second of June, Boston sent into bondage her second victim. It ought to have been fifteen days later — the Seventeenth of June. What a spectacle it was! The day was brilliant; there was not a cloud; all about Boston there was a ring

---

ceived an order which I have conceived inconsistent with my duties as an officer of the Police, until this day, at which time I have received an order, which, if performed, would implicate me in the execution of that infamous 'Fugitive Slave Bill.'

"I therefore resign the office which I now hold as a Captain of the Watch and Police, from this hour, 11 A. M.

"Most respectfully yours,

"JOSEPH K. HAYES."

of happy, summer loveliness; the green beauty of June; the grass, the trees, the heaven, the light; and Boston itself was the theatre of incipient civil war!

What a day for Boston! Citizens applauding that a man was to be carried into bondage! Drunken soldiers, hardly able to stand in the street, sung their ribald song—"Oh! carry me back to old Virginia!" *

---

* I copy this from one of the newspapers:—

"*The pay of the Boston Military for their Aid in the Rendition of Anthony Burns.*

"We write with an 'iron pen' for the benefit of some future historian, that in the year of our Lord eighteen hundred and fifty-four, in the city of Boston, there was received for their aid in consigning to the bondage of American chattel slavery one Anthony Burns,—by the grace of God and his own efforts a freeman,—by the independent volunteer militia of said city, the following sums:—

"National Lancers, Capt. Wilmarth,	$820.00
Boston Light Dragoons, Capt. Wright,	1,128.00
Fifth Regiment of Artillery, by Col. Cowdin, for himself, staff, and regiment,	3,946.00
Boston Light Infantry, Capt. Rogers,	460.00
New England Guards, Capt. Henshaw,	432.00
Pulaski Guards, Capt. Wright,	328.00
Boston Light Guard, Capt. Follett,	500.00
Boston City Guard, Capt. French,	488.00
(of which $190 was paid by order to George Young, for 'refreshments.')	
Boston Independent Fusileers, Capt. Cooley,	320.00
Washington Light Infantry, Capt. Upton,	536.00
Mechanic Infantry, Capt. Adams,	428.00
National Guard, Lieut. Harlow commanding,	416.00
Union Guard, Capt. Brown,	476.00
Sarsfield Guard, Capt. Hogan,	308.00
Boston Ind. Cadets, Capt Amory,	1,136.00

Daniel Webster lies buried at Marshfield; but his dead hand put the chain on Anthony Burns. Last winter it was proposed to build him a monument. He needs it not. Hancock has none; Samuel Adams sleeps in a nameless grave; John Adams has

---

Boston Light Artillery, Capt. Cobb, ...	168.00
Major General Edmands, and staff, ...	715.00
Major Pierce and staff, of the First Battalion Light Dragoons, ...	146.00
Col. Holbrook and staff, of the First Regiment of Light Infantry, ...	26.00
Brigadier General Andrews and staff, of the First Brigade	107.50
Major Burbank and staff, of the Third Battalion of Light Infantry, ...	76.00
William Read, hardware and sporting apparatus dealer, for ammunition, ...	155.28
Total,	$13,115.78"

The sum paid to the *civil officers* of Boston for their services, has not yet been made public!

Mr. Burns was subsequently sold to David McDaniel, of Nash County, N. C., on condition that he "*should never be sold to go North.*" A most piteous letter was received from him in January, 1855, full of pious gratitude to all who sought to preserve for him the unalienable Right to Life, Liberty, and the Pursuit of Happiness.

Presently after Commissioner Loring had accomplished his "legal" kidnapping he tried to purchase a piece of meat of a noble-hearted butcher in Boylston market. I will take that pig, said the Commissioner. "You can't have it!" replied the butcher. What, is it sold? "No, Sir! But you can't buy your meat of me. I want none of your blood-money. It would *burn my pocket!*"

Rev. Nehemiah Adams, D. D., subsequently sent to the Commissioner, a presentation copy of his South Side View of Slavery, with the author's regards!

not a stone. We are their monuments; the homage of the people is their epitaph. Daniel Webster also had his monument last Friday. It was the Court House crowded with two hundred and twenty United States soldiers and flanked with a cannon. His monument reached all the way from John Hancock's house, in Court Street, to the T wharf; nay, it went far out to sea in the Revenue Cutter, and is borne seaward or shoreward. Conquer your prejudices! No Higher Law! On the brass cannon you could read, I STILL LIVE.

Mr. Burns was seized on that day which the Christian church has consecrated to two of the Martyrs, Saints Donatian and Rogatian. They seem to have been put to death by Rictius Varus, the Commissioner of Belgic and Celtic Gaul. They suffered death at Nantes. They were impeached for professing themselves Christians. Simple death was not torment enough for being a Christian in the year 287. They were put to the rack first. Their bodies, still held in great veneration, now sleep their dusty slumber in the great cathedral of the town. The antiquarian traveller wonders at the statues of those two martyrs still standing at the corner of the Money-Changers' Street, and telling the tale of times when the Christians only suffered persecution. St. Rogatian's day was not an unfitting time for Puritanic Boston to steal a man!

The day on which Mr. Burns was sent from Boston into Alexandrian Bondage, is still more marked in the Christian church. It is consecrated to a noble army of martyrs who tasted death at Vienna, in Gaul, — now Vienne, in the South of France — in the year 178 after Christ. I shall never forget the little town, once famous and eminent, where the dreadful event took place. A letter written, it is said, by St. Irenæus himself details the saddening history. It begins, "We the Servants of Christ, [Mr. Everett might translate it '*Slaves*,'] dwelling at Vienna and Lyons in Gaul to the Brethren in Asia and Phrygia who have the same faith and hope with us. Peace, and Grace, and Glory, from God the Father, and from our Lord Jesus Christ." The whole letter is a most touching memorial of the faithful piety of the Christians in days when it cost life to be religious. Anybody may read what remains of it in Eusebius. Here is the story in short: —

A law was passed forbidding Christians to appear out of their own houses "in any place whatsoever." The most cruel punishments were denounced against all persons who professed the Christian religion.

The Governor, who was also a Commissioner appointed for persecuting and murdering the Christians, had the most prominent members of the Church arrested and brought before him. In the "examination" they were treated with such cruelty that Vettius Epagathus, a Christian of distinguished family undertook their defence, a man so exactly virtuous, that though young he won the honor of old Zacharias — "walking in all the commandments and ordinances of the Lord blameless." The Commissioner asked him, "Art thou also a Christian?" Epagathus made his "admission" in a loud voice, and shared the fate of the martyrs. The Christians called him the Comforter of Christians, — "for he had the Comforter, the Spirit, in him, more than Zacharias himself;" — a title as hateful then as Friend of the Slave now is in the Court or the Church of Kidnappers in Boston.

Sanctus, the Deacon; Maturus, a new convert; Attalus, from Asia Minor, one of the pillars of the Church; Blandina, a female Slave; Pothinus, ninety years old and Bishop of Lyons, hard by, were put to the most cruel tortures. Four of them were exposed to the wild beasts in the Amphitheatre to divert the spectators! Blandina was fastened to a post to be eaten up by the beasts, and when they left her untouched, the Marshal haled her to prison again. "But last of all St. Blandina, like a well-born mother who has nursed her children and sent them victorious to the King, hastened after them, rejoicing and leaping for joy at her departure; thrown indeed to the wild beasts she went as if invited to a bridal feast, and after the scourging, after the exposure to wild beasts, after the chair of fire, she was wrapped in a net, and tossed by a bull — and at last killed."

Others fell with them: Ponticus, a boy of fifteen; Alexander the Phrygian, and many more. They were tortured with cudgels, with whips, with wild beasts, and redhot plates of iron; at last they died, one by one. The tormentors threw their dead bodies to the dogs; some raged and gnashed their teeth over the dead, seeking to take yet more abundant vengeance thereon; others laughed and made mockery thereof. And others more gentle, seeming to sympathize as much as they dared, made grievous reproaches and said, "Where is now their God, and of what profit is their piety which they loved better even than their own life? Now we shall see if they will ever rise from the dead, and if their God can help and deliver them out of our hands!"

So things went at Allobrogian Vienna on the second of June, sixteen hundred and seventy-six years ago last Friday. The murder of those Christians was just as "legal" as the rendition of Anthony Burns. It would be curious to know what the "respectable" men of the town said thereupon: to see the list of fifteen hundred citizens volunteering their aid; to read the letter of nine hundred and eighty-seven men thanking the Commissioner for touching their conscience. The preaching of the priests must have been edifying:—"I would drive a Christian away from my own door! I would murder my own mother!"

Doubtless some men said, The statute which commands the torturous murder of men, women, and children for no crime but piety, "if constitutional, is wicked and cruel." And doubtless some Heathen "Chief-Justice Parker" choked down the rising conscience of mankind, and answered: "Whether the statute is a harsh one or not, it is not for us to determine." * No! it is not for the bloodhound to ask whether the victim he rends to quivering fragments is a sinner or a saint; the bloodhound is to bite, and not consider; he has teeth, not conscience. The Fugitive Slave Bill Commissioner is not to do justly, and love mercy, and walk humbly with his God; he is to kidnap men in Boston at ten dollars a head! The Pagan murder of Christians at Vienna under Aurelian, did not differ much from the Christian kidnapping of Mr. Burns in Boston, under Pierce. But alas for these times — it is not recorded of the Romans that any Heathen Judge of Probate came forward and volunteered to butcher the widows and orphans of the early church! Then the tormentor worshipped Mars and Bellona; now he sits in the church of Jesus Christ.

Boston chose a fit day to consummate her second kidnapping. St. Pothinus was a Christian preacher, so was Anthony Burns — "a minister of the Baptist

---

* Reference is here made to the words used by Commissioner Loring in his "decision," citing the words of the late Chief-Justice Parker.

denomination," "regularly ordained!" Commissioner Loring could not have done better than select this time to execute his "decision." On St. Pothinus's day, let Anthony Burns be led to a martyrdom more atrocious! The African churches of Boston may write a letter to-day, which three or four thousand years hence will sound as strange as now the Epistle of St. Irenæus. Sixteen hundred and seventy-six years hence, it may be thought the Marshal's "guard" is a fair match for the bullies who tortured Blandina. In the next world, the District Marshal may shake hands with the Heathen murderer who put the boy Ponticus to cruel death. I make no doubt there were men at the corners of the streets who clapped hands, as one by one the lions in the public square rent the Christian maidens limb from limb, and strewed the ground with human flesh yet palpitating in its severed agony. Boston can furnish mates for them. But the Judge of Probate, the Teacher of a Sunday School, the member of a church of Christ,—he may wander through all Hades peopled thick with Roman tormentors, nor never meet with a Heathen guardian of Orphans who can be his match. Let him pass by. Declamation can add nothing to his deed.

> "To gild refined gold, to paint the lily,
> To throw a perfume on the violet,
> To smooth the ice, or add another hue
> Unto the rainbow, or with taper light

> To seek the beauteous eye of heaven to garnish,
> Is wasteful and ridiculous excess."

No doubt the Commissioner for murdering the Christians at Vienna reasoned as "legally" and astutely in the second century as the Fugitive Slave Bill Commissioner at Boston in the nineteenth. Perhaps the "argument" was after this wise: —*

"This statute has been decided to be constitutional by the unanimous opinion of the Judges of the Supreme Court of the Province of Gaul after the fullest argument and the maturest deliberation to be the law of this Province as well as, and because it is a constitutional law of the Roman Empire, and the wise words of our revered Chief-Justice † may well be repeated now, and remembered always. The Chief-Justice says: —

"'The torture, persecution, and murder of Christians was not created, established, or perpetuated by the Constitution; it existed before; it would have existed if the Constitution had not been made. The framers of the Constitution could not abrogate the custom of persecuting, torturing, and murdering Christians, or the rights claimed under it. They took it as they found it, and regulated it to a limited extent. The Constitution, therefore, is not responsi-

* See the Commissioner's "decision."

† Hon. Lemuel Shaw. See his "opinion" on the constitutionality of the fugitive slave bill in 7 Cushing's Reports, p. 285, *et seq.*

ble for the origin or continuance of this custom of persecuting, torturing, and murdering Christians — the provision it contains was the best adjustment which could be made of conflicting rights and claims to persecute, torture, and murder, and was absolutely necessary to effect what may now be considered as the general pacification by which harmony and peace should take the place of violence and war. These were the circumstances, and this the spirit in which the Constitution was made — the regulation of persecution, torture, and murder of Christians so far as to prohibit Provinces by law from harboring fugitive Christians was an essential element in its formation, and the union intended to be established by it was essentially necessary to the peace and happiness and highest prosperity of all the Provinces and Towns. In this spirit, and with these views steadily in prospect, it seems to be the duty of all judges and magistrates to expound and apply these provisions in the Constitution and laws of the Roman Empire, and in this spirit it behooves all persons bound to obey the laws of the Roman Empire to consider and regard them.'

"Therefore *Christianos ad Leones* — Let the Christians be torn to pieces by the wild beasts."

Wednesday, the twenty-fourth of May, the city was all calm and still. The poor black man was at work with one of his own nation, earning an honest livelihood. A Judge of Probate, Boston born and Boston bred, a man in easy circumstances, a Professor in Harvard College, was sitting in his office, and with a single spurt of his pen he dashes off the liberty of a man — a citizen of Massachusetts. He kidnaps a man endowed by his Creator with the unalienable right to life, liberty, and the pursuit of happiness. He leaves the writ with the Marshal, and goes home to his family, caresses his children, and enjoys his cigar. The frivolous smoke curls round his frivolous head, and at length he lays him down to sleep, and, I suppose, such dreams as haunt such heads. But when he wakes next morn, all the winds of indignation, wrath, and honest scorn, are let loose. Before night, they are blowing all over this Commonwealth — ay, before another night they have gone to the Mississippi, and wherever the lightning messenger can tell the tale. So have I read in an old mediæval legend that one summer afternoon, there came up a "shape, all hot from Tartarus," from hell below, but garmented and garbed to represent a civil-suited man, masked with humanity. He walked quiet and decorous through Milan's stately streets, and scattered from his hand an invisible dust. It touched the walls; it lay on the streets; it ascended to the cross on the minster's utmost top. It went down to the beggar's den. Peacefully he walked through the streets, vanished and went home. But the next morning, the pestilence was in Milan, and ere a week had sped half her population were in their graves; and half the other half, crying that hell was clutching at their hearts, fled from the reeking City of the Plague!

Why did the Commissioner do all this? He knew the consequences that must follow. He knew what Boston was. We have no monument to Hancock and Adams; but still we keep their graves; and Boston, the dear old Mother that bore them, yet in her bosom hides the honored bones of men whom armies could not terrify, nor England bribe. Their spirit only sleeps. Tread roughly, tread roughly on the spot — their spirit rises from the ground! He knew that here were men who never will be silent when wrong is done. He knew Massachusetts; he knew Boston; he knew that the Fugitive Slave Bill had only raked the ashes over fires which were burning still, and that a breath might scatter those ashes to the winds of heaven, and bid the slumbering embers flame. Had he determined already what should happen to Anthony Burns? He knew what had befallen Thomas Sims. Did he wish another inhabitant of Boston whipped to death?

I have studied the records of crime — it is a part of my ministry. I do not find that any College Professor has ever been hanged for murder in all the Anglo-Saxon family of men, till Harvard College had that solitary shame. Is not that enough? Now she is the first to have a Professor that kidnaps men. "The Athens of America" furnished both!

I can understand how a man commits a crime of passion, or covetousness, or rage, — nay, of revenge, or of ambition. But for a man in Boston, with no passion, no covetousness, no rage, with no ambition nor revenge, to steal a poor negro, to send him into bondage, — I cannot comprehend the fact. I can understand the consciousness of a lion, not a kidnapper's heart. Once Mr. Loring defined a lawyer to be "a human agent for effecting a human purpose by human means." Here and now the Commissioner seems an inhuman agent for effecting an inhuman purpose by inhuman means.

I belong to a school that reverences the infinite perfection of God, if, indeed, there be such a school. I believe, also, in the nobleness of man; but last week my faith was somewhat sorely tried. As I looked at that miscreant crew, the kidnapper's body-guard, and read in their faces the record and the prophecy of many a crime,

> "Felons by the hand of nature marked,
> Quoted and signed to do a deed of shame,"

I could explain and not despair. They were tools, not agents. But as I looked into the Commissioner's face, mild and amiable, a face I have respected, not without seeming cause; as I remembered his breeding and his culture, his social position, his membership of a Christian church, and then thought of the crime he was committing against humanity, with no temptation, I asked myself, Can this be true? Is man thus noble, made in the dear image of the Father, God? Is my philosophy a dream: or are these facts a lie?

But there is another court. The Empsons and the Dudleys have been summoned there before; Jeffreys and Scroggs, the Kanes, and the Curtises, and the Lorings, must one day travel the same unwelcome road. Imagine the scene after man's mythologic way. "Edward, where is thy brother, Anthony?" "I know not; am I my brother's keeper, Lord?" "Edward, where is thy brother, Anthony?" "Oh, Lord, he was friendless, and so I smote him; he was poor, and I starved him of more than life. He owned nothing but his African body. I took that away from him, and gave it to another man!"

Then listen to the voice of the Crucified — "Did I not tell thee, when on earth, 'Thou shalt love the Lord thy God with all thy understanding and thy heart?'" "But I thought thy kingdom was not of this world."

"Did I not tell thee that thou shouldst love thy neighbor as thyself? Where is Anthony, thy brother? I was a stranger, and you sought my life; naked, and you rent away my skin; in prison, and you delivered me to the tormentors — fate far worse than death. Inasmuch as you did it to Anthony Burns, you did it unto me."

The liberty of America was never in greater peril than now. Hessian bayonets were not half so dangerous as the gold of the National treasury in the hands of this Administration. Which shall conquer, Slavery or Freedom? That is the question. The two cannot long exist side by side. Think of the peril; remember the rapacity of this Administration; its reckless leaders; think of Douglas, Cushing, and the rest. They aimed at the enslavement of Nebraska. The Northern majority in Congress yielded that.

Now they aim at Hayti and Cuba. Shall they carry that point? Surely, unless we do our duty. Shall Slavery be established at the North, at the West, and the East; in all the free States? Mr. Toombs told Mr. Hale — "Before long the master will sit down at the foot of Bunker Hill Monument with his Slaves." Will do it? He has done it already, and not an officer in the State of Massachusetts made the least resistance. Our laws were trod down by insolent officials, and Boston ordered out her soldiers to help the disgraceful deed. Strange that we should be asked to make the fetters which are to chain us. Mr. Suttle is only a feeler. Soon there will be other Suttles in Boston. Let them come!

It is not only wicked; it is costly. The kidnapping of Mr. Burns must have cost in all at least one hundred thousand dollars, including the loss of time and travelling expenses of our friends from the country. The publican's bill for feeding the Marshal's crew is already more than six thousand dollars!

Consider the demoralization of the people produced by such a deed. Mr. Dana was knocked down in the street by one of the Marshal's posse — as it is abundantly proved.* The blow might easily have been fatal. It is long since a bully has attacked a respectable citizen in Boston before. Hereafter I fear it will be more common. You cannot employ such a body-guard as the Marshal had about him in such business without greatly endangering the safety of the persons and the property of the town. We shall hear from them again. What a spectacle it was; the army of the United States, the soldiers of Boston sending an innocent man into Slavery! What a lesson to the children in the Sunday Schools — to the vagrant children in the streets, who have no school but the Sights of the City! What a lesson

* The culprit was held in trifling bail by the Court, one of the Marshal's gang became his surety. But the ruffian absconded, was subsequently arrested at New Orleans, and sent to the House of Correction for a year and a half.

of civilization to the Irish population of Boston! Men begin to understand this. There never was so much Anti-Slavery feeling in Boston before — never so much indignation in my day. If a law aims at Justice, though it fail of the mark we will respect the law — not openly resist it or with violence; wait a little, and amend it or repeal it. But when the law aims at Injustice, open, manifest, palpable wickedness, why, we must be cowards and fools too, if we submit.

Massachusetts has never felt so humiliated before. Soldiers of the Government enforcing a law in peaceful Boston, the most orderly of Christian cities! We have had no such thing since the Declaration of Independence! The rendition of Mr. Burns fills New England with sorrow and bitter indignation. The people tolled the bells at Plymouth. The bones of the Forefathers gave that response to the kidnappers in Boston. At Manchester and several other towns they did the same. To-day, ministers are preaching as never before. What will it all come to? Men came to Boston peacefully last week. Will they always come "with only the arms God gave?" One day in the seventeenth century five thousand country gentlemen rode into London with a "petition to the King" — with only the arms God gave them. Not long after they went thither with Oliver Cromwell at their head and other "arms" which God also had given. May such times never return in New England! *

We want no rashness, but calm, considerate action, deliberate, prudent, far-seeing. The Fugitive Slave Bill is a long wedge, thin at one end, wide at the other; it is entered between the bottom planks of our SHIP OF STATE; a few blows thereon will "enforce" more than the South thinks of. A little more, — and we shall go to pieces. Men talk wildly just now, and I do not credit what cool men say in this heat. But I see what may come — what must come, if a few more blows be struck in that quarter. It was only Mr. Webster's power to manufacture public

---

* While this Sermon is passing through the press, I find the following paragraph in a Newspaper: —

"One of the Fourth of July celebrations at Columbus, Ga., was the sale of ninety or a hundred men, women, and boys, by the order of Robert Toombs, United States Senator. Here is the advertisement: —

"'ADMINISTRATOR'S SALE. — Will be sold on the first Tuesday in July next, at the Court House door of Stewart County, within the usual hours of sale, between ninety and one hundred negroes, consisting of men, women, boys, etc. These negroes are all very likely, and between forty and fifty of the number are men and boys. Sold as the property of Henry J. Pope, deceased, in pursuance of an order of the Court of Ordinary of Stewart County, for the benefit of heirs and creditors. Terms of sale, a credit (with interest) until 25th December next.

"'ROBERT TOOMBS,

"'Adm'r of Henry J. Pope, deceased.'

"'Men, women, and boys,' bought on the Fourth of July, — paid for on Christmas!"

opinion by his giant will and immense eloquence, which made the North submit at all to the Fugitive Slave Bill. He strained his power to the utmost — and died! Now there is no Webster or Clay; not even a Calhoun; not a first rate man in the Pro-Slavery party, North or South. Slavery is not well manned — many hands, dirty, cunning, stealthy, — not a single great, able head.

The cowardice of Mr. Everett has excited the clergy of New England; of all the North. They are stung with the reproach of the people, and ashamed of their own past neglect. The Nebraska Bill opens men's eyes. Agitation was never so violent as at this day. The prospect of a war with Spain is not inviting to men who own ships, and want a clear sea and open market. Pirates, privateers, — Algerine, Greek, Spanish, Portuguese, West Indian, — are not welcome to the thoughts of men. The restoration of the Slave-Trade is not quite agreeable to the farmers and mechanics of the North. This attempt to seize a man in Boston; the display of force; the insolence of the officials; the character of the men concerned in this iniquity — all is offensive. Then there was insult, open and intentional. Mr. Burns was carried through State Street at "high change." Boston merchants feel as they never did before. All Massachusetts is incensed. The wrath of Massachusetts is slow, but she has wrath, has courage, "perseverance of the saints."

Let us do nothing rashly. What is done hastily must be done over again — it is not well done. This is what I would recommend.

1. A convention of all Massachusetts, without distinction of party, to take measures to preserve the rights of Massachusetts. For this we want some new and stringent laws for the defence of personal liberty, for punishing all who invade it on our soil. We want powerful men as Officers to execute these laws.

2. A general Convention of all the States to organize for mutual protection against this new master.

It is not speeches that we want — but action; not rash, crazy action, but calm, deliberate, systematic action — organization for the defence of personal liberty and the State Rights of the North. Now is a good time; let us act with cool energy. By all means let us do something, else the liberties of America go to ruin — then what curses shall mankind heap upon us!

"And deep, and more deep — as the iron is driven, —
Base slaves, will the whet of our agony be,
When we think, — as the damned haply think of the Heaven
They had once in their reach, — that we might have been free."

But, my friends, out of all this dreadful evil we can bring relief. The remedy is in our hearts and hands. God works no miracles. There is power in human nature to end this wickedness. God appointed the purpose, provided the means — a divine purpose, human means. Only be faithful, and in due time we shall triumph over the Destroyer. Every noble quality of man works with us; each attribute of God. We are His instruments. Let us faithfully do the appointed work! Darkness is about us! Journey forward; Light is before us!

> "Oh God, who in thy dear still heaven
> Dost sit and wait to see
> The errors, sufferings, and crimes
> Of our humanity;
> How deep must be thy Causal love,
> How Whole thy final care,
> Since Thou who rulest all above
> Canst see, and yet canst bear!" *

---

* See Appendix.

THE LAW OF GOD AND THE STATUTES OF MEN.

A

SERMON

PREACHED AT

THE MUSIC HALL, IN BOSTON,

ON

SUNDAY, JUNE 18, 1854.

SERMON.

"Thou shalt worship the Lord, thy God, and Him only shalt thou serve." — MATT. iv. 10.

LAST Sunday I spoke of Trust in God, endeavoring to show that it involved an absolute confidence in the Purposes of God, and an absolute confidence in the Means thereunto, and consequently the practical Use thereof.

There is a matter of very great consequence connected herewith, namely this, — the Relation between a Man's Religion and his Allegiance to the Church and the State. So this morning I ask your attention to a Sermon of our Duty to the Laws of God, and our Obligation to the Statutes of Men. It is a theme I have often spoken of; and what I shall say this morning may be regarded as occasional, and supplementary to the much I have said, and printed, likewise, before.

In its primitive form, Religion is a mere Emotion; it is nothing but a Sentiment, — an instinctive feeling; at first vague, shadowy, dim. In its secondary stage it is also a Thought; the emotion has travelled from the heart upwards to the head: it is an Idea, an abstract idea, the Object whereof transcends both time and space, and is not cognizable by any sense. But finally, in its ultimate form, it becomes likewise an Act. Thus it spreads over all a man's life, inward and outward too; it goes up to the tallest heights of the philosopher's speculation, down to the lowest deeps of human consciousness; it reaches to the minute details of our daily practice. Religion wraps all our life in its own wide mantle; takes note of the private conduct of the individual man, and the vast public concerns of the greatest nation and the whole race of mankind. So the sun, ninety-six million miles away, comes every morning and folds in its warm embrace each great and every little thing on the round world.

Religion is eminently connected with the Creeds and the Statutes of the people, wherein the nation comes to the consciousness of itself, and of its duty. To comprehend the relation which it bears to these creeds and statutes, let us look at the matter a little more narrowly, going somewhat into detail; and to understand it the more completely, let us go back to the first principles of things.

There is a God of Infinite Perfection, who acts as perfect Cause and perfect Providence of all things, — making the Universe from a perfect motive, of perfect material, for a perfect purpose, and as a perfect means thereunto. Of course, if the Universe be thus made, there must be power and force enough, of the right kind, in it to accomplish the purposes of God; and this must be true of both parts of the Universe, — the World of Matter, and the World of Man. Else, God is not a perfect Cause and Providence, and has not made the Universe from a perfect motive, of perfect material, for a perfect purpose, and as a perfect means thereto.

Now, there are certain natural modes of operation of these forces and powers which God has put in the Universe; the natural powers of matter and of man are meant to act in a certain way, and not otherwise. These modes of operation I will call Laws, Natural Laws; they exist in the material world and in the human world. They are a part of the Universe. These Laws must be observed and kept as means to the end that is proposed.

In the World of Matter these Laws are always kept, for the Actual of Nature and the Ideal of Nature are identical; they are just the same. When this leaf which I drop falls from my hand, it moves by the Law which the Infinite God meant it should fall by, and keeps that exactly. In Nature — the world of matter — this always takes place, and the Actual of to-day is the Ideal of eternity, — for there every thing is accomplished with no finite, private, individual will; all is mechanism, the brute, involuntary, unconscious action of matter passively obedient to the mind and will of God. There God is the only Actor; all else is tool; He is the only Workman; Nature is all engine and God the Engineer. Accordingly, in the world of matter there is a harmony of forces; but not a harmony of purpose, of will, of thought, of feeling, — because there is only one purpose, will, thought, feeling. God alone is the consciousness of the material world; matter obeys his Laws, but wills not, knows not. The ideal of Nature resides in God's consciousness; only its actual in itself. The two are one; but the material things do not know of that oneness; only God knows thereof. Nature knows nothing of God, nothing of his laws, nothing of itself; — because therein God is the only Cause, the only Providence, the only Consciousness.

On the other hand, in the Human World, man is an actor as well as a tool; he is in part engine, in part also engineer. The ideal of man's conduct, character, and destination, resides in God; but thence it is transferred to the mind of man by man's own instinct and reflection; and it is to become actual by man's thought, man's will, man's work. The human race comes to consciousness in itself, and not merely to consciousness in God. So in virtue of the superior nature and destination of man, between him and God there is to be not merely a harmony of forces, but a harmony of feeling, thought, will, purpose, and thence of act. Man is to obey the natural laws as completely as that leaf obeyed them, falling from my hand. But, unlike the leaf, man is to know that he obeys; he must will to obey. So he is to form in his own mind an ideal of the character which he should observe, and then by his own will he is to make that ideal his actual. This is the dignity of man, — he is partial cause and providence of his own affairs.

In general, man has powers sufficient to find out the natural mode of operation of all his human forces, all the natural Laws of his conduct, his natural ideal. Narrow this down to a small compass, and take one portion of these powers, — the Moral Part of man, and thereof this only, — that portion which relates to his dealing with his fellow men.

There is a moral faculty called Conscience. Its function is to inform us of the Moral Ideal; to transfer it from God's mind to our mind; to inform us what are the natural modes of operation, the rules of conduct in our relation with other men. Conscience does this in two ways.

First, by Instinctive moral action. Here conscience acts spontaneously and anticipates experience, acts in advance of history, and spontaneously projects an ideal which is derived from the moral instinct of our nature. This is the transcendent way of learning the moral Law. And let me add, it is the favorite way of young and enthusiastic persons; the favorite way, likewise, of meditative and contemplative men, who dwell apart from mankind, and look at Principles, which are the norm of action, more than at the immediate or ultimate effect of special Measures.

The other way is by Reflective moral action. Here we learn the moral Laws by experiment; by observation, trial, experience, we find out what suits the conscience of the individual and the conscience of mankind. This is the inductive way, and it is the favorite mode of the great mass of men, practical men who live in the midst of affairs.

Each of these methods has its advantage, both their special limitations and defects. We require both of these, — the process of moral instinct which shoots forward and forecasts the ideal, and the process of moral induction which comes carefully afterwards and studies the facts and sees what conduct squares with conscience, and how it looks after the act has been done as well as before.

In these two ways we learn the natural mode of operation and the natural rules of conduct which suit our moral nature; that is, we discover the Moral Laws which are writ in the nature and constitution of man, and are thence historically made known in the consciousness of man.

When they are understood, we see that they are the Laws of God, a part of the Universe, a part of the purpose of God, a part of the means which He has provided for accomplishing his purpose.

These laws are not of man's making, but of his finding made. He no more makes them than the blacksmith makes the heaviness of his iron, or the astronomer makes the moon eclipse the sun. A man may heed these laws, or heed them not; make them, or unmake them, — that is beyond his power.

Neither the individual nor the race acquires a consciousness of these Moral Laws all at once. It is done progressively by you and me; progressively by the human race, learning here a little, and there a little. The natural moral ideal is not all at once transferred from God's Mind to man's. We learn the Laws of our moral nature like the Laws of matter, slowly, — little by little. A good man is constantly making progress in the knowledge of God's natural Moral Laws; mankind does the same. The race to-day knows more of the natural Moral Laws of our constitution than the human race ever knew before. A thousand years hence no doubt, mankind will know a great deal more of this natural moral ideal than we know to-day. Accordingly, speaking after the events of history, the Moral Ideal of mankind is continually rising. It may not be always rising in the same man, who goes on for a while, then becomes idle, or old, or wicked, and goes down: nor always be rising in the same nation; that also advances for a while, then sins against God sometimes, and goes down to ruin. But, take the human race as a whole, the moral ideal of mankind is constantly rising higher and higher.

The next thing is to obey these Laws, consciously, knowing we obey them; voluntarily, willing to obey, and make the moral ideal the actual of life for the individual and the race. This also is done progressively; not all at once, but by slow degrees. The Moral Actual of the human race is constantly rising higher and higher. Just in proportion as the ideal shoots up the actual follows after it, though on slow and laborious wings. If you look microscopically, at the condition of mankind at intervals of only a hundred years, you will see that there is a moral progress from century to century; but separate your points of observation by a thousand years instead of a century, the moral progress of the race is so obvious that no unprejudiced man can fail to see it when he opens his natural eyes and looks. I will not say it is so with every special nation, for a nation may go back as well as forward; but it is so with the human race as a whole, so with mankind.

Religion — which begins in feeling, proceeds to thought, and thence to action, — in its highest form is the keeping of all the Laws which God writ in the constitution of man: in other words, it is the service of God by the normal use, discipline, development, enjoyment, and delight of every limb of the body, every faculty of the spirit, every power which we possess over matter or over mankind, — each in its due proportion, all in their complete harmony. That is the whole and complete religion.

Now leaving out of sight for a moment the matter of mere sentiment, in religion reducing itself to practice there are two things, — to wit, first, Intellectual Ideas, doctrines of the mind, things to be believed; secondly, Moral Duties, doctrines of the conscience, things to be done. Each man in his private individual capacity, as Edwin or Richard, has his own intellectual ideas, things to be believed; his own moral duties, things to be done. To be faithful to himself he must believe the one and must do the other. It is a part of his personal religion to believe the truths which he knows, to do the duties that he acknowledges.

But man is social as well as solitary. So men, in their collective capacity as churches, towns, nations, come to the conclusion that they have certain intellectual ideas which ought to be believed, certain moral duties which ought to be done. As an expression of this fact, men assembling in bodies for purposes called religious, as churches, make up a collection of ideas connected with religion which are deemed true. They call this a Creed. It is a collection of things to be believed, and so it is also a rule of intellectual conduct in matters pertaining to religion.

They likewise assemble in bodies for a purpose more directly practical, as towns, as nations, and make a collection of duties which are deemed obligatory. They call this collection of duties a Constitution or a Code of Statutes.

I will use the word Statute to mean what is commonly called a law, made by men: that is to say a rule of practical conduct devised by men in authority. I keep the word Law to describe the natural mode of operation which God wrote in the constitution of material or human nature, and the word Statute for that rule of conduct which man makes and adds thereunto.

This is a legitimate aim in making the Creed,— to preserve all known religious truth, and diffuse it amongst men. But it is not legitimate to aim at hindering the attainment of new religious truth, or to hinder efforts for the attainment of new religious truth.

This is a legitimate aim in making the Statutes, to preserve all known moral duty, and diffuse it amongst men; and thereby secure to each man the enjoyment of all his natural rights, so that he may act according to the natural mode of operation of his powers. But it is not legitimate to hinder the attainment of new moral duty, or efforts after that. The creed should aim at Truth, all truth, and should be a step towards it. The statutes should aim at Justice, all justice, to insure all the rights of each and should be a step in that direction, not away from it.

Both the creeds and statutes may be made as follows: —

First, they may be made by men who are far before the people, men who get sight of truths and duties in advance of mankind. Then these men set to mankind a hard lesson, but one which is profitable for instruction, for doctrine, for reproof, that the man of God may be thoroughly furnished to every good work. In such cases the creed or statute is educational; it is prepared for the pupil, set by a master.

Or, secondly, these creeds and statutes may be made by men who are just on a level with the average of the people. Then they are simply expressional of the moral character and attainments of the average men. They are educational to the hindmost, expressional to the middlemost, and merely protectional to the foremost, — of no service as helping them forward, only as protecting them from being disturbed, interrupted and so drawn backwards by those who are behind.

Or, thirdly, these creeds and statutes may be made by crafty men who are below the moral average of the people; made not as steps towards truth and justice, but as means for the private personal ambition of such as make the statutes or the creeds; by men who are endowed with force of body, and rule over our flesh by violence, or with force of cunning, and rule over our minds by sophistry and fraud. In this case the creed or statute is a step backwards, aims not at truth and justice, but at falsehood and wrong, and is simply debasing,—debasing to the mind and conscience. Here it is not a teacher giving lessons to the pupil; it is not a pupil undertaking to set a lesson to another who knows as much as he does; it is a scoundrel setting a lesson of wickedness to the saint and the sinner.

Laws may be made in any one of these three ways, and no more; the categories are exhaustive.

Now see the relation of each individual man to the Creed of his Nation or Church. By his moral nature man is bound to believe what to him appears true. His mind demands it as intellectual duty, his conscience demands it as moral duty; it is a part of his religion; faithfulness to himself requires this. But he is likewise morally bound to reject every thing that to him seems false. He can close his mind and not think about the matter at all, and so he may seem to believe when he does not; or he can actually think the other way and lie about it and pretend to believe. But if he is faithful, he must believe what to him seems true, and must reject what to him seems untrue.

If a man does this, the public creed of the people or church may be a help to him, because while it embodies both the truths that men know, and the errors which they likewise suppose to be true, he accepts from the creed what he deems true, and rejects what he deems false. The false that he rejects, harms him not; the true which he accepts is a blessing. But there is this trouble, — the priest, who has made, invented, or imported the creed, claims jurisdiction over the minds of men and bids the philosopher "Accept our creed." "No!" answers the philosopher, "I cannot! my reason forbids." "Then, down with your reason!" thunders the priest, "there is no truth above our creed! The priest and creed are not amenable to reason; reason is amenable to them!" What shall be done? Shall the philosopher submit, and seem to believe? Shall he think the other way, and yet pretend to believe, and lie? or shall he openly and unhesitatingly reject what seems false? Ask these prophets of the Old Testament what we shall do! ask Socrates, Anaxagoras, Paul, Luther, Jesus! ask the Puritans of England, the Huguenots of France, the Covenanters of Scotland, which we shall do! whether we shall count human Reason amenable to the priest, or the priest amenable to human Reason. Sometimes a whole nation violates its mind, and submits to the priest's creed. The many mainly give up thinking all together, — they can do it and have done it; the few think, but lie outwardly, pretending belief. Then there comes the intellectual death of the nation; the people are cut off from new accessions of truth, and intellectually they die out. "Where there is no vision the people perish," says the Old Testament; and there is not a word in the Bible more true. Tear a rose-bush from the ground and suspend it in the air, will it thrive? Just as much will man's mind thrive when plucked away from contact with Truth. Do you want historic examples? Look at Mahometan countries compared with Christian. Whilst the Koran was in advance of the Mahometans there was a progress in the nations which accepted it. There arose great men. But now when men have lived up to the Koran, and are forbidden to think further, science dies out, all original literature disappears, there is no great spiritual growth. In the whole Mahometan world this day, there is not a single man eminent for science or literature; not a great Mahometan orator, poet, or statesman, amongst all the many millions of Mahometans on the round world. Look at a Catholic in comparison with a Protestant country. Compare Catholic Spain, Portugal, Italy, with England, Scotland, Germany, noble Protestant countries, and see the odds. In the Catholic countries the priest has laid himself down at the foot of the tree, and says, "Root into me, and you shall have life." Compare Catholic Brazil with Protestant New England. Nay, in New England, go into the families of private men, families where bigotry of the various denominations, Nothingarian, Unitarian, as well as Trinitarian, — for there is also a "Nothingarian" bigotry, — has put its cold, hard hand, and forbidden freedom of thought; — compare the children born and bred there with such as are born and bred in families where freedom of thought is not only tolerated but encouraged, and see the difference. The foremost men of this country in science, literature, statesmanship, are men who have spurned that Pharisaic meanness, which chains a man's mind and fetters his conscience.

It is as important to accumulate the thoughts of many men, as to consolidate their property for building a railroad, a factory, or a town. No single man is so rich as the whole people of Massachusetts; and though before all others in some speciality, no one man is so rich in thought as mankind. To aggregate the knowledge of a hundred men, each mastering some special subject, is of great value; it embodies the result of very much thinking, which may thus be hoarded up for future use. That is a good thing; and as each truth is a means of power, it quickens other men and helps them to think. Such is the effect of the scientific associations of Christendom, from the Boston Society of Natural History, to the French Academy, — perhaps the most learned and accomplished body of men on earth. That is a legitimate function of bodies of men coming together, each dropping his special wisdom into the human treasury, for the advantage of the whole.

But on the other hand, the consolidation of the opinions of men who are not seeking for truth to liberate mankind, but for means to enthrall us withal, will embody falsehood and also retard the progress of mankind by hindering free thought. This will be the result wherever the actual creed is taken for total, — embracing all truth now known; as final, — embracing all truth that is to be known; and as unquestionable, the ultimate standard of Truth.

I just said there was not a single eminent man of science or letters in any Mahometan country; not a great scholar, philosopher, or historian. Yet there is talent enough born into Mahometan countries, — as much as in Christian nations of the same race; but it has not opportunity for development; the young Hercules is choked in his cradle. Look at the Catholics of the United States in comparison with the Protestants. In the whole of America there is not a single man born and bred a Catholic distinguished for any thing but his devotion to the Catholic Church: I mean to say there is not a man in America born and bred Catholic, who has any distinction in science, literature, politics, benevolence, or philanthropy. I do not know one; I never heard of a great philosopher, naturalist, historian, orator, or poet amongst them. The Jesuits have been in existence three hundred years; they have had their pick of the choicest intellect of all Europe,—they never take a common man when they know it,—they subject every pupil to a severe ordeal, physical and intellectual, as well as moral, in order to ascertain whether he has the requisite stuff in him to make a strong Jesuit out of. They have a scheme of education masterly in its way. But there has not been a single great original man produced in the company of Jesuits from 1545 to 1854. They absorb talent enough but they strangle it. Clipped oaks never grow large. Prune the roots of a tree with a spade, trim the branches close to the bole, what becomes of the tree? The bole itself remains thin and scant and slender. Can a man be a conventional dwarf and a natural giant at the same time? Case your little boy's limbs in metal, would they grow? Plant a chestnut in a tea-cup, do you get a tree? Not a shrub even. Put a priest, or a priest's creed as the only soil for a man to grow in; he grows not. The great God provided the natural mode of operation:—do you suppose He will turn aside and mend or mar the Universe at your or my request? I think God will do no such thing.

Now see the relation of the individual to the Statutes of men. There is a natural duty to obey every statute which is just. It is so before the thing becomes a statute. The legislator makes a decree;

it is a declaration that certain things must be done, or certain other things not done. If the things commanded are just, the statute does not make them just; does not make them any more morally obligatory than they were before. The legislator may make it very uncomfortable for me to disobey his command, when that is wicked; he cannot make it right for me to keep it when wicked. All the moral obligation depends on the justice of the statute, not on its legality; not on its constitutionality; but, on the fact that it is a part of the natural Law of God, the natural mode of operation of man. The statute no more makes it a moral duty to love men and not hate them, than the multiplication table makes twice two four: the multiplication table declares this; it does not make it. If a statute announces, "Thou shalt hate thy neighbor, not love him," it does not change the natural moral duty, more than the multiplication table would alter the fact if it should declare that twice two is three. Geometry proves that the three angles of a triangle are equal to two right angles: it does not make the equality between the two.

Now then, as it is a moral duty to obey a just statute because it is just, so it is a moral duty to disobey any statute which is unjust. If the statute squares with the Law of God, if the constitution of Morocco corresponds with the Constitution of the Universe, which God writ in my heart, — then I am to keep the constitution of Morocco; if not, disobey it, as a matter of conscience.

Here in disobedience, there are two degrees. First, there is Passive Disobedience, non-obedience, the doing nothing for the statute; and second, there is Active Disobedience, which is resistance, the doing something, not for the statute, but something against it. Sometimes the moral duty is accomplished by the passive disobedience, doing nothing; sometimes, to accomplish the moral duty, it is requisite to resist, to do something against the statute. However, we are to resist wrong by right, not wrong by wrong.

There are many statutes which relate mainly to matters of convenience. They are rules of public conduct indeed, but only rules of prudence, not of morals. Such are the statutes declaring that a man shall not vote till twenty-one; that he shall drive his team on the right hand side of the street; that he may take six per cent. per annum as interest, and not sixty; that he may catch Alewives in Taunton River on Fridays, and not on Thursdays or Saturdays. It is necessary that there should be such rules of prudence as these; and while they do not offend the conscience every good man will respect them; it is not immoral to keep them.

The intellectual value of a creed is that while it embodies truth it also represents the free thought of the believer who has come to that conclusion, either by himself alone, or as he has been voluntarily helped thitherward by some person who knows better than he. In that case his creed is the monument of te man's progress, and is the basis for future progress. It is to him, in that stage of his growth, the right rule of intellectual conduct. But when the creed is forced on the man, and he pretends to believe and believes not, or only tacitly assents, not having thought enough to deny it, — then it debases and enslaves the man.

So the moral value of a statute is, that while it embodies justice it also represents the free conscience of the nation. Then also it is a monument of the nation's moral progress, showing how far it has got on. It is likewise a basis for future progress, being a right rule for moral conduct. But when the statute only embodies injustice, and so violates the conscience, and is forced on men by bayonets, then its moral value is all gone; it is against the conscience. If the people consent to suffer it, it is because they are weak; and if they consent to obey it, it is because they are also wicked.

When the foremost moral men make a statute in advance of the people, and then attempt to enforce that law against the consent of the majority of the people, it is an effort in the right direction and is educational; then I suppose the best men will try to execute the law, and will appeal to the best motives in the rest of men. But even in such a case, if ever this is attempted, it should always be done with the greatest caution, lest the leader go too fast for his followers, undertaking to drag the nation instead of leading them. You may drag dead oxen, drive living oxen; but a nation is not to be dragged, not to be driven, even in the right direction; it is to be led. A grown father, six feet high, does not walk five miles the hour with his child two years old; if he does, he must drag his boy; if he wants to lead him he must go by slow and careful steps, now and then taking him over the rough places in his arms. That must be done when the lawmaker is very far in advance of the people; he must lead them gently to the right end.

But when a wicked statute is made by the hindmost men in morals, men far in the rear of the average of the people, and urging them in the wrong direction; when the statute offends the conscience of the people, and the rulers undertake by violence to enforce the statute, then it can be only mean men who will desire its execution, and they must appeal to the lowest motives which animate mean men, and will thus debase the people further and further.

The priest makes a creed against the mind of the people, and says, "There is no truth above my creed! Down with your reason! it asks terrible questions." So the Catholic is always taught by authority. The priest does not aim to convince the reason; not at all! He says to the philosophers, "This is the Doctrine of the Church. It is a true doctrine, and you must believe it, not because it is true, — you have no right to ask questions, — but because the church says so." The tyrant makes a statute, and says, "There is no Law above this." The subject is not to ask, "Is the statute right? does it conform to the Constitution of the Universe, to God's will reflected in my conscience?" He is only to inquire, "Is it a statute-law? what does the judge say? There is no Higher Law."

That is the doctrine which is taught to-day in almost every political newspaper in this country, Whig and Democratic; and in many of the theological newspapers. But the theological newspapers do not teach it as a Principle and all at once; they teach it in detail, as a Measure, telling us that this or that particular statute is to be observed, say conscience what it may. It is assumed that the legislator is not amenable to the rules of natural justice. He is only to be checked by the constitution of the land, not the Constitution of the Universe.

See how the principle once worked. Pharaoh made a statute that all the new-born boys of Hebrew parentage should be killed as soon as they were born. That was the statute; and instructions were given to the nurses, "If it be a son, then ye shall kill him." Did it become the moral duty of Nurse Shiprah and Nurse Puah to drown every new-born Hebrew baby in the River Nile? Was it the moral duty of Amram and Jochebed to allow Moses to be killed? It is only a legitimate application of the principle laid down by "the highest authorities" in America,—what are called the highest, though I reckon them among the lowest.

King Darius forbade prayer to any God or man except himself. Should the worshippers of Jehovah hold back their prayer to the Creator? Daniel was of rather a different opinion. A few years ago a minister of a "prominent church" in this city was told of another minister who had exhorted persons to disobey the Fugitive Slave Bill, because it was contrary to the Law of God and the principles of Right. "What do you think of it?" said the questioner, who was a woman, to the Doctor of Divinity. "Very bad!" replied he, "this minister ought to keep the statute, and he should not advise men to disobey it." "But," said the good woman, "Daniel, we are told, when the law was otherwise, prayed to the Lord! prayed right out loud three times a day, with his window wide open! Did he do right or wrong? Would not you have done the same?" The minister said, "If I had lived in those times,—I think,—I should—have shut my window." There was no Higher Law!

King Herod ordered all the young children in Bethlehem to be slain. Was it right for the magistrates to execute the order? for the Justices of the Peace to kill the babies? for the fathers and mothers to do nothing against the massacre of those innocents? The person who wrote the account of it seems to have been of rather a different opinion.

King Henry the Eighth of England, ordered that no man should read the English Bible. Reading the Bible in the Kingdom was made a felony,—punishable with death, without benefit of clergy. Was it the duty of Dr. Franklin's humble fathers to refuse to read their Bibles? They did read them, and your fathers and mine also, I trust. King Pharaoh, Darius, Herod, Henry the Eighth, could not make a wrong thing right. If a mechanic puts his wheel on the upper side of the dam, do you suppose the Merrimack is going to run up into New Hampshire to turn his mill? Just as soon as the great God will undo his own moral work to accommodate a foolish and wicked legislator.

Suppose it was not the king, a one-headed legislator, but the majority of the nation, a legislator with many heads, who made the statutes, would that alter the case? Once, when France was democratic, the democracy ordered the butchery of thousands of men and women. Was it a moral duty to massacre the people?

I know very well it is commonly taught that it is the moral duty of the officers of government to execute every statute, and of the people to submit thereto, no matter how wicked the statute may be. This is the doctrine of the Supreme Court of the United States of America, of the Executive of the

United States; I know very well it is the doctrine of the majority of the Legislature in both Houses of Congress; it is the doctrine of the churches of Commerce; — God be praised, it is not the doctrine of the churches of Christianity, and there are such in every denomination, in many a town; even in the great centres of commerce there are ministers of many denominations, earnest, faithful men, who declare openly that they will keep God's Law, come what will of man's statute. This is practical piety; the opposite is practical atheism. I have known some speculative atheists. I abhor their doctrines; but the speculative atheists that I have known, all recognize a Law higher than men's passions and calculations; the Law of some Power which makes the Universe and sways it for noble purposes and to a blessed end.

Then comes the doctrine: — While the statute is on the books it must be enforced: it is not only the Right of the legislator to make any constitutional statute he pleases, but it is the moral and religious Duty of the magistrate to enforce the statute; it is the duty of the people to obey. So in Pharaoh's time it was a moral duty to drown the babies in the Nile; in Darius' time to pray to King Darius, and him only; in Herod's time to massacre the children of Bethlehem; in Henry the Eighth's time to cast your Bible to the flames. Iscariot only did a disagreeable duty.

It is a most dreadful doctrine; utterly false! Has a legislator, Pharaoh, Darius, Herod, Henry the Eighth, a single tyrant, any moral right to repudiate God, and declare himself not amenable to the moral Law of the Universe? You all answer, No! Have ten millions of men out of nineteen millions in America a right to do this? Has any man a moral right to repudiate justice and declare himself not amenable to conscience and to God? Where did he get the right to invade the conscience of mankind? Is it because he is legislator, magistrate, governor, president, king? a right to do wrong!

Suppose all the voluptuaries of America held a congress of lewdness at New Orleans, and said, "There is no Law higher than the brute instinctive passion of lust in men," — then would the pimps and bawds and lechers have the moral right to repudiate conscience and crush purity out of the nation?

Imagine that all the misers and sharpers and cheats held a convention of avarice at New York or Boston, and made statutes accordingly, declaring "There is no Law higher than covetousness," — would they have the moral right to lie and steal and cheat, and "crush out" all the honest men?

Fancy all the ruffians and man-killers assembled in San Francisco, — it would be a fit place, for there were twelve hundred murders committed there in less than four years, — held a convention of violence, and sought to organize murder, and declared, "There is no Law higher than the might of the lifted arm," — would they have the moral right to kill, stab, butcher whomsoever they pleased?

But that is supposing all this wickedness done without the form of an elected legislature. Then suppose the actual legislatures of the nation should revise the Constitution and delegate the power to those persons to do that work and make statutes for the protection of lewdness, fraud, and butchery, — would it then be the moral duty of the rulers to enforce those statutes; and of the people to submit? Just as much as it is the moral duty of men to enforce any wicked statute made under the present Constitution of the United States and by the present legislators. The principle is false. It is only justified on the idea that there is no God, and this world is a chaos. But yet it is taught; and only last Sunday the minister of a "prominent church" taught that every law must be executed, right or wrong, and thanked the soldiers who, with their bayonets, forced an innocent man to slavery. No matter how unjust a statute is, it must be enforced and obeyed so long as it is on the Law Book!

Human law in general is a useful and indispensable instrument; but because a special statute has been made for injustice, is it to be used for injustice? Massachusetts has some thousands of muskets in the arsenal at Cambridge; but because they were made to shoot with, shall I take them to kill my neighbors; shall the governor order the soldiers to shoot down the citizens? It is no worse to do injustice with a gun than to do injustice with a statute. It is not merely the means by which the wicked end is reached that is wicked, it is the end itself; and if the means is a thing otherwise good, the wicked end makes its use atrocious. What is the statute in the one case but a tool, and the gun a tool in the other case? The instrument is not to be blamed, and the statute is no more to be used for a wicked purpose than the gun; a State statute no more than a State gun. Medicine is a very useful thing. But will you, therefore, go into an apothecary's shop and take his drugs at random? If you are killed by a poison it is no better because called "medicine."

But the notion that every statute must be enforced is historically false. Who enforces the Sunday law in Massachusetts? Every daily newspaper you will read to-morrow morning violates the statutes of Massachusetts to-day. It would not be possible to enforce them. Of all the sixty millions of bank capital in Massachusetts, within twelve months, every dollar has violated the statute against Usury. Nobody enforces these acts. Half the statutes of New England are but sleeping lions to wait for the call of the people; nobody wakes them up every day. Some have been so long fast asleep that they are dead.

When the nation will accept every creed which the priest makes, because it is made for them, then they are tools for the priest, intellectually dead; and they are fit to have Catholic tyrants rule over them in the church. When the nation is willing to accept a statute which violates the nation's conscience, the nation is rotten. If a statute is right, I will ask how I can best obey it. When it is wrong, I will ask how I can best disobey it, — most safely, most effectually, with the least violence. When we make the priest the keeper of our creed, the State the master of our conscience, then it is all over with us.

Sometimes a great deal of sophistry is used to deceive the consciences of men and make them think a wicked law is just and right. There are two modes of procedure for reaching this end.

One is to weaken the man's confidence in his own moral perceptions by debasing human nature, declaring that "conscience is a most uncertain guide for the individual," and showing that all manner of follies and even wickedness have been perpetrated in its name. So all manner of follies have been taught in the name of Reason, and foolish undertakings have been set a going by prudent and practical men. But is that sufficient argument for refusing to trust the science of the philosopher and the common sense of practical men?

The other way is to pretend that the obnoxious statute is "consistent with morality and religion."

Thus the most wicked acts have been announced in the name of God. The Catholics claimed divine authority for the Inquisition; the Carthaginians alleged the command of God as authority for sacrificing children to Melkarte. In the Law Library at Cambridge, a copy of the English Bible in Folio was once the first book in the collection: a Professor then used often to point to the Bible and say, "That is the foundation of the law. It all rests on the word of God!" So every wicked statute, each "ungodly custom become a law," had divine authority! The same experiment is often tried with the Fugitive Slave Bill — it is declared "divine," having "the sanction of the Law, the Prophets, and the Gospel."

With these two poisons do men corrupt the public fountains of morality!

Religion is the only basis for every thing. It must go everywhere, into the man's shop, into the seamstress' work-room, must steer the sailor's ship. Reverence for the Infinite Mind, and Conscience, and Heart, and Soul, who is Cause and Providence of this world, — that must go up to the highest heights of our speculation, down to the lowest deeps of our practice. Take that away, and there is nothing on which you can depend, even for your money; or for your liberty and life. Without a reverence for the Higher Law of God every thing will be ruled by interest or violence. The Church will collapse into nothing, the State will go down to ruin!

All around us are monuments of men who, in the name of Truth broke the priest's creed, defied the king's statute in the spirit of Justice. Look at them! There is a little one at Acton where two men gave their lives for their country; another at Concord; one at Lexington, — a little pile of dear old mossy stone, "Sacred to Liberty and the Rights of Mankind;" another at West Cambridge; another at Danvers, — all commemorative of the same deed; and on yonder hill there is a great stone finger pointing to God's Higher Law, and casting its shadow on the shame of the two sister cities. All New England is a monument to the memory of those men who trusted God's Higher Law, and for its sake put an ocean three thousand miles wide between them and their mothers' bones. It is this which makes Plymouth Rock so dear. Our calendar is dotted all over with days sacred to the memory of such men. What are the First of August, the Twenty-second of December, the Nineteenth of April, the Seventeenth of June, the Fourth of July, but bright, red-letter days in our calendar, marked by the memory of men who were faithful to God, say the statutes of tyrants what they may say? Nay, what else are these venerable days, called Christmas, Easter, Pentecost, and the Catholic Saints' days throughout the Christian year?

There is one thing which this Bible teaches in almost every page, and that is reverence for the Higher Law of God. The greatest men who wrote here were only men; to err is human, we all learn by experiment, and they were mistaken in many things; but all teach this, from the littlest to the greatest, from Genesis to Revelation,—RELIGION BEFORE ALL OTHER THINGS, REVERENCE FOR GOD ABOVE ALL! It was that for which Jesus bowed his head on the Cross, and "sat down at the right hand of God."

There is an Infinite God! You and I owe allegiance to Him, and our service of Him is the keeping of every Law which He made;—keeping it faithfully, earnestly, honestly. That is Religion, and to those who do it, on every thundering cloud which passes over their heads, He will cast his rainbow, girdling it with sevenfold magnificence of beauty, and on that cloud take them to His own Kingdom of Heaven, to be with Him forever and forever.

A

SERMON

OF THE

DANGERS WHICH THREATEN THE RIGHTS OF MAN IN AMERICA.

PREACHED AT THE MUSIC HALL,

ON

SUNDAY, JULY 2, 1854.

SERMON.

And he gave them their request; but sent leanness into their soul.— PSALM cvi. 15.

NEXT Tuesday will be the seventy-eighth anniversary of American Independence. The day suggests a national subject as theme for meditation this morning. The condition of America makes it a dark and a sad meditation. I ask your attention, therefore, to a Sermon of the Dangers which threaten the Rights of Man in America.

The human race is permanent as the Mississippi, and like that is fed from springs which never dry; but the several nations are as fleeting as its waves. In the great tide of humanity, States come up, one after the other, a wave or a bubble; each lasts its moment, then dies — passed off, forgot;

> "Or like the snow-falls in the river,
> A moment white — then melts forever,"

while the great stream of humanity rolls ever forward, from time to eternity: — not a wave needless; not a snow-flake, no drop of rain or dew, no ephemeral bubble, but has its function to perform in that vast, unmeasured, never-ending stream.

How powerless appears a single man! He is one of a thousand million men; the infinitessimal of a vulgar fraction; one leaf on a particular tree in the forest. A single nation, like America, is a considerable part of mankind now living; but when compared with the human race of all time, past and to come, it seems as nothing; it is but one bough in the woods. Nay, the population of the earth, to-day, is but one tree in the wide primeval forest of mankind, which covers the earth and outlasts the ages. The leaf may fall and not be missed from the bough; the branch may be rudely broken off, and its absence not marked; the tree will die and be succeeded by other trees in the forest, green with summer beauty, or foodful and prophetic with autumnal seed. Tree by tree, the woods will pass away, and, unobserved, another forest take its place, arising, also, tree by tree.

How various the duration of States or men — dying at birth, or lasting long periods of time! For more than three thousand years, Egypt stood the queen of the world's young civilization, invincible as her own pyramids, which yet time and the nations alike respect. From Romulus, the first half-mythologic king of the seven-hilled city, to Augustulus, her last historic Emperor, it is more than twelve centuries. At this day, the Austrian, the Spanish, the French and German sovereigns sit each on a long-descended throne. Victoria is "daughter of a hundred kings." Pope Pius the Ninth claims two hundred and fifty-six predecessors, canonical and "infallible." His chair is reckoned more than eighteen hundred years old; and it rests on an Etrurian platform yet ten centuries more ancient. The Turkish Throne has been firmly fixed at Constantinople for four hundred years. Individual tyrants, like summer flies, are short-lived; but tyranny is old and lasting. The family of ephemera, permanent amid the fleeting, is yet as old as that of elephants, and will last as long.

But free governments have commonly been brief. If the Hebrew people had wellnigh a thousand years of independent national life, their Commonwealth lasted but about three centuries; the flower of their literature and religion was but little longer. The historic period of Greece begins 776 B. C.; her independence was all over in six hundred and thirty years. The Roman deluge had swallowed it up. No Deucalion and Pyrrha could repeople the land with Men. Her little States — how brief was their hour of Freedom for the people! From the first annual archon of Athens to her conquest by Philip, and the death of her Liberty, it was only two hundred and forty-five years! Her tree of Freedom grew in a narrow field of time, and briefly bore its age-outlasting fruit of Science, Literature, and Art. Now the tree is dead; its fragments are only curious Athenian stone. The Grecian colonies in the East, Ætolian, Dorian, Ionian — how fair they flourished in the despotic waste of Asia! how soon those liberal blossoms died! Even her colonies in the advancing West had no long independent life. Cyrene, Syracusa, Agrigentum, Crotona, Massilia, Saguntum, — how soon they died! — flowers which the savage winter swiftly nipped.

The Roman Commonwealth could not endure five hundred years. Her theocratic Tarquin the Proud must be succeeded by a more despotic Dictator, with the style of Democrat, and Rome, abhorring still the name of King, see all her liberties laid low. The red sea of despotism opened to let pass one noble troop — the Elder Brutus at the head, the Younger bringing up the rear, — then closed again and swallowed up that worse than Ægyptian host, clamoring only for "bread and games!"

The Republics of Italy in the Middle Ages were no more fortunate. The half-Grecian Commonwealths, Naples, Amalphi, Gaëta, — what promise they once held forth; and what a warning fate! They were only born to die. A similar destiny befell the towns of more Northern Italy, where Freedom later found a home, — Milan, Padua, Genoa, Verona,

Venice, Bologna, Florence, Pisa. Nay, in the midnight of the dark ages, seven hundred years ago, in the very city of the Popes and Cæsars, in the centre of that red Roman sea of despotism, there was a momentary spot of dry free land; and Arnaldo da Brescia eloquently spoke of "Roman Liberty." The "Roman Republic" and "Roman Senate" became once more familiar words. Italian Liberty, Lombard Republics, — how soon they all went down! No city — not even Florence — kept the people's freedom safe three hundred years. Silently the wealthy nobles and despotic priests sapped the walls. Party spirit blinded the else clear eyes: "the State may perish; let the faction thrive." The Republicans sought to crush the adjacent feeble States. They forgot Justice, the Higher Law of God: unworthy of Liberty, they fell and died! Let the Tyrant swallow up the Italian towns; they were unfit for Freedom. "A generous disdain of one man's will is to Republics what chastity is to woman;" they spurned this austere virtue. Let them serve their despots. "Liberty withdrew from a people who disgraced her name." Let Dante burn his poetic brand of infamy into the forehead of his countrymen. But while Freedom lasted, how fair was her blossom, how rich and sweet her fruit! What riches, what beauty, what Science, Letters, Art, came of that noble stock! Italy was the world's wonder — for a day; its sorrow ever since. So the cactus flowers into one gorgeous ecstasy of bloom; then the excessive blossom, with withering collapse, swoons and dies of its voluptuous and tropical delight.

Liberty wanders from the North, through Italy the fairest of all earthly lands; then sits sadly down on the tallest of the Alps, and once more reviews those famous towns; the jewels that adorn the purple robe of history — all tarnished, shattered, spoiled. Slowly she turns her face Northward and longs for hope. But even the Teutonic towns, where Freedom ever wore a sober dress, were only spots of sunshine in a day of wintry storm. Swiss, German, Dutch, they were brief as fair. In Novogorod and in Poland, how soon was Slavonian Freedom lost!

So in a winter day in the country have I seen a little frame of glass, screening from the Northern snow and ice a nicely sheltered spot, where careful hands tended little delicate plants, for beauty and for use. How fair the winter garden seemed amid the wildering snow, and else all-conquering frost! The little roses lifted up their face and kissed the glass which sheltered from the storm. But anon, some rude hand broke the frail barrier down, and in an hour the plants were frozen, stiff and dead; and the little garden was all filled with snow and ice; — a garden now no more!

How often do you see in a great city a man perish in his youth, bowed down by lusts of the body. The graves of such stand thick along the highway of our mortal life, — numberless, nameless, or all too conspicuously marked. Other men we see early bowed down by their ambition, and they live a life far worse than merely sensual death — themselves the ghastliest monuments, beacons of ruin! And so, along the highway that mankind treads, there are the open sepulchres of nations, which perished of their sin; or else transformed to stone, the gloomy sphinxes sit there by the way-side — a hard, dread, awful lesson to the nations that pass by. Let America,

"The Heir of all the ages! and the youngest born of time!"

gather up every jewel which the prodigal scattered from his hand, look down into his grave, and then confront these gloomy, awful sphinxes, and learn what lessons of guidance they have; or of warning, if it alone is to be found! Even the sphinx has a riddle which we needs must learn, or else perish.

The greater part of a nation's life is not delight; it is discipline. A famous political philosopher, who has survived two revolutionary storms in France, has just now written, "God has made the condition of all men more severe than they are willing to believe. He causes them at all times to purchase the success of their labors and the progress of their destiny at a dearer price than they had anticipated."

The merchant knows how difficult it is to acquire

a great estate; the scholar, youthful and impatient, well understands that the way of science or of letters is steep and hard to climb; the farmer knowing the stern climate of New England, her niggard soil, rises early and retires late, and is never off his guard. These men all thrive. But, alas, the people of America do not know on what severe conditions alone national welfare is to be won. Human Nature is yet only a New England soil and climate for Freedom to grow in.

Nations may come to an end through the Decay of the Family they belong to; and thus they may die out of old age,—for there is an infancy, manhood, and old age to a nation as well as to a man. Then the nation comes to a natural end, and like a shock of corn fully ripe, in its season it is gathered to its people. But I do not find that any State has thus lived out its destiny, and died a natural death.

Again, States may perish by outward Violence, military conquest,—for as the lion in the wilderness eateth up the wild ass, so the strong nations devour the weak. But this happened most often in ancient times, when men and States were more rapacious even than now.

Thirdly, States may perish through their own vice, moral or political. Their national institutions may be a defective machine which works badly, and fails of producing national welfare of body or spirit. It may not secure national unity of action — there being no national gravitation of the great masses which fly asunder; or it may fail of individual variety of action — having no personal freedom; excessive national gravitation destroys individual cohesion, and pulls the people flat; the men are Slaves; they cannot reach the moral and spiritual welfare necessary for a nation's continuous life. In both these cases the vice is political; the machinery is defective, made after false ideas. Or when the institutions are good and capable of accommodating the nation's increase and growth, the vice may be moral, lying deeper in the character of the people. They may have a false and unimprovable form of religion, which suits not the nature of man or of God, and which consequently produces a false system of morals, and so corrupts the nation's heart. They may become selfish, gross, cowardly, atheistic, and so decay inwardly and perish. If left all alone such a people will rot down and die of internal corruption. Mexico is in a perishing condition to-day; so is Spain; so are some of the young nations of South America, and some of the old of Asia and Europe. Nothing can ever save Turkey, — not all the arms of all the allied West; and though Protestant and Catholic join hands, Christendom cannot propagate Mahometanism, nor keep it from going down.

Leave these nations to their fate and they will die.

But commonly, they are not left to themselves; other people rush in and conquer. The wild individual man is rapacious by instinct. The present nations are rapacious also by calculation; they prey on feeble States. The hooded crow of Europe watches for the sickly sheep. In America, the wolves prowl round the herd of buffaloes and seize the sickly, the wounded, and the old. And so there are scavengers of the nations, — fillibusters, the flesh-flies and carrion-vultures of the world, who have also their function to perform. Wealth and power are never left without occupants. Rome was corrupt, her institutions bad, her religion worn out, her morals desperate; Northern nations came upon her. "Wheresoever the body is thither the eagles will be gathered together."

In Europe, there are nations in this state of decay, from moral or political vice. All the Italo-Greek populations, most of the Celto-Roman, all the Celtic, all the old Asiatic populations — the Hungarians and Turks. The Teutonic and Slavic families alone seem to prosper, full of vigorous, new life, capable of making new improvements, to suit the altered phases of the world.

In America, there is only one family in a condition of advance, of hardy health. Spanish America is in a state of decay; she has a bad form of religion, and bad morals; her republics only "guarantee the right of assassination;" an empire is her freest state.

But in the North of North America the Anglo-Saxon British colonies rapidly advance in material and spiritual development, and one day doubtless they will separate from the parent stem and become an independent tree. The roots of England run under the ocean; they come up in Africa, India, Australia, America, in many an island of all the seas. Great, fresh, living trunks grow up therefrom. One day these offshoots will become self-supporting, with new and independent roots, and ere long will separate from the parent stem; then there will be a great Anglo-Saxon trunk in Australia, another in India, another in Africa, another in the North of our own Continent, and yet others scattered over the manifold islands of the sea, an Anglo-Saxon forest of civilization.

But in the centre of the North American Continent, the same Anglo-Saxons have passed from their first condition of scattered and dependent colonies, and become a united and independent nation, five-and-twenty millions strong. Our fellow-countrymen here in America compose one fortieth part of all the inhabitants of the globe. We are now making the greatest political experiment which the sun ever looked down upon.

First, we are seeking to found a State on Industry, and not War. All the prizes of America are rewards of toil, not fighting. We are ruled by the constable, not by the soldier. It is only in exceptional cases, when the liberal institutions of America are to be trodden underfoot, that the constable disappears, and the red arm of the soldier clutches at the people's throat. That is the first part of our scheme — we are aiming to found an Industrial State.

Next, the national Theory of the government is a Democracy — the government of all, by all, for all. All officers depend on election, none are foreordained. There are to be no special privileges, only natural, universal rights.

It would be a fair spectacle, — a great industrial Commonwealth, spread over half the continent, and folding in its bosom one fortieth of God's whole family! It is a lovely dream; nor Athenian Plato, nor English Thomas More, nor Bacon, nor Harrington ever dared to write on paper so fair an ideal as our fathers and we have essayed to put into men. I once thought this dream of America would one day become a blessed fact! We have many elements of national success. Our territory for quantity and quality is all we could ask; our origin is of the Caucasian's best. No nation had ever so fair a beginning as we. The Anglo-Saxon is a good hardy stock for national welfare to grow on. To my American eye, it seems that Human Nature had never any thing so good for popular liberty to be grafted into. We are already strong, and fear nothing from any foreign power. The violent cannot take us by force. No nation is our enemy.

But the question now comes, Is America to live or to die? If we live, what life shall it be? Shall we fall into the sepulchre of departed States — a new debauchee of the nations? Shall we live petrified to stone, a despotism many-headed, sitting — another sphinx — by the way-side of history, to scare young nations in their march and impede their progress? Or shall we pursue the journey, — a great, noble-hearted Commonwealth, a nation possessing the continent, full of riches, full of justice, full of wisdom, full of piety, and full of peace? It depends on ourselves. It is for America, for this generation of Americans, to say which of the three shall happen. No fate holds us up. Our character is our destiny.

I am not a timid man; I am no excessive praiser of times passed by; I seldom take counsel of my fears, often of my hopes; — but now I must say that since '76 our success was never so doubtful as at this time. England is in peril; the despots on the continent hate her free Parliament, which makes laws for the people — just laws; they hate her free speech, which tells every grievance at home or abroad; they hate her free soil, which offers a home to every exile, republican or despotic. England is in peril, for every tyrant hates her. Russia is in danger, for the two strongest powers of Christendom have just clasped hands, and sworn an oath to fight against that great marauding empire of the East. Their armies threaten her cities; her sovereign deserts his capital; her treasure is carried a thousand miles inward; the Western fleets blockade her ports and sweep her navies from the sea. But Russia has no peril like ours; England has no danger so great as that which threatens us this day. In the darkest periods of the American Revolution, when Washington's army, without blankets, without coats, without shoes, fled through the Jerseys, when they marked the ice of the Delaware, and left Revolutionary tracks in frozen blood, we were not in such peril as to-day. When General Gage had the throat of Boston in his hand, and perfidiously disarmed the people, we were not in such danger. Yea, when four hundred houses in yonder town went up in one great cloud of smoke towards heaven, the liberties of America were not in such peril as they are to-day. Then we were called to fight with swords — and when that work was to be done, was America ever found wanting? Then our adversary was the other side of the sea, and wicked statutes were enacted against us in Westminster Hall. Now our enemy is at home; and something far costlier than swords is to be called into service.

Look at some of these dangers. I shall pass by all that are trifling. I find four great perils. Here they are: —

I. There comes the Danger from our exclusive devotion to Riches.

II. The Danger from the Roman Catholic Church, established in the midst of us.

III. The Danger from the Idea that there is no Higher Law above the Statutes which men make.

IV. The Danger from the Institution of Slavery, which is based on that atheistic idea last named.

I. Of the Danger which comes from our Exclusive Devotion to Riches.

Power is never left without a possessor: when it fell from the theocratic and military classes, from the priest, the noble, and the king, it passed to the hands of the capitalists. In America, ecclesiastical office is not power; noble or royal birth is of small value. If Madison or Jefferson had left any sons but Mulattoes, their distinguished birth would avail them nothing. The son of Patrick Henry lived a strolling schoolmaster, and a pauper's funeral was asked for his body. Money is power; the only permanent and transmissible power: it goes by device. Money "can ennoble sots and slaves and cowards."

It gives rank in the Church. The millionaire is always a saint. The priests of Commerce will think twice before damning a man who enhances their salary and gives them dinners. In one thing the American Heaven resembles the New Jerusalem: — its pavement is "of fine gold." The capitalist has the chief seat in our Christian synagogue. It is a rare minister who dares assail a vice which has riches on its side. Is there a clergyman at the South who speaks against the profitable wickedness which chains three million American men? How few at the North! European gentility is ancient power; American is new money hot from the stamping.

In Society, money is genteel; it is always respectable. The high places of society do not belong to ecclesiastical men, as in Rome; to military men, as in St. Petersburg; to men of famous family, as in England and Spain; to men of Science and Literature, men of Genius, as in Berlin; but to rich men.

Money gives distinction in Literature, so far as the literary class can control the public judgment. The colleges revere a rich man's son; they name professorships after such as endow them with money, not mind. Critics respect a rich man's book; if he has not brains, he has brass, which is better. The capitalist is admitted a member of the Academies of Arts and Sciences, of collegiate societies; if he cannot write dissertations, he can give suppers, and there must be a material basis for Science. At anniversaries, he receives the Honorary degree. "'Tis easier to weigh purses, sure, than brains." A dull scholar is expelled from college for idleness, and twenty years later returns to New England with half a million of money, and gets his degree. As he puzzles at the Latin diploma, he asks, "If I had come home poor, I wonder how long it would have taken the 'Alma Mater' to find out that I was ever a 'good scholar,' and now 'merited an honorary degree' — facts which I never knew before!"

In politics, money has more influence than in Turkey, Austria, Russia, England, or Spain. For in our politics the interest of property is preferred before all others. National legislation almost invariably favors capital, and not the laboring hand. The Federalists feared that riches would not be safe in America — the many would plunder the wealthy few. It was a groundless fear. In an Industrial Commonwealth, property is sure of popular protection. Where all own hay-ricks no one scatters firebrands. Nowhere in the world is property so secure or so much respected; for it rests on a more natural basis than elsewhere. Nowhere is wealth so powerful in Church, Society, and State. In Kentucky and elsewhere, it can take the murderer's neck out of the halter. It can make the foolish "wise;" the dull man, "eloquent;" the mean man, "honorable, one of our most prominent citizens;" the heretic, "sound orthodox;" the ugly, "fair;" the old man, a "desirable young bridegroom." Nay, vice itself becomes virtue, and man-stealing is Christianity!

Here, nothing but the voter's naked ballot holds money in check: there are no great families with their historic tradition, as in all Europe; no bodies of literary or scientific men to oppose their Genius to mere material Gold. The church is no barrier, only its servant, for when the minister depends on the wealth of his parish for support, you know the common consequence. Lying rides on Obligation's back. The minister respects the hand that feeds him: "the ox knoweth his owner, and the ass his master's crib." Yet now and then a minister looks starvation in the face and continues his unpopular service of God. No political institutions check the authority of wealth; it can bribe and buy the venal; the brave it sometimes can intimidate and starve. Money can often carry a Bill through the legislature — state or national. The majority is hardly strong enough to check this pecuniary sway.

In the "most democratic" States, gold is most powerful. Thus, in fifteen States of America, three hundred thousand proprietors own thirteen hundred millions of money invested in men. In virtue thereof they control the legislation of their own States, making their institutions despotic, and not republican; they keep the poor white man from political power, from comfort, from the natural means of education and religion; they destroy his self-respect, and leave him nothing but his body; from the poorest of the poor, they take away his body itself. Next they control the legislation of America; they make the President, they appoint the Supreme Court, they control the Senate, the Representatives; they determine the domestic and foreign policy of the Nation. Finally, they affect the laws of all the other sixteen States — the Southern hand coloring the local institutions of New Haven and Boston.

That is only one example — one of many. Russia is governed by a long-descended Czar; England by a Queen, Nobles, and Gentry, — men of ancient family, with culture and riches. America is ruled by a troop of men with nothing but new money and what it brings — three hundred thousand slave-holders and their servants, North and South. Boston is under their thumb; at their command the Mayor spits in the face of Massachusetts law, and plants a thousand bayonets at the people's throat. They make ball cartridges under the eaves of Faneuil Hall.

Accordingly, money is the great object of desire and pursuit. There are material reasons why this is so in many lands: — in America there are also social, political, and ecclesiastical reasons for it. "To be rich is to be blessed: Poverty is damnation:" that is the popular creed.

The public looks superficially at the immediate effect of this opinion, at this exceeding and exclusive desire for riches; they see its effect on Israel and John Jacob, on Stephen, Peter, and Robert: it makes them rich, and their children respectable and famous. Few ask, What effect will this have on the nation? They foresee not the future evil it threatens. Nay, they do not consider how it debauches the institutions of America — ecclesiastical, academic, social, political; how it corrupts the hearts of the people, making them prize money as the end of life, and manhood as only the means thereto, making money master, and human nature its tool or servant, but no more.

The political effect of this unnatural esteem for riches is not at all well understood. History but too plainly tells of the dangerous power of priests or nobles consolidated into a class, and their united forces directed by a single able head. The power of allied kings, concentrating whole realms of men and money on a single point; the effect of armies and navies collected together and marshalled by a single will; is all too boldly written in the ruin of many a State. We have often been warned against the peril from forts, and castles, and standing armies. But the power of consolidated riches, the peril which accumulated property may bring upon the liberties of an industrial Commonwealth, though formidably near, as yet is all unknown, all unconsidered too. Already the consolidated property of one eightieth part of the population controls all the rest.

Two special causes, both exceptional and fleeting, just now stimulate the acquisitiveness of America almost to madness.

One is the rapid development of the art of manufacturing the raw materials gathered from the bosom or the surface of the earth. The invention of printing made education and freedom possible on a large scale; one of the immediate results thereof is this — the head briefly performs the else long-protracted labor of the hand. Wind, water, fire, steam, lightning, have become pliant forces to manufacture wood, flax, cotton, wool, and all the metals. This result is nowhere so noticeable as in New England, where education is almost universal. The New England school-house is the machine-shop of America. What the State invests in slates and teachers pays dividends in hard coin. This new power over the material world, the first and unexpected commercial result of the public education of the people, gives a great and perhaps lasting stimulus to the pursuit of wealth. It affects the most undisciplined portions of the world, — for the educated man leaves much rough labor for the ignorant, and enhances the demand for the results of their toil. The thinking head raises the wages of all mere hands. Hence arises the increased value of Slaves at the South, and the rapid immigration of the most ignorant Irishmen to the North. They are to the thoughtful projector what the Merrimack is to the cotton-spinner — a rude force pliant before his will. Dr. Faustus is the unconscious pioneer of many a pilgrimage.

The other cause is the discovery of gold in California and then in Australia. This doubles or trebles the pecuniary momentum of America. Its stimulating influence on our covetousness, accumulation, and luxury, is obvious. What further and ultimate effects it will produce, I shall not now pause to inquire. When a whirlwind rises all men can see that dust is mounting to the sky.

Besides, the form of American industry is changed. Once, New England and all the North were chiefly agricultural; manufactures and commerce were conducted on a small scale; and therein each man wrought on his own account. There was a great deal of individual activity, individuality of character. Few men worked for wages. Now, New England is mainly manufacturing and commercial. Vermont is the only farming State. Mechanics, men and women, work for wages; many in the employment of a single man; thousands in the pay of one company, organized by superior ability. The workman loses his independence, and is not only paid but governed also by his employer's money. His opinions and character are formed after the prescribed pattern, by the mill he works in. The old military organizations for defence or aggression brought freedom of body distinctly in peril: the new industrial organizations jeopardize spiritual individuality, all freedom of mind and conscience. New England is a monumental proof thereof.

Another change also follows: the military habits

of the North are all gone. Once, New England had more firelocks than householders; every man was a soldier and a marksman. Now, the people have lost their taste for military discipline, and neither keep nor bear arms. Of course a few holiday soldiers, called out by a doctor and commanded by an apothecary, can overawe the town.

The Northern, and especially the Eastern and Middle States, are the great centre of this industrial development. Here, and especially in New England, the desire for riches has become so powerful that a very large proportion of our men of the greatest practical intellect have almost exclusively turned their attention to purely productive business, to commerce and manufactures. They rarely engage in the work of politics — unprofitable and distasteful to the individual, and at first sight merely preservative and defensive to the community. This they shun or neglect, as the mass of men avoid military discipline.

The statutes must be made and administered by politicians. Here they are not able men. Of the forty-one New England delegates in Congress, of the six governors, of the many other professional leaders in politics, how many first-rate men are there? how many middle-sized second-rate men? The control of the national affairs passes out of the fingers of the North — which has yet three fifths of the population, and more than four fifths of the speculative and practical intelligence and material wealth. The Nation is controlled by the South, whose ablest men almost exclusively attend to politics. Besides, the State politics of the North fall into the hands of men quite inadequate to such a weighty trust. This mistake is as fatal as it would be in time of war to send all the able-bodied men to the plough, and the women and children to the camp. We are mismanaged at home, and dishonorably routed in the Federal Capital. In the present state of the world, I think no nation would be justified in turning non-resistant, tearing down its forts, disbanding its armies, melting up its guns and swords; and I am sure the North suffers sadly from devoting so large a part of its masterly, practical men to the productive work of commerce and manufactures. Her politicians are not strong enough for her own defence. In American politics, the great battle of Ideas and Principles, yea of Measures, is to be fought. Shall we keep our Washingtons surveying land?

The national effect of this estimate and accumulation of riches is to produce a great and rapid development of the practical understanding; a great love for vulgar finery which pleases the palate or the eye; great luxury of dress, ornament, furniture. You see this in the hotels and public carriages on land and sea, in the costume of the nation, at public and private tables. Along with this there comes a certain refinement of the public taste.

But there is no proportionate culture of the higher intellectual faculties — of the Reason and Imagination; still less of yet nobler powers — moral, affectional, and religious. From the common school to the college, the chief things taught are Arithmetic and Elocution; not the art to reason and create, but the trade to calculate and express. Every thing is measured by the money standard. "The protection of property is the great object of government." The politician must suit the pecuniary interest of his constituency, though at the cost of Justice; the writer, author, or editor, the pecuniary interest of his readers, though at the sacrifice of Truth; the minister, the pecuniary interest of his audience, though Piety and Morality both come to the ground: Mammon is a profitable god to worship — he gives dinners!

I think it must be confessed in the last eighty years the general moral and religious tone of the People in the free States has improved. This change comes from the natural forward tendency of mankind, the instinct of development, quickened by our free institutions. But at the same time it is quite plain to me that the moral and religious tone of American politicians, writers, and preachers, has proportionately and absolutely gone down. You see this in the great towns: if Boston were once the "Athens of America," she is now only the "Corinth." Athens has retreated to some inland Salamis.

But, in general, this peril from the excessive pursuit of riches comes unavoidably from our position in time and space, and our consequent political institutions. It belongs to the period of transition from the old form of vicarious rule by theocratic, military, and aristocratic governments, to the personal administration of an industrial Commonwealth. I do not much fear this peril, nor apprehend lasting evil from it. One of the great things which mankind now most needs is, Power over the material world as the basis for the higher development of our Spiritual faculties. Wealth is indispensable; it is the material pulp around the Spiritual seed. No nation was ever too rich, too well fed, clad, housed, and comforted. The human race still suffers from poverty, the great obstacle to our progress. Doubtless we shall make many errors in our national attempt to organize the productive forces into an industrial State, as our fathers, — thousands of years ago, — in organizing their destructive powers into a military state. Once, man cut his fingers with iron, he now poisons them with gold. All Christendom shares this peril, though America feels it most. She is now like a thriving man, who gets rich fast, and thinks more than he ought of his money, and less of his manhood. Some misfortune, the ruin of a prodigal son perishing in quicksands of gold, will by and by convince him that riches is not the only thing in life.

II. Of the Danger which comes from the Roman Catholic Church.

The Roman Catholic Church claims infallibility for itself, and denies Spiritual Freedom, Liberty of Mind or Conscience, to its members. It is therefore the foe to all progress; it is deadly hostile to Democracy. To mankind this is its first command — Submit to an external authority; subordinate your human nature to an element foreign and abhorrent thereto! It aims at absolute domination over the body and the spirit of man. The Catholic Church can never escape from the consequences of her first principle. She is the natural ally of tyrants, and the irreconcilable enemy of Freedom. Individual Catholics in America, as elsewhere, are inconsistent, and favor the progress of mankind. Alas! such are exceptional; the Catholic Church has an iron logic, and consistently hates Liberty in all its forms — free thought, free speech.

I quote the words of her own authors in America, recently uttered by the press. "Protestantism . . . has not and never can have any rights where Catholicity is triumphant." "We lose all the breath we expend in declaiming against bigotry and intolerance, and in favor of religious liberty." "Religious liberty [in America] is merely endured until the opposite can be carried into execution without peril to the Catholic world." "Catholicity will one day rule in America, and then religious liberty is at an end."

"The very name of Liberty . . . ought to be banished from the very domain of religion." "No man has a right to choose his religion." "Catholicism is the most intolerant of creeds. It is intolerance itself, for it is the truth itself." *

The Catholic population is not great in numbers. In 1853, there were in America 1,712 churches, 1,574 priests, 396 theological students, 32 bishops, 7 archbishops, church property worth about $10,000,000, and 1,728,000 Catholics. But most of them are of the Celtic stock, which has never much favored Protestantism or individual liberty in religion; and in this respect is widely distinguished from the Teutonic population, who have the strongest ethnological instinct for personal freedom.

Besides, the Catholics are governed with absolute rigor by their clergy, who are celibate priests, a social caste by themselves, not sympathizing with mankind, but emasculated of the natural humanities of our race. There are exceptional men amongst them, but such seems to be the rule with the class of Catholic priests in America. They are united into one compact body, with complete corporate unity of action, and ruled despotically by their bishops, archbishops, and Pope. The Catholic worshipper is not

---

* The above, and many more similar declarations, may be found in a little pamphlet—"Familiar Letters to John B. Fitzpatrick, the Catholic Bishop of Boston, by an Independent Irishman. Boston, 1854.

to think, but to believe and obey; the priest not to reason and consider, but to proclaim and command; the voter is not to inquire and examine, but to deposit his ballot as the ecclesiastical authority directs. The better Religious Orders do not visit America: the Jesuits, the most subtle enemies of humanity, come in abundance; some are known, others stealthily prowl about the land, all the more dangerous for their disguise. They all act under the direction of a single head. One shrewd Protestant minister may be equal to one Jesuit, but no ten or forty Protestant ministers is a match for a combination of ten Jesuits, bred to the business of deception, knowing no allegiance to Truth or Justice, consciously disregarding the Higher Law of God, with the notorious maxim that "the end justifies the means," bound to their order by the most stringent oath, and devoted to the worst purposes of the Catholic Church.

All these priests owe allegiance to a foreign head. It is not an American Church; it is Roman, not free, individual, but despotic; nay, in its designs not so much human as merely papal.

The Catholic Church opposes every thing which favors Democracy and the natural rights of man. It hates our free churches, free press, and above all our free schools. No owl more shuns the light. It hates the rule of majorities, the voice of the people; it loves violence, force, and blood.

The Catholic clergy are on the side of Slavery. They find it is the dominant power, and pay court thereto that they may rise by its help. They love Slavery itself; it is an institution thoroughly congenial to them, consistent with the first principles of their church. Their Jesuit leaders think is is "an ulcer which will eat up the Republic," and so stimulate and foster it for the ruin of Democracy, the deadliest foe of the Roman hierarchy.

Besides, most of the Catholics are the victims of oppression, poor, illiterate, oppressed, and often vicious. Their circumstances have ground the humanity out of them. No sect furnishes half so many criminals — victims of society before they become its foes; no sect has so little philanthropy; none is so greedy to oppress. All this is natural. The lower you go down the coarser and more cruel do you find the human being.

I am told there is not in all America a single Catholic newspaper hostile to Slavery; not one opposed to tyranny in general; not one that takes sides with the oppressed in Europe. There is not in America a man born and bred in the Catholic Church, who is eminent for Philosophy, Science, Literature, or Art; none distinguished for Philanthropy! The water tastes of the fountain.

Catholic votes are in the market; the bishops can dispose of them — politicians will make their bid.

Shall it be the sacrifice of the free schools? of other noble institutions? In some States it seems not unlikely.

I do not think our leading men see all this danger. But the baneful influence of the Church of the Dark Ages begins to show itself in the press, in the schools, and still more in the politics of America. Yet I am glad the Catholics come here. Let America be an asylum for the poor and the down-trodden of all lands; let the Irish ships, reeking with misery, land their human burdens in our harbors. The continent is wide enough for all. I rejoice that in America there is no national form of religion; — let the Jew, the Chinese Buddhist, the savage Indian, the Mormon, the Protestant, and the Catholic have free opportunity to be faithful each to his own conscience. Let the American Catholic have his bishops, his archbishops, and his Pope, his Jesuits, his convents, his nunneries, his celibate priesthood of hard drinkers, if he will. Let him oppose the public education of the people; oppose the press, the meeting-house, and the ballot-box; nay, oppose temperance and religion, if he likes. If, with Truth and Justice on our side, the few Catholics can overcome the many Protestants, we deserve defeat. We should be false to the first principles of our democratic theory, if we did not grant them their unalienable rights. Let there be no tyranny; let us pay the Catholics good for ill; and cast out

Satan by the finger of God, not by the Prince of Devils. This peril is easily mastered. The Catholic Church has still many lessons to offer the Protestants.

III. Of the Danger from the Idea that there is no Higher Law above the Statutes of Men.

Of late years, it has been industriously taught in America that there is no Law of Nature superior to the Statutes which men enact; that Politics are not amenable to Conscience or to God. Accordingly, the American Congress knows no check in legislation but the Constitution of the United States and the Will of the Majority; none in the Constitution of the Universe and the Will of God. The atheistic idea of the Jesuits, that the End justifies the Means, is made the first principle in American politics. Hence it has been repeatedly declared by "prominent clergymen" that politics should not be treated of in the pulpit; they are not amenable to religion; Christianity has nothing to do with making or administering the laws. When the Pharisees and Sadducees have silenced the Prophet and the Apostle, it is not difficult to make men believe that Machiavelli is a great saint, and Jesuitism the revealed religion of politics! Let the legislators make what wicked laws they will against the Rights of Man; the priest of commerce is to say nothing. Nay, the legislators themselves are never to refer to Justice and the Eternal Right, only to the expediency of the hour.

Then when the Statute is made, the magistrate is not to ask if it be just, he is only to execute it; the people are to obey and help enforce the wicked enactment, never asking if it be right. The highest virtue in the people is — "unquestioning submission to the Constitution;" or, when the Statute violates their conscience, to do "a disagreeable duty!" Thus the political action of the people is exempted from the jurisdiction of God and his natural moral law! "Christianity has nothing to do with politics!"

Within a few years this doctrine has been taught in a great variety of forms. At first it came in with evil laws, simply as the occasional support of a measure; at length it is announced as a Principle. It has taken a deep hold on the educated classes of the community; for our "superior education" is almost wholly of the intellect, and of only its humbler powers. It appears among the lawyers, the politicians, the editors, and the ministers. Some deny the natural distinction between right and wrong. "Justice," is a matter of convention; things are not "true," but "agreed upon;" not "right," only "assented to." There is no "moral obligation." Government rests on a compact, having its ultimate foundation on the caprice of men, not in their moral nature. What are called Natural

Rights are only certain conveniences agreed upon amongst men; legal fictions — their recognition is their essence, they are the creatures of a compact. Property has no foundation in the nature of things; it may consist of whatever the legislature determines — land, cattle, food, clothing; or of men, women, and children. Dives may own Lazarus as well as the dogs who serve him at the gate. There is no political morality, only political economy.

This conclusion arises from the philosophy of Hobbes and Filmer; yes, from the first principles of Locke and Rousseau. It is one of the worst results of materialism and practical atheism. It takes different forms in different nations. In a monarchy it has for its axiom, "The King can do no wrong; he is the Norm of Law — *Vox Regis vox Dei*." In a Democracy, "The majority can do no wrong; they are the Norm of Law — *Vox Populi vox Dei*." So the Statute becomes an idol; loyalty takes the place of Religion, and despotism becomes enthroned on the necks of the people.

It is not surprising that this doctrine should be taught from the pulpit in Catholic countries — it is conformable to the general conduct of the Roman Church. It belongs also with the sensational philosophy which has yet done so much to break to pieces the theology of the Dark Ages; — and does not astonish one in the sects which build thereon. But at first sight it seems amazing that American

Christians of the Puritanic stock, with a philosophy that transcends sensationalism, should prove false to the only principle which at once justifies the conduct of Jesus, of Luther, and the Puritans themselves. For certainly if obedience to the established law be the highest virtue, then the Patriots and Pilgrims of New England, the Reformers of the Church, the glorious company of the Apostles, the goodly fellowship of the Prophets, and the noble army of martyrs, nay, Jesus himself, were only criminals and traitors. To appreciate this denial of the first principle of all religion, it would be necessary to go deep into the theology of Christendom, and touch the fatal error of all the three parties just referred to. For that there is now no time.

One of the consequences of this atheistic denial of the natural foundation of human laws is, the Preponderance of Parties. An opinion before it becomes a law, while it is yet a tendency, becomes organized into a faction, or party. Members of the party feel the same loyalty thereto which narrow patriots feel for their nation, or bigots for their sect; they give up their mind and conscience to their party. So fidelity to their party, right or wrong, is deemed a great political virtue; the individual member is bound by the party opinion. Thus is the private conscience still further debauched, by the second act in this atheistic popular tragedy.

Thus both national and party politics are taken

out of the jurisdiction of morals, declared not amenable to conscience: in other words, are left to the control of political Jesuits. An American may read the natural result of such principles in the downfall of the Grecian and Italian Republics, or wait to behold it in his own land.

IV. Of the Dangers from the Institution of Slavery which rests on this False Idea.

Slavery is the child of Violence and Atheism. Brute material force is its father: the atheistic idea that there is no Law of God above the passions of men — that is the mother of it. I have lately spoken so long, so often, and with such publicity, both of speech and print, respecting the extent of Slavery in America, and its constant advance since 1788, that I shall pass over all that theme, and speak more directly of the present danger it brings upon our Freedom.

There can be no national welfare without national Unity of Action. That cannot take place unless there is national Unity of Idea in fundamentals. Without this a nation is a "house divided against itself;" of course it cannot stand. It is what mechanics call a figure without equilibrium; the different parts thereof do not balance.

Now, in the American State there are two distinct ideas — Freedom and Slavery.

The Idea of Freedom first got a national expression seventy-eight years ago next Tuesday. Here it is. I put it in a philosophic form. There are five points to it.

First, All men are endowed by their Creator with certain natural rights, amongst which is the right to life, liberty, and the pursuit of happiness.

Second, These rights are unalienable; they can be alienated and forfeited only by the possessor thereof; the father cannot alienate them for the son, nor the son for the father; nor the husband for the wife, nor the wife for the husband; nor the strong for the weak, nor the weak for the strong; nor the few for the many, nor the many for the few; and so on.

Third, In respect to these all men are equal; the rich man has not more, and the poor less; the strong man has not more, and the weak man less: — all are exactly equal in these rights, however unequal in their powers.

Fourth, It is the function of government to secure these natural, unalienable, and equal rights to every man.

Fifth, Government derives all its divine right from its conformity with these ideas, all its human sanction from the consent of the governed.

That is the Idea of Freedom. I used to call it "the American Idea;" it was when I was younger than I am to-day. It is derived from human nature; it rests on the immutable Laws of God; it is part of the natural religion of mankind. It demands a government after natural Justice, which is the point common between the conscience of God and the conscience of mankind, the point common also between the interests of one man and of all men.

Now this government, just in its substance, in its form must be democratic: that is to say, the government of all, by all, and for all. You see what consequences must follow from such an idea, and the attempt to reënact the Law of God into political institutions. There will follow the freedom of the people, respect for every natural right of all men, the rights of their body, and of their spirit — the rights of mind and conscience, heart and soul. There must be some restraint — as of children by their parents, as of bad men by good men; but it will be restraint for the joint good of all parties concerned; not restraint for the exclusive benefit of the restrainer. The ultimate consequence of this will be the material and spiritual welfare of all — riches, comfort, noble manhood, all desirable things.

That is the Idea of Freedom. It appears in the Declaration of Independence; it reappears in the Preamble to the American Constitution, which aims "to establish Justice, insure domestic tranquillity, provide for the common defence, promote the general welfare, and secure the blessings of Liberty." That is a religious idea; and when men pray for the "Reign of Justice" and the "Kingdom of Heaven" to come on earth politically, I suppose they mean that there may be a Commonwealth where every man has his natural rights of mind, body, and estate.

Next is the Idea of Slavery. Here it is. I put it also in a philosophic form. There are three points which I make.

First. There are no natural, unalienable, and equal rights, wherewith men are endowed by their Creator; no natural, unalienable, and equal right to life, liberty, and the pursuit of happiness.

Second. There is a great diversity of powers, and in virtue thereof the strong man may rule and oppress, enslave and ruin the weak, for his interest and against theirs.

Third. There is no natural law of God to forbid the strong to oppress the weak, and enslave and ruin the weak.

That is the Idea of Slavery. It has never got a national expression in America; it has never been laid down as a Principle in any act of the American people, nor in any single State, so far as I know. All profess the opposite; but it is involved in the measures of both State and Nation. This Idea is founded in the selfishness of man; it is atheistic.

The idea must lead to a corresponding government; that will be unjust in its substance,— for it will depend not on natural right, but on personal force; not on the Constitution of the Universe, but on the compact of men. It is the abnegation of God in the universe and of conscience in man. Its form will be despotism,—the government of all, by a part, for the sake of a part. It may be a single-headed despotism, or a despotism of many heads; but whether a Cyclops or a Hydra, it is alike "the abomination which maketh desolate." Its ultimate consequence is plain to forsee—poverty to a nation, misery, ruin.

At first, Slavery came as a Measure; nothing was said about it as a Principle. But in a country full of schoolmasters, legislatures, newspapers, talking men, —a measure without a principle to bear it up is like a single twig of willow cast out on a wooden floor; there is nothing for it to grow by; it will die. So of late the principle has been boldly avowed. Mr. Calhoun denied the self-evident truths of the Declaration of Independence; denied the natural, unalienable, and equal rights of man. Many since have done the same—political, literary, and mercantile men, and, of course, ecclesiastical men; there are enough of them always in the market. All parts of the Idea of Slavery have been affirmed by prominent men at the North and the South. It has been acted on in the formation of the Constitution of every Slave State, and in the passage of many of its laws. It lies at the basis of a great deal of national legislation.

Hear the opinions of some of our Southern Patriots: "Slavery is coeval with Society:" "it was commended by God's chosen Theocracy, and sanctioned by His Apostles in the Christian Church." All ancient literature "is the literature of Slave-holders;" "Rome and Greece owed their literary and national greatness exclusively to the institution of Slavery;" "Slavery is as necessary for the welfare of the Southern States as sunshine is for the flowers of the prairies;" "a noble and necessary institution of God's creation." * "Nature is the mother and protector of Slavery;" "Domestic Slavery is not only *natural* and *necessary*, but a great blessing." "Free Society is a sad and signal failure;" "it does well enough in a new country." "Free Society has become diseased by abolishing Slavery. It can only be restored to pristine health, happiness, and prosperity, by reinstituting Slavery." "Slavery may be administered under a new name." "Free Society is a monstrosity. Like all monsters, it will be short-lived. We dare and do vindicate Slavery in the abstract." The negro "needs a master to protect and govern him; so do the ignorant poor in old countries." †

"There is no moral wrong in Slavery;" it "is the normal condition of human society." "The benefits and advantages which so far have resulted from this institution we take as lights to guide us to the

---

* Richmond Examiner for June 30, 1854.
† Ibid. June 23, 1854.

brighter truths of its future history." "We belong to that society of which Slavery is the distinguishing element, and we are not ashamed of it. We find it marked by every evidence of divine approval." *

These two Ideas are now fairly on foot. They are hostile; they are both mutually invasive and destructive. They are in exact opposition to each other, and the nation which embodies these two is not a figure of equilibrium. As both are active forces in the minds of men, and as each idea tends to become a fact — a universal and exclusive fact, — as men with these ideas organize into parties as a means to make their idea into a fact, — it follows that there must not only be strife amongst philosophical men about these antagonistic Principles and Ideas, but a strife of practical men about corresponding Facts and Measures. So the quarrel, if not otherwise ended, will pass from words to what seems more serious; and one will overcome the other.

So long as these two Ideas exist in the nation as two political forces, there is no national Unity of Idea, of course no Unity of Action. For there is no centre of gravity common to Freedom and Slavery. They will not compose an equilibrious figure. You may cry "Peace! Peace!" but so long

* Charleston Standard, (S. C.,) June 21, 1854.

as these two antagonistic Ideas remain, each seeking to organize itself and get exclusive power, there is no peace; there can be none.

The question before the nation to-day is, Which shall prevail — the Idea and Fact of Freedom, or the Idea and the Fact of Slavery; Freedom, exclusive and universal, or Slavery, exclusive and universal? The question is not merely, Shall the African be bond or free? but, Shall America be a Democracy or a Despotism? For nothing is so remorseless as an idea, and no logic is so strong as the historical development of a national idea by millions of men. A measure is nothing without its Principle. The idea which allows Slavery in South Carolina will establish it also in New England. The bondage of a black man in Alexandria imperils every white woman's daughter in Boston. You cannot escape the consequences of a first Principle more than you can "take the leap of Niagara and stop when half-way down." The Principle which recognizes Slavery in the Constitution of the United States would make all America a Despotism; while the principle which made John Quincy Adams a free man would extirpate Slavery from Louisiana and Texas. It is plain America cannot long hold these two contradictions in the national consciousness. Equilibrium must come.

Now there are three possible ways of settling the

quarrel between these two Ideas; only three. The categories are exhaustive.

This is the first: The discord may rend the nation asunder, and the two elements separate and become distinct nations — a Despotism with the Idea of Slavery, a Democracy with the Idea of Freedom. Then each will be an equilibrious figure. The Anglo-Saxon Despotism may go to ruin on its own account, while the Anglo-Saxon Democracy marches on to national welfare. That is the first hypothesis.

Or, second: The Idea of Freedom may destroy Slavery, with all its accidents — attendant and consequent. Then the nation may have unity of idea, and so a unity of action, and become a harmonious whole, a Unit of Freedom, a great industrial Democracy, reënacting the laws of God, and pursuing its way, continually attaining greater degrees of freedom and prosperity. That is the second hypothesis.

Here is the third: The Idea of Slavery may destroy Freedom, with all its accidents — attendant and consequent. Then the nation will become an integer; only it will be a Unit of Despotism. This involves, of course, the destructive revolution of all our liberal institutions, State as well as national. Democracy must go down; the free press go down; the free church go down; the free school go down. There must be an industrial despotism, which will soon become a military despotism. Popular legislation must end; the Federal Congress will be a club of officials, like Nero's senate, which voted his horse first consul. The State legislature will be a knot of commissioners, tide-waiters, postmasters, district-attorneys, deputy-marshals. The town-meeting will be a gang of government officers, like the "Marshal's Guard," revolvers in their pockets, soldiers at their back. The *Habeas Corpus* will be at an end; trial by jury never heard of, and open courts as common in America as in Spain or Rome. Commissioners Curtis, Loring, and Kane, will not be exceptional men; there will be no other "judges;" all courts, courts of the kidnapper; all process summary; all cases decided by the will of the government; arbitrary force the only rule. The constable will disappear, the soldier come forth. All newspapers will be like the "Satanic press" of Boston and New York, like the Journal of St. Petersburg or the Diario Romano, which tell lies when the ruler commands, or tell truth when he insists upon it. Then the wicked will walk on every side, for the vilest of men will be exalted, and America, become the mock and scorn and hissing of the nations, will go down to worse shame than was ever heaped upon Sodom; for with her lust for wealth, land, and power, she also will have committed the crime against nature. Then America will be another Italy, Greece, Asia Minor, yea, like Gomorrah — for the Dead Sea will have settled down upon us with nothing living in its breast, and the rulers will proclaim Peace where they have made solitude.

Which of these three hypotheses shall we take?

I. Will there be a Separation of the two elements, and a formation of two distinct States, — Freedom with Democracy, and Slavery with a tendency to despotism? That may save one half the nation, and leave the other to voluntary ruin. Certainly it is better to enter into life halt or maimed, rather than having two hands and two feet to be cast into everlasting fire.

Now, I do not suppose it is possible for the Anglo-Saxons of America to remain as one nation for a great many years. Suppose we become harmonious and prosper abundantly: when there are a hundred millions on the Atlantic slope, another hundred millions in the Mississippi Valley, a third hundred millions on the Pacific slope, and a fourth hundred millions in South America, — it is not likely that all these will hold together. We shall be too wide spread. And, besides, it is not according to the disposition of the Teutonic family to aggregate into one great State any very large body of men; division, not conglomeration, is after the ethnologic instinct and the historical custom of the Teutonic family, and especially of its Anglo-Saxon tribe. We do not like centralization of power, but have such strong individuality that we prefer local self-government; we are social, not gregarious like the Celtic family. I, therefore, do not look on the union of the States as a thing that is likely to last a great length of time, under any circumstances. I doubt if any part of the nation will desire it a hundred years hence.

True, there are causes which tend to keep us united: community of ethnologic origin — fifteen millions are Anglo-Saxon; — unity of language, literature, religion; historic and legal traditions, and commercial interest. But all these may easily be overcome, and doubtless will be. So a dissolution of the great Anglo-Saxon State seems likely to take place, when the territory is spread so wide that there is a practical inconvenience in balancing the nation on a single governmental point; when the numbers are so great that we require many centres of legislative and administrative action in order to secure individual freedom of the parts as well as national unity of the whole; or when the Federal Government shall become so corrupt that the trunk will not sustain the limbs. Then the branches which make up this great American Banyan-tree will separate from the rotten primeval trunk, draw their support from their own local roots, and spread into great and independent trees. All this may take place without fighting. Massachusetts and Maine were once a single State; now friendly sisters.

But I do not think this "dissolution of the Union" will take place immediately, or very soon. For America is not now ruled — as it is commonly thought, — either by the mass of men who follow their national, ethnological, and human instincts; or by a few far-sighted men of genius for politics, who consciously obey the Law of God made clear in their own masterly mind and conscience, and make statutes in advance of the calculation or even the instincts of the people, and so manage the Ship of State that every occasional tack is on a great circle of the Universe, a right line of Justice, and therefore the shortest way to welfare: but by two very different classes of men; — by Mercantile men, who covet money, actual or expectant Capitalists; and by Political men, who want power, actual or expectant office-holders. These appear diverse; but there is a strong unanimity between the two; — for the mercantile men want money as a means of power, and the political men power as a means of money. There are noble men in both classes, exceptional, not instantial, men with great riches even, and great office. But as a class, these men are not above the average morality of the people, often below it; they have no deep, religious faith, which leads them to trust the Higher Law of God. They do not look for Principles that are right, conformable to the Constitution of the Universe, and so creative of the nation's permanent welfare; but only for expedient

Measures, productive to themselves of selfish money or selfish power. In general, they have the character of adventurers, the aims of adventurers, the morals of adventurers; they begin poor, and of course obscure, and are then "democratic," and hurrah for the people: "Down with the powerful and the rich" is the private maxim of their heart. If they are successful and become rich, famous, attaining high office, they commonly despise the people: "Down with the people!" is the axiom of their heart — only they dare not say it; for there are so many others with the same selfishness, who have not yet achieved their end, and raise the opposite cry. The line of the nation's course is a resultant of the compound selfishness of these two classes.

From these two, with their mercantile and political selfishness, we are to expect no comprehensive Morality, which will secure the Rights of mankind; no comprehensive Policy, which will secure expedient measures for a long time. Both will unite in what serves their apparent interest, brings money to the trader, power to the politician, — whatever be the consequence to the country.

As things now are, the Union favors the schemes of both of these classes of men; thereby the politician gets power, the trader makes money.

If the Union were to be dissolved and a great Northern Commonwealth were to be organized, with the Idea of Freedom, three quarters of the Politicians, Federal and State, would pass into contempt and oblivion; all that class of Northern demagogues who scoff at God's Law, such as filled the offices of the late Whig administration in its day of power, or as fill the offices of the Democratic administration to-day — they would drop down so deep that no plummet would ever reach them; you would never hear of them again.

Gratitude is not a very common virtue; but gratitude to the hand of Slavery, which feeds these creatures, is their sole and single moral excellence; they have that form of gratitude. When the hand of Slavery is cut off, that class of men will perish just as caterpillars die when, some day in May, the farmer cuts off from the old tree a great branch to graft in a better fruit. The caterpillers will not vote for the grafting. That class of men will go for the Union while it serves them.

Look at the other class. Property is safe in America: and why? Because we have aimed to establish a government on natural rights, and property is a natural right; say oligarchic Blackstone and socialistic Proudhon what they may, property is not the mere creature of compact, or the child of robbery; it is founded in the Nature of Man. It has a very great and important function to perform. Nowhere in the world is it so much respected as here.

But there is one kind of property which is not

safe just now: — Property in Men. It is the only kind of property which is purely the creature of violence and law; it has no root in itself.

Now, the Union protects that "property." There are three hundred thousand Slave-holders, owning thirteen hundred millions of dollars invested in men. Their wealth depends on the Union; destroy that, and their unnatural property will take to itself legs and run off, seeking liberty by flight, or else stay at home and, like an Anglo-Saxon, take to itself fire-brands and swords, and burn down the master's house and cut the master's throat. So the Slave-holder wants the Union; he makes money by it. Slavery is unprofitable to the nation. No three millions earn so little as the three million Slaves. It is costly to every State. But it enriches the owner of the Slaves. The South is agricultural; that is all. She raises cotton, sugar, and corn; she has no commerce, no manufactures, no mining. The North has mills, ships, mines, manufactures; buys and sells for the South, and makes money by what impoverishes the South. So all the great commercial centres of the North are in favor of Union, in favor of Slavery. The instinct of American trade just now is hostile to American Freedom. The Money Power and the Slave Power go hand in hand. Of course such editors and ministers as are only the tools of the Money Power, or the Slave Power, will be fond of "Union at all hazards." They will sell their mothers to keep it. Now these are the controlling classes of men; these ministers and editors are the mouth-pieces of these controlling classes of men; and as these classes make money and power out of the Union, for the present I think the Union will hold together. Yet I know very well that there are causes now at work which embitter the minds of men, and which, if much enforced, will so exasperate the North that we shall rend the Union asunder at a blow. That I think not likely to take place, for the South sees the peril and its own ruin.

II. The next hypothesis is, Freedom may triumph over Slavery. That was the expectation once, at the time of the Declaration of Independence; nay, at the formation of the Constitution. But only two national steps have been taken against Slavery since then — one the Ordinance of 1787, the other the abolition of the African Slave-Trade; really that was done in 1788, formally twenty years after. In the individual States, the white man's freedom enlarges every year; but the Federal Government becomes more and more addicted to Slavery. This hypothesis does not seem very likely to be adopted.

III. Shall Slavery destroy Freedom? It looks very much like it. Here are nine great steps, openly taken since '87, in favor of Slavery. First, America put Slavery into the Constitution. Second, out of old soil she made four new Slave States. Third, America, in 1793, adopted Slavery as a Federal institution, and guaranteed her protection for that kind of property as for no other. Fourth, America bought the Louisiana territory in 1803, and put Slavery into it. Fifth, she thence made Louisiana, Missouri, and then Arkansas Slave States. Sixth, she made Slavery perpetual in Florida. Seventh, she annexed Texas. Eighth, she fought the Mexican War, and plundered a feeble sister republic of California, Utah, and New Mexico, to get more Slave Soil. Ninth, America gave ten millions of money to Texas to support Slavery, passed the Fugitive Slave Bill, and has since kidnapped men in New England, New York, New Jersey, Pennsylvania, Ohio, Michigan, Wisconsin, Illinois, Indiana, in all the East, in all the West, in all the Middle States. All the great cities have kidnapped their own citizens. Professional Slave-hunters are members of New England Churches; kidnappers sit down at the Lord's table in the city of Cotton, Chauncey, and Mayhew. In this very year, before it is half through, America has taken two more steps for the destruction of freedom. The repeal of the Missouri Compromise and the enslavement of Nebraska: that is the tenth step. Here is the eleventh : The Mexican Treaty, giving away ten millions of dollars and buying a little strip of worthless land, solely that it may serve the cause of Slavery.

Here are eleven great steps openly taken towards the ruin of Liberty in America. Are these the worst? Very far from it! Yet more dangerous things have been done in secret.

I. Slavery has corrupted the Mercantile Class. Almost all the leading merchants of the North are Pro-Slavery men. They hate freedom, hate your freedom and mine! This is the only Christian country in which commerce is hostile to freedom.

II. See the corruption of the Political Class. There are forty thousand officers of the Federal Government. Look at them in Boston, — their character is as well known as this Hall. Read their journals in this city, — do you catch a whisper of freedom in them? Slavery has sought its menial servants, — men basely born and basely bred: it has corrupted them still further, and put them in office. America, like Russia, is the country for mean men to thrive in. Give him time and mire enough, a worm can crawl as high as an eagle flies. State rights are sacrificed at the North; centralization goes on with rapid strides; State laws are trodden underfoot.* The Northern President is all for Slavery. The

* While this volume is passing through the press, another example of this same corruption appears. The Senate passes a bill to protect United States officers engaged in kidnapping citizens of the free States, from the justice of the People. Such kidnappers are to be tried in the kidnappers' court.

Northern Members of the Cabinet are for Slavery; in the Senate, fourteen Northern Democrats were for the enslavement of Nebraska; in the House of Representatives, forty-four Northern Democrats voted for the bill, — fourteen in the Senate, forty-four in the House; fifty-eight Northern men voted against the conscience of the North and the Law of God. Only eight men out of all the South could be found friendly to justice and false to their own local idea of injustice. The present administration, with its supple tools of tyranny, came into office while the cry of "No Higher Law" was echoing through the land!

III. Slavery has debauched the Press. How many leading journals of commerce and politics in the great cities do you know that are friendly to Freedom and opposed to Slavery? Out of the five large daily commercial papers in Boston, Whig or Democratic, I know of only one that has spoken a word for freedom this great while. The American newspapers are poor defenders of American liberty. Listen to one of them, speaking of the last kidnapping in Boston: "We shall need to employ the same measures of coercion as are necessary in monarchical countries." There is always some one ready to do the basest deeds. Yet there are some noble journals — political and commercial; such as the New York Tribune and Evening Post.

IV. Then our Colleges and Schools are corrupted by Slavery. I do not know of five colleges in all the North which publicly appear on the side of freedom. What the hearts of the presidents and professors are, God knows, not I. The great crime against humanity, practical atheism, found ready support in Northern colleges, in 1850 and 1851. Once, the common reading books of our schools were full of noble words. Read the school-books now made by Yankee peddlers of literature, and what liberal ideas do you find there? They are meant for the Southern market. Slavery must not be offended!

V. Slavery has corrupted the Churches! There are twenty-eight thousand Protestant clergymen in the United States. There are noble hearts, true and just men among them, who have fearlessly borne witness to the truth. I need not mention their names. Alas! they are not very numerous; I should not have to go over my fingers many times to count them all. I honor these exceptional men. Some of them are old, far older than I am; older than my father need have been; some of them are far younger than I; nay, some of them younger than my children might be:—and I honor these men for the fearless testimony which they have borne—the old, the middle-aged, and the young. But they are very exceptional men. Is there a minister in the South who preaches against Slavery? How few in all the North!

Look and see the condition of the Sunday Schools. In 1853, the Episcopal Methodists had 9,438 Sunday Schools; 102,732 Sunday School teachers; 525,008 scholars. There is not an Anti-Slavery Sunday School in the compass of the Methodist Episcopal Church. Last year, in New York, they issued, on an average, two thousand bound volumes every day in the year, not a line against Slavery in them. They printed also two thousand pamphlets every day; there is not a line in them all against Slavery; they printed more than two hundred and forty million pages of Sunday School books, not a line against Slavery in them all; not a line showing that it is wicked to buy and sell a man, for whom, according to the Methodist Episcopal Church, Christ died!

The Orthodox Sunday School Union spent last year $248,201; not a cent against Slavery, our great National Sin. They print books by the million. Only one of them contains a word against Slavery; that is Cowper's Task, which contains these words — my mother taught them to me when I was a little boy, and sat in her lap: —

"I would not have a Slave to till my ground,
To carry me, to fan me when I sleep,
And tremble when I wake, for all the wealth
That sinews, bought and sold, have ever earned!"

You all know it: if you do not, you had better learn and teach it to your children. That is the only Anti-Slavery work they print. Once they published a book written by Mr. Gallaudet, which related the story, I think, of the selling of Joseph: at any rate, it showed that Egyptian Slavery was wrong. A little girl in a Sunday School in one of the Southern States one day said to her teacher, "If it was wrong to make Joseph a Slave, why is it not wrong to make Dinah, and Sambo, and Chloe Slaves?" The Sunday School teacher and the Church took the alarm and complained of the Sunday School Union: "You are poisoning the South with your religion, telling the children that Slavery is wicked." It was a serious thing, "dissolution of the Union," "levying war," or at least, "misdemeanor," for aught I know "obstructing an officer of the United States." What do you think the Sunday School Union did? It suppressed the book! It printed one Sunday School book which had a line against Egyptian Slavery and then suppressed it; and it cannot be had to-day! Amid all their million books, there is not a line against Slavery, save what Cowper sung. There are five million Sunday School scholars in the United States, and there is not a Sunday School manual which has got a word against Slavery in it.

You all know the American Tract Society. Last year the American Tract Society in Boston spent

$79,983.46; it visited more than fourteen thousand families; it distributed 3,334,920 tracts — not a word against Slavery in them all. The American Tract Society in New York last year visited 568,000 families, containing three million persons; it spent for home purposes $406,707; for foreign purposes $422,294; it distributed tracts in English, French, German, Dutch, Danish, Swedish, Norwegian, Italian, Hungarian, and Welch — and it did not print one single line, nor whisper a single word against this great national sin of Slavery! Nay, worse: — if it finds English books which suit its general purpose, but containing matter adverse to Slavery, it strikes out all the Anti-Slavery matter, then prints and circulates the book. Is the Tract Society also managed by Jesuits from the Roman Church?

At this day, 600,000 Slaves are directly and personally owned by men who are called "professing Christians," "members in good fellowship" of the churches of this land; 80,000 owned by Presbyterians, 225,000 by Baptists, 250,000 owned by Methodists; — 600,000 Slaves in this land owned by men who profess themselves Christians, and in churches sit down to take the Lord's Supper, in the name of Christ and God! There are ministers who own their fellow men — "bought with a price."

Does not this look as if Slavery were to triumph over Freedom?

VI. Slavery corrupts the Judicial Class. In America, especially in New England, no class of men has been so much respected as the judges; and for this reason: we have had wise, learned, excellent men for our judges; men who reverenced the Higher Law of God, and sought by human statutes to execute Justice. You all know their venerable names, and how reverentially we have looked up to them. Many of them are dead; some are still living, and their hoary hairs are a crown of glory on a judicial life, without judicial blot. But of late Slavery has put a different class of men on the benches of the Federal Courts — mere tools of the government; creatures which get their appointment as pay for past political service, and as pay in advance for iniquity not yet accomplished. You see the consequences. Note the zeal of the Federal Judges to execute iniquity by statute and destroy Liberty. See how ready they are to support the Fugitive Slave Bill, which tramples on the spirit of the Constitution, and its letter too; which outrages Justice and violates the most sacred principles and precepts of Christianity. Not a United States Judge, Circuit or District, has uttered one word against that "bill of abominations." Nay, how greedy they are to get victims under it! No wolf loves better to rend a lamb into fragments than these judges to kidnap a Fugitive Slave, and punish any man who dares to speak against it. You know what has happened in Fugitive Slave Bill Courts. You remember the "miraculous" rescue of Shadrach: the peaceable snatching of a man from the hands of a cowardly kidnapper was "high treason;" it was "levying war." You remember the "trial" of the rescuers! Judge Sprague's charge to the Grand Jury that if they thought the question was which they ought to obey, the law of man or the Law of God, then they must "Obey both!" serve God and Mammon, Christ and the Devil, in the same act! You remember the "trial," the "ruling" of the Bench, the swearing on the stand, the witness coming back to alter and "enlarge his testimony" and have another gird at the prisoner! You have not forgotten the trials before Judge Kane at Philadelphia, and Judge Grier at Christiana and Wilkesbarre.

These are natural results of causes well known. You cannot escape a Principle. Enslave a negro, will you? — you doom to bondage your own sons and daughters, by your own act.

Do you forget the Union meeting in Faneuil Hall, November 26, 1850, the Tuesday before Thanksgiving Day? It was called to indorse the Fugitive Slave Bill — a meeting to promote the stealing of men in Boston, of your fellow worshippers and my parishioners. Do you remember the Democratic Herods and Whig Pilates, who were made friends that day, melted into one Unity of Despotism, in order that they might enslave men? They had Unity of Idea and Unity of Action, that day. Do you remember the speeches of Mr. Curtis and Mr. Hallett; their yelp against the unalienable rights of men; their howl at God's Higher Law? The worser half of that platform is now the United States Court;—the Fugitive Slave Bill Judge, the United States Attorney. They got their offices for their political services past and for their character—very fitting reward to very fitting men! A man professes a fondness for kidnapping, hurrahs for it in Faneuil Hall:—give him the United States Judgeship; make him United States Attorney—fit to fit! When Slavery dispenses offices, every service rendered to despotism is well paid. Men with foreheads of brass, with iron elbows, with consciences of gum elastic, whose chief commandment of their Law, their Prophets, and their Gospel, is to

> "—— crook the pregnant hinges of the knee,
> Where thrift may follow fawning,"

verily they shall have their reward! They shall become Fugitive Slave Bill Judges; yea, Attorneys of the United States!

In 1836, a poor Slave girl named Med, who had been brought from Louisiana to Boston by her master, sued for her freedom in the Courts of Massachusetts. Mr. Benjamin R. Curtis appeared as the Slave-hunter's counsel, long, and stoutly, and learnedly contending that she should not receive her freedom by the laws, constitution, and usages of this Commonwealth, but should be sent back to eternal bondage.* On the 7th of March, 1850, Mr. Webster made his Speech against freedom, so fatal to himself, but soon after found such a fire in his rear that he must return to Massachusetts to rescue his own popularity — then apparently in great peril. On the 29th of April, the same Mr. Curtis, faithful to his proclivities towards Slavery, made a public address to the apostate Senator, at the Revere House, and expressed his "abounding gratitude for the ability and fidelity" which Mr. Webster had "brought to the defence of the Constitution and the Union," praising him as "eminently vigilant, wise, and faithful to our country, without shadow of turning." At the Union meeting in Faneuil Hall, (Nov. 26th,) Mr. Curtis declared the fugitive slaves "a class of foreigners," "with whose rights Massachusetts has

* The girl was set free, and the principle laid down that Slaves coming to a free State with the consent of their masters, secured their freedom. An account of the case was published in the Boston Daily Advertiser of August 29, 1836, and introduced with the following editorial comment: — "In some of the States there is, we believe, legislative provision for cases of this sort, [namely, allowing the master to bring and keep Slaves in bondage,] and it would seem that some such provision is necessary in this State, unless we would prohibit citizens of the Slave-holding States from travelling in this State with their families, and unless we would permit such of them as wish to emancipate their Slaves, to throw them at their pleasure upon the people of this State."

nothing to do. It is enough for us that they have no right to be *here*." Other services, similar or analogous, which he has rendered to the cause of inhumanity, I here pass by.

This is a world in which "men do nothing for nothing;" the workman is worthy of his hire; in due time Mr. Curtis received his reward.

He has lately, (June 7th,) "charged" the Grand Jury of the Circuit Court of the United States, pointing out their duty in respect to recent events in Boston. A federal enactment of 1790 provides that if any person shall wilfully obstruct, resist, or oppose any officer of the United States in executing any legal writ or process thereof, he shall be imprisoned not more than twelve months, and fined not more than three hundred dollars. Mr. Curtis charges that the offence is "a misdemeanor:" to constitute the crime it is "not necessary to prove the accused used or even threatened active violence." "If a multitude of persons should assemble, even in a public highway, with the design to stand together, and thus prevent the officer from passing freely along the way, . . . this would of itself, and without any active violence, be such an obstruction as is contemplated by this law."

So much for what constitutes the crime. Now see who are criminals: "All who are present and actually obstruct, resist, or oppose, are of course guilty. So are all who are present, leagued in the common design, and so situated as to be able, in case of need, to afford assistance to those actually engaged, though they do not actually obstruct, resist, or oppose." That is, they are guilty of a misdemeanor, because they are in the neighborhood of such as oppose a constable of the United States, and are "able" "to afford assistance." "If they are present for the purpose of affording assistance, though no overt act is done by them, they are still guilty under this law." They are guilty of a misdemeanor, not merely as accessory before the fact, but as principals, for "in misdemeanors all are principals."

"Not only those who are present, but those who though absent when the offence was committed, did procure, counsel, command, or abet others to commit the offence, are indictable as principals." But what amounts to such counselling as constitutes a misdemeanor? "Evincing an express liking, approbation, or assent to another's criminal design." "It need not appear that the precise time, or place, or means advised, were used." So all who evinced "an express liking, approbation, or assent" to the rescue of Mr. Burns are guilty of a misdemeanor; if they evinced "an express liking" that he should be rescued by a miracle wrought by Almighty God,—and some did express "approbation" of that "means,"—they are indictable, guilty of a "misdemeanor;" "it need not appear that the precise time, or place, or means advised, were used!" If any colored woman, during the wicked week—which was ten days long—prayed that God would deliver Anthony, as it is said his angel delivered Peter, or said "amen" to such a prayer, she was "guilty of a misdemeanor;" to be indicted as a "principal."

So every man in Boston who, on that bad Friday, stood in the streets of Boston between Court Square and T Wharf, was "guilty of a misdemeanor," liable to a fine of three hundred dollars, and to jailing for twelve months. All who at Faneuil Hall stirred up the minds of the people in opposition to the Fugitive Slave Bill; all who shouted, who clapped their hands at the words or the countenance of their favorites, or who expressed "approbation" by a whisper of "assent," are "guilty of misdemeanor." The very women who stood for four days at the street corners, and hissed the infamous Slave-hunters and their coadjutors; they, too, ought to be punished by fine of three hundred dollars and imprisonment for a year! Well, there were fifteen thousand persons "assembled" "in the highway" of the City of Boston that day opposed to kidnapping; half the newspapers in the country towns of Massachusetts "evinced an express liking" for freedom, and opposed the kidnapping; they are all "guilty of a misdemeanor;" they are "Principals." Nay, the few ministers all over the State, who preached that kidnapping was a sin; those who read brave words out of the Old Testament or the New; those who prayed that the victim might escape; they, likewise, were "guilty of a misdemeanor," liable to be fined three hundred dollars and jailed for twelve months. Excellent Fugitive Slave Bill Judge! Mr. Webster did wisely in making that appointment! He chose an appropriate tool. The charge was worthy of the worst days of Jeffreys and the second James!

We all know against whom this judicial iniquity was directed — against men who, at Faneuil Hall, under the pictured and sculptured eyes of John Hancock and the three Adamses, appealed to the spirit of humanity, not yet crushed out of your heart and mine, and lifted up their voices in favor of Freedom and the Eternal Law of God. If he had called us by our names, he could not have made the thing plainer. You know the zeal of the United States Attorney, you have heard of the swearing before the Grand Jury and at the Grand Jury. Did the Judge's lightning only glow with judicial ardor and zeal for the Fugitive Slave Bill? — or was it also red with personal malignity and family spleen? Judge you!

But, alas! there was a Grand Jury, and the Salmonean thunder of the Fugitive Slave Bill Judge fell harmless — quenched, conquered, disgraced, and brutal, — to the ground. Poor Fugitive Slave Bill Court! it can only gnash its teeth against freedom of speech in Faneuil Hall; only bark and yelp against the unalienable rights of man, and howl against the Higher Law of God! it cannot bite! Poor, imbecile, malignant Court! What a pity that the Fugitive Slave Bill Judge was not himself the Grand Jury, to order the indictment! what a shame that the Attorney was not a petty jury to convict! Then New England, like Old, might have had her "bloody assizes," and Boston streets might have streamed with the heart's gore of noble men and women; and human heads might have decked the pinnacles all round the town; and Judge Curtis and Attorney Hallett might have had their place with Judge Jeffreys and John Boilman of old. What a pity that we have a Grand Jury and a traverse jury to stand between the malignant arm of the Slave-hunter and the heart of you and me! Perhaps the Court will try again, and find a more pliant Grand Jury, easier to intimidate. Let me suggest to the Court that the next time it should pack its Jurors from the Marshal's "guard." Then there will be unity of Idea; of action, too — the Court a figure of equilibrium.*

At a Fugitive Slave Bill meeting in Faneuil Hall, it is easy to ask a minister a question designed to be insulting, and not dare listen to the proffered

---

* The experiment was made; the brother-in-law of the Fugitive Slave Bill Judge was put on the Jury, and indictments were found in October and November.

reply; easy to bark at Justice, and howl at the unalienable rights of man; easy to yelp out the vengeance of a corrupt administration of Slave-hunters upon all who love the Higher Law of God; but He Himself has so fashioned the hearts of men that we instinctively hate all tyranny, all oppression, all wrong; and the hand of history brands ineffaceable disgrace on the brass foreheads of all such as enact iniquity by statute, and execute wickedness as law. The memory of the wicked shall rot. Scroggs and Jeffreys also got their appointment as pay for their service and their character — fitting bloodhounds for a fitting king. For near two hundred years, their names have been a stench in the face of the Anglo-Saxon tribe. Others as unscrupulous may take warning by their fate.

Thus has Slavery debauched the Federal Courts.

VII. Alas me! Slavery has not ended yet its long career of sin. Its corruption is seven-fold. It debauches the elected officers of our City, and even our State. In the Sims time of 1851, the laws of Massachusetts were violated nine days running, and the Free Soil Governor sat in the State House as idle as a feather in his chair. In the wicked week of 1854, the Whig Governor sat in the seat of his predecessor; Massachusetts was one of the inferior counties of Virginia, and a Slave-hunter had eminent domain over the birthplace of Franklin and the burial-place of Hancock! Nay, against our own laws the Free Soil Mayor put the neck of Boston in the hands of a "trainband captain" — the people "wondering much to see how he did ride!" Boston was a suburb of Alexandria; the Mayor a a Slave-catcher for our masters at the South! You and I were only fellow Slaves!

All this looks as if Slavery was to triumph over Freedom. But even this is not the end. Slavery has privately emptied her seven vials of wrath upon the nation — committing seven debaucheries of human safeguards of our Natural Rights. That is not enough — there are other seven to come. This Apocalyptic Dragon, grown black with long-continued deeds of shame and death, now meditates five further steps of crime. Here is the programme of the next attempt — a new political Tragedy in five acts.

I. — The acquisition of Dominica — and then all Hayti — as new Slave Territory.

II. — The acquisition of Cuba, by purchase, or else by private fillibustering and public war, — as new Slave Territory.

III. — The reëstablishment of Slavery in all the Free States, by Judicial "decision" or legislative enactment. Then the Master of the North may "sit down with his Slaves at the foot of Bunker Hill Monument!"

IV.—The restoration of the African Slave-Trade, which is already seriously proposed and defended in the Southern Journals. Nay, the Senate Committee on Foreign Relations recommend the first step towards it—the withdrawal of our fleet from the coast of Africa. You cannot escape the consequence of your first principle: if Slavery is right, then the Slave-trade is right; the traffic between Guinea and New Orleans is no worse than between Virginia and New Orleans; it is no worse to kidnap in Timbuctoo than in Boston.

V.—A yet further quarrel must be sought with Mexico, and more Slave Territory be stolen from her.

Who shall oppose this five-fold wickedness? The Fugitive Slave Bill Party;—the Nebraska Enslavement Party? Northern servility has hitherto been ready to grant more than Southern arrogance dared to demand!

All this looks as if the third hypothesis would be fulfilled, and Slavery triumph over Freedom; as if the nation would expunge the Declaration of Independence from the scroll of time, and instead of honoring Hancock and the Adamses and Washington, do homage to Kane and Grier and Curtis and Hallett and Loring. Then the preamble to our Constitution might read — "to establish injustice, insure domestic strife, hinder the common defence, disturb the general welfare, and inflict the curse of bondage on ourselves and our posterity." Then we shall honor the Puritans no more, but their Prelatical tormentors; nor reverence the great Reformers, only the Inquisitors of Rome. Yea, we may tear the name of Jesus out of the American Bible; yes, God's name; worship the Devil at our Lord's table, Iscariot for Redeemer!

See the steady triumph of Despotism! Ten years more like the ten years past, and it will be all over with the liberties of America. Every thing must go down, and the heel of the tyrant will be on our neck. It will be all over with the Rights of Man in America, and you and I must go to Austria, to Italy, or to Siberia for our freedom; or perish with the liberty which our fathers fought for and secured to themselves, — not to their faithless sons! Shall America thus miserably perish? Such is the aspect of things to-day!

But are the people alarmed? No, they fear nothing; only the tightness in the money market! Next Tuesday at sunrise every bell in Boston will ring joyously; every cannon will belch sulphurous Welcome from its brazen throat. There will be processions, — the Mayor and the Aldermen and the Marshal and the Naval Officer, and, I suppose, the "Marshal's Guard," very appropriately taking their places. There is a chain on the Common to-day: it is the same chain that was around the Court House in 1851; it is the chain that bound Sims; now it is a festal chain. There are mottoes about the Common — "They mutually pledged to each other their lives, their fortunes, and their sacred honor." I suppose it means that the mayor and the kidnappers did this. "The spirit of '76 still lives." Lives, I suppose, in the Supreme Court of Fugitive Slave Bill judges. "Washington, Jefferson, and their compatriots! — their names are sacred in the heart of every American." That, I suppose, is the opinion of Thomas Sims and of Anthony Burns. And opposite the great Park Street Church, — where a noble man is this day, I trust, discoursing noble words, for he has never yet been found false to freedom — "Liberty and Independence, our Fathers' Legacy! — God forbid that we their sons should prove recreant to the trust!" It ought to read, "God forgive us that we their sons have proved so recreant to the trust!" So they will celebrate the Fourth of July, and call it "Independence Day!" The foolish press of France, bought and beaten and trodden on by Napoleon the Crafty, is full of talk about the welfare of the "Great Nation!" Philip of Macedon was conquering the Athenian allies town by town; he destroyed and swept off two-and-thirty cities, selling their children as Slaves. All the Cassandrian eloquence of Demosethenes could not rouse degenerate Athens from her idle sleep. She also fell — the fairest of all free States; corrupted first — forgetful of God's Higher Law. Shall America thus perish, all immature!

So was it in the days of old: they ate, they drank, they planted, they builded, they married, they were given in marriage, until the day that Noah entered into the ark, and the Flood came and devoured them all!

Well, is this to be the end? Was it for this the Pilgrims came over the sea? Does Forefathers' Rock assent to it? Was it for this that the New England clergy prayed, and their prayers became the law of the land for a hundred years? Was it for this that Cotton planted in Boston a little branch of the Lord's vine, and Roger Williams and Higginson — he still lives in an undegenerate son — did the same in the city which they called of Peace, Salem? Was it for this that Eliot carried the Gospel to the Indians? that Chauncey, and Edwards, and Hopkins, and Mayhew, and Channing, and Ware labored and prayed? for this that our fathers fought — the Adamses, Washington, Hancock? for this that there was an eight years' war, and a thousand battle fields? for this the little monuments at Acton, Concord, Lexington, West Cambridge, Danvers, and the great one over there on the spot which our fathers' blood made so red? Shall America become Asia Minor? New

England, Italy? Boston such as Athens — dead and rotten? Yes! if we do not mend, and speedily mend. Ten years more, and the Liberty of America is all gone. We shall fall — the laugh, the byword, the proverb, the scorn, the mock of the nations, who shall cry against us. Hell from beneath shall be moved to meet us at our coming, and in derision shall it welcome us; —

"The Heir of all the ages, and the youngest born of time!"

We shall lie down with the unrepentant prodigals of old time, damned to everlasting infamy and shame.

Would you have it so? Shall it be?

To-day, America is a debauched young man, of good blood, fortune, and family, but the companion of gamesters and brawlers; reeking with wine; wasting his substance in riotous living; in the lap of harlots squandering the life which his mother gave him. Shall he return? Shall he perish? One day may determine.

Shall America thus die? I look to the past, — Asia, Africa, Europe, and they answer, "Yes!" Where is the Hebrew Commonwealth; the Roman Republic; where is liberal Greece, — Athens, and many a far-famed Ionian town; where are the Commonwealths of Mediæval Italy; the Teutonic free cities — German, Dutch, or Swiss? They have all perished. Not one of them is left. Parian Statues of Liberty, sorely mutilated, still remain; but the

Parian rock whence Liberty once hewed her sculptures out — it is all gone. Shall America thus perish? Greece and Italy both answer, "Yes!" I question the last fifty years of American history, and it says, "Yes." I look to the American pulpit, I ask the five million Sunday School scholars, and they say, "Yes." I ask the Federal Court, the Democratic Party, and the Whig, and the answer is still the same.

But I close my eyes on the eleven past missteps we have taken for Slavery; on that sevenfold clandestine corruption; I forget the Whig party; I forget the present Administration; I forget the Judges of the Courts; — I remember the few noblest men that there are in society, Church and State; I remember the grave of my father, the lessons of my mother's life; I look to the Spirit of this Age — it is the nineteenth century, not the ninth; — I look to the history of the Anglo-Saxons in America, and the history of Mankind; I remember the story and the song of Italian and German Patriots; I recall the dear words of those great-minded Greeks — Ionian, Dorian, Ætolian; I remember the Romans who spoke, and sang, and fought for truth and right; I recollect those old Hebrew Prophets, earth's nobler sons, Poets and Saints; I call to mind the greatest, noblest, purest soul that ever blossomed in this dusty world; — and I say, "No!" Truth shall triumph, Justice shall be law! And if America fail, though she is one fortieth of God's family, and it is a great loss, there are other nations behind us; our Truth shall not perish, even if we go down.

But we shall not fail! I look into your eyes — young men and women, thousands of you, and men and women far enough from young! I look into the eyes of fifty thousand other men and women, whom, in the last eight months, I have spoken to, face to face, and they say, "No! America shall not fail!"

I remember the women, who were never found faithless when a sacrifice was to be offered to great principles; I look up to my God, and I look into my own heart, and I say, We shall not fail! We shall not fail!

This, at my side, it is the willow;* it is the symbol of weeping: — but its leaves are deciduous; the autumn wind will strew them on the ground; and beneath, here is a perennial plant; it is green all the year through. When this willow branch is leafless, the other is green with hope, and its buds are in its bosom; its buds will blossom. So it is with America.

Did our fathers live? are we dead? Even in our ashes live their holy fires! Boston only sleeps; one day she will wake! Massachusetts will stir again! New England will rise and walk! the van-

* Referring to the floral ornaments that day on the desk.

ished North be found once more, queenly and majestic! Then it will be seen that Slavery is weak and powerless in itself, only a phantom of the night.

Slavery is a "Finality," is it? There shall be no "Agitation," — not the least, — shall there? There is a Hispaniola in the South, and the South knows it. She sits on a powder magazine, and then plays with fire, while Humanity shoots rockets all round the world. To mutilate, to torture, to burn to death revolted Africans whom outrage has stung to crime — that is only to light the torches of San Domingo. This Black Bondage will be Red Freedom one day; nay, Lust, Vengeance, redder yet. I would not wait till that Flood comes and devours all.

When the North stands up, manfully, united, we can tear down Slavery in a single twelvemonth; and when we do unite, it must be not only to destroy Slavery in the territories, but to uproot every weed of Slavery throughout this whole wide land. Then leanness will depart from our souls; then the blessing of God will come upon us; we shall have a Commonwealth based on righteousness, which is the strength of any people, and shall stand longer than Ægypt, — National Fidelity to God our age-outlasting Pyramid!

How feeble seems a single nation; how powerless a solitary man! But one of a family of forty, we can do much. How much is Italy, Rome, Greece, Palestine, Ægypt to the world? The solitary man — a Luther, a Paul, a Jesus — he outweighs millions of coward souls! Each one of you take heed that the Republic receive no harm!

SOME ACCOUNT OF MY MINISTRY.

TWO SERMONS

PREACHED BEFORE THE

TWENTY-EIGHTH CONGREGATIONAL SOCIETY IN BOSTON,

ON THE 14TH AND 21ST OF NOVEMBER, 1852,

ON LEAVING THEIR OLD AND ENTERING A NEW
PLACE OF WORSHIP.

SERMON I.

"I have not shunned to declare unto you all the counsel of God."
ACTS xx. 27.

ON the twenty-second of January, 1845, at a meeting of gentlemen in Boston, which some of you very well remember, it was " *Resolved*, that the Rev. Theodore Parker shall have a chance to be heard in Boston."

That resolution has been abundantly backed up by action; and I have had "a chance to be heard." And this is not all: I have had a long and patient, a most faithful and abundant hearing. No man in the last eight years in New England has had so much. I mean to say, no minister in New England has done so much preaching, and had so much hearing. This is the result of your resolution, and your attempts to make your thought a thing.

As this seems likely to be the last time I shall stand within these walls, it is not improper that I should give some little account of my stewardship whilst here; and therefore you will pardon me if I speak considerably of myself, — a subject which has been before you a long time, very much in your eye, and I think also very much in your heart.

I must, in advance, ask your indulgence for the character of this sermon. I have but just returned from an expedition to Ohio, to lecture and to preach; whither I went weary and not well, and whence I have returned still more weary and no better. It is scarcely more than twenty-four hours since I came back, and accordingly but a brief time has been allowed me for the composition of this sermon. For its manner and its matter, its substance and its form, therefore, I must ask your indulgence.

When I spoke to you for the first time on that dark, rainy Sunday, on the 16th of February, 1845, I had recently returned from Europe. I had enjoyed a whole year of leisure: it was the first and last I have ever had. I had employed that time in studying the people and institutions of Western Europe; their social, academical, political, and ecclesiastical institutions. And that leisure gave me an opportunity to pause, and review my scheme of philosophy and theology; to compare my own system with that of eminent men, as well living as dead, in all parts of Europe, and see how the scheme would fit the wants of Christendom, Protestant and Catholic. It was a very fortunate thing that at the age of three and thirty I was enabled to pause, and study myself anew; to reëxamine what I had left behind me, and recast my plans for what of life might yet remain.

You remember, when you first asked me to come here and preach, I doubted and hesitated, and at first said, No; for I distrusted my own ability to make my idea welcome at that time to any large body of men. In the country I had a small parish, very dear to me still, wherein I knew every man, woman, and child, and was well known to them: I knew the thoughts of such as had the habit of thinking. Some of them accepted my conclusions because they had entertained ideas like them before I did, perhaps before I was born. Others tolerated the doctrine because they liked the man, and the doctrine seemed part of him, and, if they took my ideas at all, took them for my sake. You, who knew little of me, must hear the doctrine before you could know the man; and, as you would know the doctrine only as I had power to set it forth in speech, I doubted if I should make it welcome. I had no doubt of the truth of my idea; none of its ultimate triumph. I felt certain that one day it would be "a flame in all men's hearts." I doubted only of its immediate success in my hands.

Some of you had not a very clear notion of my Programme of Principles. Most of you knew this, — that a strong effort was making to exclude me from the pulpits of New England; not on account of any charge brought against my character, but simply on account of the ideas which I presented; ideas which, as I claimed, were bottomed on the Nature of Man and the Nature of God: my opponents claimed that they were not bottomed on the Bible. You thought that my doctrine was not fairly and scientifically met; that an attempt was making, not to put it down by reason, but to howl it down by force of ecclesiastical shouting; and that was true. And so you passed a resolve that Mr. Parker should have "a chance to be heard in Boston," because he had not a chance to be heard anywhere else, in a pulpit, except in the little village of West Roxbury.

It was a great Principle, certainly, which was at stake; the great Protestant Principle of free Individuality of Thought in Matters of Religion. And that, with most of you, was stronger than a belief in my peculiar opinions; far stronger than any personal fondness for me. Therefore your resolution was bottomed on a great idea.

My Scheme of Theology may be briefly told. There are three great doctrines in it, relating to the Idea of God, the Idea of Man, and of the Connection or Relation between God and Man.

First, of the Idea of God. I have taught the Infinite Perfection of God; that in God there are united all conceivable perfections, — the perfection of being, which is self-existence; the perfection of power, almightiness; the perfection of wisdom, all-knowingness; the perfection of conscience, all-righteousness; the perfection of the affections, all-lovingness; and the perfection of soul, all-holiness; — that He is perfect Cause of all that He creates, making every thing from a perfect motive, of perfect material, for a perfect purpose, as a perfect means; — that He is perfect Providence also, and has arranged all things in his creation so that no ultimate and absolute evil shall befall any thing which He has made; — that, in the material world, all is order without freedom, for a perfect end; and in the human world, the contingent forces of human freedom are perfectly known by God at the moment of creation, and so balanced together that they shall work out a perfect blessedness for each and for all his children.

That is my idea of God, and it is the foundation of all my preaching. It is the one idea in which I differ from the antichristian sects, and from every Christian sect. I know of no Christian or antichristian sect which really believes in the infinite God. If the infinity of God appears in their synthetic definition of Deity, it is straightway brought to nothing in their analytic description of the divine character, and their historic account of his works and purposes.

Then, of the Idea of Man. I have taught that God gave mankind powers perfectly adapted to the purpose of God;—that the Body of Man was just what God meant it to be; had nothing redundant, to be cut off sacramentally; was not deficient in any thing, to be sacramentally agglutinated thereunto;—and that the Spirit of man was exactly such a spirit as the good God meant to make; redundant in nothing, deficient in nothing; requiring no sacramental amputation of an old faculty, no sacramental imputation of a new faculty from another tree;—that the Mind and Conscience and Heart and Soul were exactly adequate to the function that God meant for them all; that they found their appropriate objects of satisfaction in the universe; and as there was food for the body,—all Nature ready to serve it on due condition,—so there was satisfaction for the spirit, truth and beauty for the Intellect, justice for the Conscience; human beings—lover and maid, husband and wife, kith and kin, friend and friend, parent and child—for the Affections; and God for the Soul;—that man can as naturally find satisfaction for his soul, which hungers after the infinite God, as for his heart, which hungers for a human friend, or for his mouth, which hungers for daily bread;—that mankind no more needs to receive a miraculous revelation of things pertaining to religion than of things pertaining to housekeeping, agriculture, or manufactures; for God made the religious faculty as adequate to its function as the practical faculties for theirs.

In the development of man's faculties, I have taught that there has been a great progress of mankind, — outwardly shown in the increased power over Nature, in the increase of comfort, art, science, literature; and this progress is just as obvious in religion as in agriculture or in housekeeping. The progress in man's idea of God is as remarkable as the progress in building ships; for, indeed, the difference between the popular conception of a jealous and angry God, who said his first word in the Old Testament, and his last word in the New Testament, and who will never speak again "till the last day," and then only damn to everlasting ruin the bulk of mankind, — the difference between that conception and the idea of the Infinite God is as great as the difference between the "dug-out" of a Sandwich Islander and a California clipper, that takes all the airs of heaven in its broad arms, and skims over the waters with the speed of wind. I see no limit to this general power of progressive development in man; none to man's power of religious development. The progress did not begin with Moses, nor end with Jesus. Neither of these great benefactors was a finality in benefaction. This power of growth, which belongs to human nature, is only definite in the historical forms already produced, but quite indefinite and boundless in its capabilities of future expansion.

In the human faculties, this is the order of rank: I have put the body and all its powers at the bottom of the scale; and then, of the spiritual powers, I put the Intellect the lowest of all; Conscience came next higher; the Affections higher yet; and highest of all, I have put the Religious Faculty. Hence I have always taught that the religious faculty was the natural ruler in all this Commonwealth of man; yet I would not have it a tyrant, to deprive the mind or the conscience or the affections of their natural rights. But the importance of religion, and its commanding power in every relation of life, that is what I have continually preached; and some of you will remember that the first sermon I addressed to you was on this theme, — The Absolute Necessity of Religion for safely conducting the life of the Individual and the life of the State. I dwelt on both of these points, — religion for the individual, and religion for the State. You know very well I did not begin too soon. Yet I did not then foresee that it would soon be denied in America, in Boston, that there was any Law of God higher than an Act of Congress.

Woman I have always regarded as the equal of man, — more nicely speaking, the equivalent of man; superior in some things, inferior in some other; inferior in the lower qualities, in bulk of body and bulk of brain; superior in the higher and nicer qualities, in the moral power of conscience, the loving power of affection, the religious power of the soul: equal, on the whole, and of course entitled to just the same rights as man; to the same rights of mind, body, and estate; the same domestic, social, ecclesiastical, and political rights as man, and only kept from the enjoyment of these by might, not right; yet herself destined one day to acquire them all. For, as in the development of man, the lower faculties come out and blossom first, and as accordingly, in the development of society, those persons who represent the lower powers first get elevated to prominence; so Man, while he is wanting in the superior quality, possesses brute strength and brute intellect, and in virtue thereof has had the sway in the world. But as the finer qualities come later, and the persons who represent those finer qualities come later into prominence; so Woman is destined one day to come forth and introduce a better element into the family, society, politics, and church, and to bless us far more than the highest of men are yet aware. Out of that mine the fine gold is to be brought which shall sanctify the church, and save the State.

That is my idea of man; and you see how widely it differs from the popular ecclesiastical idea of him.

Then a word for the Idea of the Relation between God and Man.

I. First, of this on God's part. God is perfect Cause and perfect Providence, Father and Mother of all men; and He loves each with all of his Being, all of his almightiness, his all-knowingness, all-righteousness, all-lovingness, and all-holiness. He knew at the beginning all the future history of mankind, and of each man, — of Jesus of Nazareth and Judas Iscariot; and prepared for all, so that a perfect result shall be worked out at last for each soul. The means for the purposes of God in the human world are the natural powers of man, his faculties; those faculties which are fettered by instinct, and those also which are winged by freewill. Hence while, with my idea of God, I am sure of the end, and have asked of all men an infinite faith that the result would be brought out right by the forces of God, — with my idea of man, I have also pointed out the human means; and, while I was sure of the end, and called for divine faith, I have also been sure of the means, and called for human work. Here are two propositions: first, that God so orders things in his providence, that a perfect result shall be wrought out for each; and, second, that He gives a certain amount of freedom to every man. I believe both of these propositions; I have presented both as strongly as I could. I do not mean to say that I have logically reconciled these two propositions, with all their consequences, in my own mind, and still less to the minds of others. There may seem to be a contradiction. Perhaps I do not know how to reconcile the seeming contradiction, and yet I believe both propositions.

From this it follows that the history of the world is no astonishment to God; that the vice of a Judas, or the virtue of a Jesus, is not a surprise to Him. Error and sin are what stumbling is to the child; accidents of development, which will in due time be overcome. As the finite mother does not hate the sound and strong boy, who sometimes stumbles in learning to walk; nor the sound, but weak boy, who stumbles often; nor yet the crippled boy, who stumbles continually, and only stumbles;—but as she seeks to help and teach all three, so the Infinite Mother of us all does not hate the well-born, who seldom errs; nor the ill-born, who often transgresses; nor yet hate the moral idiot, even the person that is born organized for kidnapping;—but will, in the long run of eternity, bring all these safely home,—the first murderer and the last kidnapper, both reformed and blessed. Suffering for error and sin is a fact in this world. I make no doubt it will be a fact in all stages of development in the next world. But mark this: It is not from the anger or weakness of God that we suffer; it is for purposes worthy of his perfection and his love. Suffering is not a devil's malice, but God's medicine. I can never believe that Evil is a finality with God.

II. Then see the relation on Man's part. Providence is what God owes to man; and man has an absolutely unalienable right to the infinite providence of God. No sin ever can alienate and nullify that right. To say that it could, would seem to me blasphemy against the Most High God; for it would imply a lack of some element of perfection on God's part; a lack of power, of wisdom, of justice, of love, or of holiness, — fidelity to Himself. It would make God finite, and not infinite.

Religion is what man owes to God, as God owes Providence to man. And with me religion is something exceedingly wide, covering the whole surface, and including the whole depth of human life.

The internal part I have called Piety. By that I mean, speaking synthetically, the love of God as God, with all the mind and conscience, heart and soul: speaking analytically, the love of truth and beauty, with the intellect; the love of justice, with the conscience; the love of persons, with the affections; the love of holiness, with the soul. For all these faculties find in God their perfect Object, — the all-true, all-beautiful, all-just, all-loving, and all-holy God, the Father and Mother of all.

The more external part of religion, I have called Morality; that is, keeping all the natural laws which God has writ for the body and spirit, for mind and conscience and heart and soul; and I consider that it is just as much a part of religion to keep every law which God has writ in our frame, as it is to keep the "Ten Commandments;" and just as much our duty to keep the law which He has thus published in human nature, as if the voice of God spoke out of heaven, and said, "Thou shalt," and "Thou shalt not." Man's consciousness proclaims God's law. It is Nature on which I have endeavored to bottom my teachings. Of course this morality includes the subordination of the body to the spirit, and, in the spirit, the subordination of the lower faculties to the higher; so that the religious element shall correct the partiality of affection, the coldness of justice, and the shortsightedness of intellectual calculation; and, still more, shall rule and keep in rank the appetites of the body. But in this the soul must not be a tyrant over the body; for, as there is a holy spirit, so there is likewise a holy flesh; all its natural appetites are sacred; and the religious faculty is not to domineer over the mind, nor over the conscience, nor over the affections of man. All these powers are to be coördinated into one great harmony, where the parts are not sacrificed to the whole, nor the whole to any one part. So, in short, man's religious duty is to serve God by the normal use, development, and enjoyment of every limb of the body, every faculty of the spirit, every particle of power which we progressively acquire and possess over matter or over man.

The ordinances of that religion are, inwardly, prayer of penitence and aspiration, the joy and delight in God and his gifts; and, outwardly, they are the daily works of life, by fireside and street-side and field-side, — "the charities that soothe and heal and bless." These are the ordinances, and I know no other.

Of course, to determine the religiousness of a man, the question is not merely — What does he believe? but — Has he been faithful to himself in coming to his belief? It may be possible that a man comes to the conviction of Atheism, but yet has been faithful to himself. It may be that the man believes the highest words taught by Jesus, and yet has been faithless to himself. It is a fact which deserves to be held up everlastingly before men, that religion begins in faithfulness to yourself. I have known men whom the world called Infidels, and mocked at, who yet were faithful among the faithfulest. Their intellectual conclusions I would have trodden under my feet; but their faithfulness I would fall on my knees to do honor to.

Then the question is not how a man dies, but how he lives. It is very easy for a dying man to be opiated by the doctor and minister to such a degree that his mouth shall utter any thing you will; and then, though he was the most hardened of wretches, you shall say "he died a saint!" The common notion of the value of a little snivelling and whimpering on a death-bed is too dangerous, as well as too poor, to be taught for science in the midst of the nineteenth century.

I have taken it for granted also, that religion gave to men the highest, dearest, and deepest of all enjoyments and delights; that it beautified every relation in human life, and shed the light of heaven into the very humblest house, into the lowliest heart, and cheered, and soothed, and blessed the very hardest lot and the most cruel fate in mortal life. This is not only my word, but your hearts bear witness to the truth of that teaching, and all human history will tell the same thing.

These have been the chief doctrines which I have set forth in a thousand forms. You see at once how very widely this differs from the common scheme of theology in which most of us were born and bred. There is a vast difference in the Idea of God, of Man, and of the Relation between the two.

Of course I do not believe in a devil, eternal torment, nor in a particle of absolute evil in God's world or in God. I do not believe there ever was a miracle, or ever will be: everywhere I find law,—the constant mode of operation of the infinite God. I do not believe in the miraculous inspiration of the Old Testament or the New Testament. I do not believe that the Old Testament was God's first word, nor the New Testament his last. The Scriptures are no finality to me. Inspiration is a perpetual fact. Prophets and Apostles did not monopolize the

Father: He inspires men to-day as much as heretofore. In nature, also, God speaks for ever. Are not these flowers new words of God? Are not the fossils underneath our feet, hundreds of miles thick, old words of God, spoken millions of millions of years before Moses began to be?

I do not believe the miraculous origin of the Hebrew Church, or the Buddhist Church, or the Christian Church; nor the miraculous character of Jesus. I take not the Bible for my master, nor yet the church; nor even Jesus of Nazareth for my master. I feel not at all bound to believe what any church says is true, nor what any writer in the Old or New Testament declares true; and I am ready to believe that Jesus taught, as I think, eternal torment, the existence of a devil, and that he himself should ere long come back in the clouds of heaven. I do not accept these things on his authority. I try all things by the human faculties,—intellectual things by the intellect, moral things by the conscience, affectional things by the affections, and religious things by the soul. Has God given us any thing better than our nature? How can we serve Him and his purposes but by its normal use?

But, at the same time, I reverence the Christian Church for the great good it has done for mankind; I reverence the Mahometan Church for the good it has done,—a far less good. I reverence the Scriptures for every word of truth they teach,—and they are crowded with truth and beauty, from end to end. Above all men do I bow my face before that august personage, Jesus of Nazareth, who seems to have had the strength of man and the softness of woman, — man's mighty, wide-grasping, reasoning, calculating, and poetic mind; and woman's conscience, woman's heart, and woman's faith in God. He is my best historic ideal of human greatness; not without errors, not without the stain of his times, and, I presume, of course not without sins, — for men without sins exist in the dreams of girls, not in real fact; you never saw such a one, nor I, and we never shall. But Jesus of Nazareth is my best historic ideal of a religious man, and revolutionizes the vulgar conception of human greatness. What are your Cæsars, Alexanders, Cromwells, Napoleons, Bacons, and Leibnitz, and Kant, and Shakspeare, and Milton even, — men of immense brain and will, — what are they all to this person of large and delicate intellect, of a great conscience, and heart and soul far mightier yet?

With such Ideas of Man, of God, and of the Relation between them, how all things must look from my point of view! I cannot praise a man because he is rich. While I deplore the vulgar rage for wealth, and warn men against the popular lust of gold, which makes money the tri-une deity of so many men, I yet see the function of riches, and have probably preached in favor of national and individual accumulation thereof more than any other man in all New England, as I see the necessity of a material basis for the spiritual development of man; but I never honor a live man because he is rich, and should not think of ascribing to a dead one all the Christian virtues because he died with a large estate, and his faith, hope, and charity were only faith in money, hope for money, and love of money. I should not think such a man entitled to the praise of all the Christian virtues.

And again, I should never praise or honor a man simply because he had a great office, nor because he had the praise of men; nor should I praise and honor a man because he had the greatest intellect in the world, and the widest culture of that intellect. I should take the intellect for what it was worth; but I should honor the just conscience of a man who carried a hod up the tallest ladder in Boston; I should honor the loving heart of a girl who went without her dinner to feed a poor boy; the faith in God which made a poor woman faithful to every daily duty, while poverty and sickness stared her in the face, and a drunken husband smote her in the heart, — a faith which conquered despair, and still kept loving on! I should honor any one of these things more than the intellect of Cæsar and Bacon and Hannibal all united into one: and you see why; because I put intellect at the bottom of the scale, and these higher faculties at the other end.

I put small value on the common "signs of religion." Church-going is not morality: it is compliance with common custom. It may be grievous self-denial, and often is. Reading the Bible daily or weekly is not piety: it may help to it. The "sacraments" are no signs of religion to me: they are dispensations of water, of wine, of bread, and no more. I do not think a few hours of crying on a sick-bed proves that a notorious miser or voluptuary, a hard, worldly fellow, for fifty years, has been a saint all that time, any more than one mild day in March proves that there was no ice in Labrador all winter.

With such views, you see in what esteem I must be held by society, church, and state. I cannot be otherwise than hated. This is the necessity of my position, — that I must be hated; and, accordingly, I believe there is no living man in America so widely, abundantly, and deeply hated as I have been, and still continue to be. In the last twelve years, I fear there has been more ecclesiastical preaching in the United States against me than against war and slavery. Those that hate any particular set of reformers hate me because I am with that particular set; with each and with all. I do not blame men for this; not so much as some others have done on my account. I pity very much more than I blame; not with the pity of contempt, I hope, but with the pity of appreciation, and with the pity of love. I see in the circumstances of men very much to palliate the offences of their character; and I long ago learned not to hate men who hated me. It was not hard to learn; I began early, — I had a mother who taught me.

You know the actual condition of the American Church, — I mean all the ecclesiastical institutions of the land — that it has a Theology which cannot stand the test of reason; and accordingly it very wisely resolved to throw reason overboard before it began its voyage. You know that all Christendom, with a small exception, professes a belief in the devil, in eternal torment; and, of course, all Christendom, with scarce any exception, professes a belief in a God who has those qualities which created a devil and eternal torment.

You know the Morality of the American Church. The clergy are a body of kindly and charitable men. Some virtues, which are not very easy to possess, they have in advance of any other class of men amongst us; they are the virtues which belong to their position. I believe they are, as a body, a good deal better than their creed. I know men often say a man is not so good as his creed; I never knew a minister who was half so bad as Calvinism. I surely have no prejudice against John Calvin, when

I say he was an uncommonly hard man, with a great head and a rigorous conscience; but John Calvin himself was a great deal better than the Calvinistic idea of God. I should give up in despair with that idea of God: I should not cast myself on his mercy, for there would be no mercy in Him.

But the preaching of the churches is not adapted to produce the higher kinds of morality. Certain humble but needful forms thereof the church helps, and very much indeed. On the whole it blocks the wheels of society backwards, so that society does not run down hill; but, on the other hand, it blocks them forward, so that it is harder to get up; and, while you must run over the church to get far down hill, you must also run over it to get up. It favors certain lower things of morality: higher things it hinders.

Here are two great forms of vice, — natural forms. One comes from the Period of Passion; and, when it is fully ripe, it is the vice of the Debauchee: the other comes from the Period of Calculation; and, when it is fully rotten, it is the sin of the Hunker.* Now, the churches are not very severe on the first kind of vice. They are very severe on unpopular degrees of it, not on the popular degree. They do service, however, in checking the unpopular degree. But the sin of the Hunkers, I think, the

* I do not use this word in its political sense, but to denote a man thoroughly selfish on calculation.

churches uniformly uphold and support. The popular sins of calculation are pretty sure to get the support of the pulpit on their side. Why so? They can pay for it in money and in praise! I know but few exceptions to that rule.

Then there are certain other merely ecclesiastical vices, mere conventional vices; not sins, not transgressions of any natural law. These the churches regard as great sins. Such are doubt and disbelief of ecclesiastical doctrine; neglect of ecclesiastical ordinances, — of the "Sabbath day," as it is called; neglect of the great bodily sacrament, church-going, and the like. All these offences the churches preach against with great power.

Accordingly the churches hinder the highest morality, favor the lower. The highest morality is thought superfluous in society, contemptible in politics, and an abomination in the church.

Just now, I learned through the newspapers that John Wesley's pulpit has been brought to America, and it is thought a great gain. But if John Wesley's voice, declaring aloud that slavery is "the sum of all villanies," were to be brought, it would presently be excommunicated from the Methodist Church. I understand that the chair in which the "Shepherd of Salisbury Plains" once sat has likewise arrived in America; and the tub, I think it is, which belonged to the "Dairyman's Daughter," has also immigrated; and these will be thought much more valuable ecclesiastical furniture than the Piety of the Shepherd of Salisbury Plains, and the Self-denial of the Dairyman's Daughter. It is popular to sprinkle babies with water from the Jordan; unpopular to baptize men with the spirit of Jesus, and with fire from the Holy Ghost.

My preaching has been mainly positive, of truth and duty in their application to life; but sometimes negative and critical, even militant. This was unavoidable; for I must show how my scheme would work when brought face to face with the church, society, and the State.

So I have sometimes preached against the evil doctrines of the Popular Theology; its false idea of God, of man, and of religion. This popular theology contains many excellent things: but its false things, taken as a whole, are the greatest curse of the nation; a greater curse than drunkenness, than the corruption of political parties; greater than slavery. It stands in the way of every advance. Would you reform the criminal, — along comes theology, with its "Whoso sheddeth man's blood, by man shall his blood be shed." Would you improve the church, — men say, "You must listen to the church, but not reform it; it must reform you, and not you it." Would you elevate woman to her rights, — the popular theology quotes St. Paul till you are almost sick of his name. Would you refuse obedience to a wicked law, and quote Jesus, and every great martyr from the beginning of the world, — the popular theology meets you with "Whoso resisteth the powers that be, resisteth the ordinance of God." If you wish to abolish slavery, — ministers come out with the old story of Ham and Noah, and justify American bondage on an old mythology, writ three thousand years ago, nobody knows where, nobody knows by whom, nobody knows for what purpose. All the garments possessed by the children of Shem and Japheth are too scant to hide the shame of the popular theology. At this day it bears the same relation to human progress, that Heathenism and Judaism bore in the first and second and third and fourth centuries after Christ. I confess, that, while I respect the clergy as much as any class of men, I hate the false ideas of the popular theology, and hate them with my body and with my spirit, with my mind and my conscience, with my heart and my soul; and I hate nothing so much as I hate the false ideas of the popular theology. They are the greatest curse of this nation.

Then I have preached against Slavery; and to me slavery appears in two views.

First, it is a Measure to be looked on as a part of the national housekeeping. We are to ask if it will pay; what its effect will be on the material earnings of the nation. And when we propose to extend slavery to a new territory, this is the question: Will you have slavery, and your land worth five dollars an acre, as in South Carolina; or will you have freedom, and your land worth thirty dollars an acre, as in Massachusetts? Will you have slavery, and the average earnings of all the people one dollar a week; or freedom, and the average earnings four dollars a week? Will you have slavery, and the worst cultivated lands, the rudest houses, and the poorest towns; or will you have freedom, and the nicest agriculture, the best manufactures, the richest houses, and the most sumptuous towns? Looking at it barely as a part of housekeeping, if I were a monarch I should not like to say to California, Texas, and New Mexico: "You might have institutions that would make your land worth thirty dollars an acre, and enable your people to earn four dollars a week; but you shall have institutions that will make your land worth five dollars an acre, and the average earnings of the people one dollar a week." I like money too well to take off three dollars from every four that might be earned, and twenty-five dollars from every acre of land worth thirty. I should think twice, if I were the President of the United States, before I did any thing to bring about that result.

That is not all. Slavery is a Principle, to be looked on as a part of our national religion: for our actions are our worship of God, if pious; of the "devil," if impious. It is to be estimated by its conformity to Natural Law. From my point of view it is against all natural right, all natural religion, and is, as John Wesley said, "the sum of all villanies." When the question comes up, Shall we introduce Slavery into a new territory? this is the question to be asked, Shall the laboring population be reduced to the legal rank of cattle; bought, bred, branded as cattle? Shall the husband have no right to his wife's society? Shall the maiden have no protection for her own virtue? Shall the wife be torn from her husband? Shall a mother be forced to cut the throats of four of her children, or else see them sold into Slavery?—a case that has actually happened. If I were a monarch, I should not like to levy such a tax on any people under my dominion. If I were President of the United States, I should not like to say to California, New Mexico, or old Mexico, "I intend to reduce you to that position;" and I think if I did, and stood up before you afterwards, you would have something to say about it. I should not like to do this for the sake of being President of the United States.

Now, I must confess that I hate Slavery; and I do not hate it any the less since it has become so popular in Boston, and, after a belief in the finality of the Compromise Measures has been made the *sine qua non* of a man's social, political, and ecclesiastical respectability. I always hated it, and hate it all the worse to-day for what it has done.

Then I have preached against Oppression in every form: the tyranny of man over woman; of popular opinion over the individual reason, conscience, and soul. I have preached against the tyranny of public law, when the law was wicked. Standing in a pulpit, preaching in the name of God, could I call on you to blaspheme the name of God for the sake of obeying a wicked statute which men had made? When I do that, may my right arm drop from my shoulder, and my tongue cleave to the roof of my mouth! I have preached against the tyranny which takes advantage of men's misfortunes, and with the sponge of illegal usury sucks up the earnings of honest men; against the tyranny of the few over the many in Europe, and of the many over the few in America. I love freedom of thought and of action; and I claim for every man the right to think, not as I do, but as he must or may.

Then I have preached against Intemperance, against making rum, selling rum, and drinking rum. The evil of intemperance has been under my eyes every Sunday. There is not a man before me, not a woman before me, not a girl or boy before me, but has lost some dear and valued relative, within not many years, slain by this monstrous

Vampire, which sucks and poisons the body of America. The poor men that I feed have been made paupers by rum; of the funerals that I attend, rum, with its harsh hammer, has often nailed down the coffin-lid; and of the marriages that I have helped to solemnize, how often has the wife been left worse than a widow! Since intemperance has become so popular in Boston; since it has got the mayor and aldermen on its side, and while every thirty-fifth voter in Boston is a licensed seller of rum; when it is invested with such strength, and gets possession of the House of Representatives, — I have preached against it all the more. I know, from the little town where I was born, as well as this large one, what a curse and blight drunkenness is.

Then I have preached against War, and I suppose, before long, I shall have a new occasion to lift up my voice against it once more.

Now, with such ideas, and such a style of preaching, I could not be popular. Hated I must needs be. How could it be otherwise? Men who knew no God but a jealous God; no human nature but total depravity; no religion but the ordinances of baptism, the Lord's Supper, and reverence for ancient words of holy men, and the like; no truth but public opinion; no justice but public law; no earthly good above respectability, — they must needs hate me, and I do not wonder at it. I fear there is not a theological newspaper in the land that has not delivered its shot in my face. You know how the pulpits, at various times, have rung out with indignation against me, and what names you and I have been called.

Well, I have not yet fired a shot in my own defence. Not one. I have replied to no attack, to no calumny. I have had too much else to do. In comparison with the idea which I endeavor to set forth, I am nothing, and may go to the ground, so that the truth goes on.

When I first came to stand in this place, many of my Unitarian brethren of the city, and elsewhere, complained publicly and privately, that they were held responsible for my theological opinions, which they did not share; and that they had no opportunity to place themselves right before the public. To give them an opportunity and occasion for developing the theological antithesis betwixt their doctrines and my own, and to let the public see in what things they all agreed, and in what they unitedly differed from me, I published "a Letter to the Boston Association of Congregational Ministers, touching certain Matters of their Theology." But, alas! they have not answered the letter, nor informed the public of the things in which they "all agree with each other," and wherein they all differ from me.

Men predicted our defeat. I believe, six months

was the longest space allotted to us to live and repent: that was the extent of our "mortal probation." We ought not to think harshly of men for this. I suppose they did the best they could with their light. But we went on, and continued to live. It is a little curious to notice the reasons assigned, by the press and the pulpit, for the audience that came together. For the first six months, I took pains to collect the opinions of the theological press and pulpit. I would say, that, with this exception, I have seldom read the various denunciations which have been written against you and me, and which have been sent, I hope with the best intentions, from all parts of the United States. When I have received them, and seen their character from a line or two, — and the postage was seldom paid,* — I have immediately put them in the safest of all places, — committed them to the flames. But, for this period of six months, during which our ecclesiastical existence was likely to continue, I inquired what the opinions of the press and pulpit were.

The first reason assigned for the audience coming together was this: They came from vain curiosity, having itching ears to hear "what this babbler sayeth."

* Here I must make one exception. Abusive letters from South Carolina have been uniformly post-paid. Such anonymous letters I never read.

Then it was said men came here because I taught "utter irreligion, blank immorality;" that I had "no love of God, no fear of God, no love of man;" and that you thought, if you could get rid of your conscience and soul, and trample immortality underfoot, and were satisfied there was no God, you should "have a very nice time of it here and hereafter." Men read history very poorly. It is not ministers who falsify the word of God that are ever popular with the great mass of men. Never, never! Not so. The strictest, hardest preacher draws crowds of men together, when he speaks in the name of Religion and God's Higher Law; but eloquent Voltaire gets most of his admirers of scoffing among the cultivated, the refined, and the rich: Atheism is never democratic.

Then it was declared that I was a shrewd, practical man, perfectly "well posted up" in every thing which took place; knew how to make investments, and get very large returns: unluckily, it has not been for myself that this has been true. And it was said that I collected large-headed, practical men to hear me, and that you were a "boisterous assembly."

Then, that I was a learned man, and gave learned discourses on ecclesiastical history or political history, — things which have not been found very attractive in the churches hitherto.

Then again, that I was a philosopher, with a wise

head, and taught men "theological metaphysics;" and so a large company of men seemed all at once smitten with a panic for metaphysics and abstract preaching. It was never so before.

Then it was reported that I was a witty man, and shot nicely feathered arrows very deftly into the mark; and that men came to attend the sharp-shooting of a wit.

Then there was a seventh thing, — that I was an eloquent man; and I remember certain diatribes against the folly of "filling churches with eloquence."

Then again, it was charged against me that I was a philanthropist, and taught the love of men, but did "not teach at all the love of God;" and that men really loved to love one another, and so came.

Then it was thought that I was a sentimentalist, and tickled the ears of "weak women," who came to delight themselves, and be filled full of "poetry and love."

The real thing they did not seem to hit; that I preached an Idea of God, of Man, and of Religion, which commended itself to the nature of mankind.

From the churches in general, I expected little; but I have found much deep and real kindness from fellow ministers of all denominations, — Unitarian, Universalist, Baptist, Methodist, Calvinist, and Christian. On the whole, — I am sorry to say it, — I have had less friendship shown me by the Unitarian sect in America, all things considered, than by the other sects. The heartiest abuse has come from my own brethren, and the stingiest testimonials for any merit. That was to be expected. I was a Unitarian: that is, I utterly rejected the Trinitarian theology; I associated chiefly with Unitarian clergymen. When my theological opinions became known to the wider public, some twelve years ago, they were declared "unsafe" and "dangerous" by the stricter sects. So an outcry was raised, not only against me, but also against the Unitarian sect. In self-defence, many Unitarian ministers, who had long been accused of being "hag-ridden by the orthodox," turned round, and denounced both my opinions and me, sometimes in the bitterest and most cruel fashion. They said, "He must be put down." They sought to "silence" me, to exclude me from the journals and the pulpits of the sect, to dissuade lyceum committees from asking me to lecture, and to prevent my speaking in Boston. Nay, some took pains to prevent my parishioners at West Roxbury from attending service there; they tried to hinder booksellers from publishing my works; and twelve years ago I could not find a publisher to put his name to the title-page of the first edition of my "Discourse of the Transient and Permanent in Christianity," — the Swedenborgian printers generously volunteered their name! The commonest courtesies of life were carefully withheld. I was treated like a leprous Jew. Studious attempts at deliberate insult were frequently made by Unitarian clergymen. I soon found, that, if theological Odium had been legally deprived of the arrows in its ancient quiver, it had yet lost none of the old venom from its heart. The Unitarians denied the great principle they had so manfully contended for, — free spiritual individuality in religion. I must say, I think they made a mistake. As a Measure, their conduct was inexpedient; as a Principle, it was false and wrong; as priestcraft, it was impolitic; as ethics, it was wicked: they hurt their own hand in breaking the Golden Rule over my head. But there were some very honorable exceptions in the denomination; men who lost sectarian favor by adhering to a universal principle of morals; and let me say, that I think no sect in Christendom would, in such a case, have treated a "heretic" in their own bosom with so little harshness as the Unitarians have shown to me. They have at least the tradition of liberality, which no other sect possesses. In England they have met my opinions with philosophical fairness, if not with partiality, and treated me with more consideration and esteem than I ever ventured to claim for myself.

All over the land I have found kindly and warm-hearted men and women, who have shed their dew-drop of sympathy upon me, just when my flower hung its head and collapsed, and seemed ready to perish. There is one clergyman to whom I owe an especial obligation. He has often stood in this place, and, for conscience' sake, has made greater and more difficult sacrifices than I. He began as an evangelist to the poor in Boston; carrying them the body's bread in his left hand, and Heaven's own manna in his right; and he now sheds broader charity from the same noble and generous heart. "A friend in need is a friend indeed;" and, if his face were not before me at this moment, I should say what his modesty would be pained to hear; but it is what none of you need to be told.*

It is eight years since first we came together; and that is a long time in American history. America has gained four new States in that time; a territory bigger than the old thirteen; and got all this new country by wickedness. We have spread Slavery anew over a country larger than the empire of France; have fought the Mexican war, so notorious for its iniquity. We have seen both political parties become the tools of Slavery; the Democratic perhaps a little worse than the Whig. We have seen the Fugitive Slave Bill welcomed in Boston, a salute of one hundred guns fired to honor its passage; and a man kidnapped out of the birthplace of Samuel Adams, to the delight of the controlling men thereof! You and I have repeatedly transgressed

---

* If this sermon should fall into the hands of a stranger, he may be glad to know that I refer to the Rev. JOHN T. SARGENT.

the laws of the land, in order to hinder "Unitarian Christians" of Boston, supported by their clergy, from sending our fellow worshippers into the most hideous slavery in the world!

Great men have died, — Jackson, Adams, Taylor, Calhoun, Clay, Webster. What changes have taken place in Europe in this brief eight years! The old Pope has died. The new Pope promised to be a philanthropist, and turned out what we now see. All of royalty, all of the king, "was carried out from Paris in a single street cab;" and, a few days later, "Napoleon the Little" came in, furnished with nothing but "a tame eagle and a pocketful of debts." We have seen France rise up to the highest point of sublimity, and declare government to be founded on the unchanging law of God; and the same France, with scarcely the firing of a musket, drop down to the bottom of the ridiculous, and become the slave of the stupidest and vulgarest even of vulgar kings. We have seen all Western Europe convulsed with revolutions; the hope of political freedom brightening in men's hearts; and now see a heavier despotism as the present result of the defeated effort. Kossuth is an exile; and a ruined debauchee is the "imperial representative of morality" on the throne of Saint Louis.

I have been your minister almost eight years. Some of our members have withdrawn, and walk no more with us. I trust they were true to their conscience, and went where wiser and abler and better men can feed their souls as I cannot. I have never thought it a religious duty for any man to listen to my poor words; how poor nobody knows so well as I.

In myself there are many things which I lament. It has been a great grief to me, as I have looked upon your faces, that I was no worthier to speak to you; that I had not a larger intellectual power, by birth and culture, to honor the ideas withal; and, still more, that, in conscience and heart and soul, I was so poor.

One thing in my ministry has troubled me a good deal. Coming from a little country parish, with the habits of a country minister; knowing every man, woman, and child therein; knowing the thoughts of all that had any thoughts, and the doubts of such as had strength to raise a doubt, — I have found it painful to preach to men whom I did not know in the intimacy of private life. For the future, I hope it will be possible for me to know you better, and more intimately in your homes.

I must have committed many errors. When an old man, I trust I shall see them, and some time point them out, that others may be warned by my follies. You must know my character better than I know it. My private actions I know best; but you see me in joy and sorrow, in indignation and penitence, in sermon and in prayer, when there is no concealment in a man's face. Hold a medal, worn smooth, before the fire, and the old stamp comes out as before. Concealment lifts her veil before any strong emotion which renews the face. You must know me better than I know myself. I also know you. I have tasted your kindness in public and private; not only from women, — who have always shown the readiest sympathy for a new religious development, from the time when Pharaoh's daughter drew a slave's child out of the Nile, to that day when a woman poured the box of ointment over the head of Jesus, — but also from men; not only from young men, but from those whose heads have blossomed anew with the venerable flowers of age.

You, my friends, have been patient with my weaknesses, kind and affectionate. I think no man ever had truer, warmer, or more loving friends. As I have looked round on your faces, before the commencement of service; as I have sat and seen the young and the old, the rich and the poor, the joyous and the sad, come together; as I have gathered up the outward elements of my morning prayer from the various faces and dissimilar histories, which, at a single glance, stood before me, — my friends, I have thanked my God it was my lot to stand here; and yet have reproached myself again and again, that I was no worthier of the trust, and have asked before God, "Who is sufficient for these things?"

I know how often I must have wounded your

feelings, in speaking of the political conduct of America; for I have endeavored to honor what was right, and expose to censure what was wrong, in both parties, and in the third party during its existence. I have not passed over the sins of trade. I have preached on all the exciting and agitating topics of the day. I wonder not that some friends were offended. I only wonder that such a multitude has still continued to listen. Verily, there is little to attract you in these surroundings: public opinion pronounced it infamous to be here. It was the Ideas of Absolute Religion that drew you here through ill report. The highest and the best things I have had to offer, have always found the warmest welcome in your heart.

We must bid farewell to these old walls. They have not been very comfortable. All the elements have been hostile. The winter's cold has chilled us; the summer's heat has burned us; the air has often been poisoned with contaminations, a whole week long in collecting; and the element of earth, the dirt, that was everywhere. As I have stood here, I have often seen the spangles of opera-dancers, who beguiled the previous night, lying on the floor beside me; and have picked them up in imagination, and woven them into my sermon and psalm and prayer. The associations commonly connected with this hall have not been of the most agreeable character.

Dancing monkeys, and "Ethiopian Serenaders" making vulgar merriment out of the ignorance and the wretchedness of the American slave, have occupied this spot during the week, and left their marks, their instruments, and their breath, behind them on the Sunday. Could we complain of such things? I have thought we were very well provided for, and have given God thanks for these old, but spacious walls. The early Christians worshipped in caverns of the ground. In the tombs of dead men did the only live religion find its dwelling-place at Rome. The star of Christianity "first stood still over a stable!" These old walls will always be dear and sacred to me. Even the weather stains thereon are to me more sacred than the pictures which the genius of Angelo painted in the Sistine Chapel, or those with which Raphael adorned the Vatican. To me they are associated with some of the holiest aspirations and devoutest hours of my mortal life, and with the faces which welcomed every noble word I ever learned to speak.

Well, we must bid them farewell. Yonder clock will no more remind me how long I have trespassed on your patience, when your faces tell no such tale. We will bid these old walls, these dusty lights, farewell. Our old companion, the organ, has gone before us; and again shall we hear its voice.

But what have I been to you in all this time?

You have lent me your ears: I have taken your hearts too, I believe. But let me ask this of you: Have I done you good, or harm? Have I taught you, and helped you, to reverence God the more; to have a firmer and heartier faith in Him; to love Him the deeper, and keep his laws the better; to love man the more? If so, then indeed has my work been blessed, and I have been a Minister to you. But, if it has not been so; if your reverence and faith in God grow cold under my preaching, and your zeal for man dwindles and passes away,—then turn off from me, and leave me to the cold gilding and empty magnificence of our new place of worship; and go you and seek some other, who, with a loftier aspiring mind, shall point upwards towards God, and, with a holier heart, shall bid you love Him. But, above all things, let me entreat you that no reverence for me shall ever blind your eyes to any fault of mine, to any error of doctrine. If there are sins in my life, copy them not. Remember them at first, drop the tear of charity on them, and blot them out.

SERMON II.

OF THE POSITION AND DUTY OF A MINISTER.

"I know whom I have believed." — 2 TIMOTHY i. 12.

IN the development of mankind, all the great desires get some instrument to help achieve their end — a machine for the private hand, an institution for the mind and conscience, the heart and soul, of millions of men. Thus all the great desires, great duties, great rights, become organized in human history; provided with some instrument to reach out and achieve their end. This is true of the finite desires; true also of the infinite.

Man would be fed and clothed: behold the tools of agriculture and the arts, — the plough and the factory. He would be housed and comforted: behold the hamlet and the town. Man and maid would love one another: see the home and the family, — the instrument of their love. Thousands want mutual succor: there is society, with its neighborly charities, and duties every day. Millions of men ask defence, guidance, unity of action: behold the State, with its constitutions and its laws, its officers, and all its array of political means. These are finite; a lengthening of the arm, a widening of the understanding; tools for the conscience and the heart. Thereby I lay hold of matter and lay hold of man, and get the uses of the material world and of my brother men.

These are finite, for to-day. But the same rule applies to the infinite desires. Man would orient himself before his God; and hence, along-side of the field and the factory, in the midst of the hamlet and the town, beside the State House and the Market House, there rises up the Church, its finger pointing to the sky. This is to represent to man the infinite desire, infinite duty, infinite right. Thereby mankind would avail itself of the forces of God, and be at home in His world. Man is so much body, that the mouth goes always: he never forgets to build and plant. But the body is so full of soul, that no generation ever loses sight of God. In this ship of the body, cruising oft in many an unholy enterprise, standing off and standing on, tacking and veering with the shifting wind of circumstance and time, there is yet a little needle that points up, which has its dip and variations;

"But, though it trembles as it lowly lies,
Points to the light that changes not in heaven."

Man must have his institution for the divine side of him, and hence comes the church. Man has a priest before he has a king; and the progress in his idea of priest marks the continual advance of the human race.

The minister is to serve the Infinite Duties of man, minister to his Infinite Rights; and is to betake himself to the work of Religion, as the farmer to agriculture, the housewright to building. But his function will depend on his Idea of Religion, of what religion is; that on his Idea of God, of what God is.

Now, in all the great historical forms of religion, both before and after Christ, priest and people have regarded God as imperfect in power, in wisdom, in justice, in love, or in holiness; as a finite God, and often with a dark background of evil to Him. Therefore, while they have worshipped before the Father, they have trembled before the devil, and deemed the devil mightier than God. Hence religion has been thought the service of an imperfect God, and of course a service with only a part of the faculties of man; those faculties not in their perfect action, but in their partial development and play.

Thus the function of the minister has been a very different thing in different ages of mankind. Let me sum up all these in three great forms.

I. First, the priest was to appease the Wrath of God. He was to stand between offended Deity and offending man, to propitiate God and appease Him, to make Him humane. The priest was a special mediator between God on the one side, and Man on the other; and it was taught that God would not listen to Silas and Daniel: He would hear the word of Abner. So Abner must propitiate the Deity for Silas and Daniel.

The priest attempts this, first, by sacrifice, which the offending offers to the Offended; and the sacrifice is an atonement, a peace-offering, a bribe to God to buy off his anger. Next, he attempts it by prayers, which, it is thought, alter the mind of God and his purpose; for the priest is supposed to be more humane than the God who made humanity. But God, it is thought, will not hear the prayer of the profane People, nor accept their sacrifice; only that of the sacred Priest.

This, then, was the function of the Heathen and Hebrew priest for a long time. Without sacrifice by the priest's hand, there was no salvation. That was the rule. "Come not empty-handed before the Lord," says the priest, "else He will turn you off." Then, the offering of a sacrifice was thought to be religion, and the priest's function was to offer it. That is the rudest form.

II. Next, the function of the priest is to reconcile

the offended God to offending men by ritual action, and then to communicate Salvation to Men by outward means, — baptism, penitence, communion, absolution, extreme unction, and the like. Here the priest is no longer merely a sacrificer: he is a communicator of salvation already achieved; he does not make a new deposit of salvation, but only draws on the established fund. That is the chief function of the Catholic priest at this day. But still, like the Hebrew and Heathen priests, he makes "intercession with God" for the living and the dead. "Out of the range of the sacraments of the church," says he, "there is no salvation: the wrath of God will eat you up." The Catholic priest does not make a new and original sacrifice; for the one great sacrifice has been made once for all, and God has been appeased towards mankind in general. But the priest is to take that great sacrifice, and therewith redeem this and the other particular man; communicating to individuals the general salvation which Christ has wrought. With the Catholic, therefore, to take the sacraments is thought to be religion, and the great thing of religion.

III. Then, as a third thing, the priest aims to communicate and explain a Miraculous Revelation of the Will of God; and the worshippers are to believe that miraculous revelation of the will of God, and have faith in it. That is the only means of salvation with them. So, in this third form, to take the Scriptures and believe them is thought to be religion. This is the chief official function of the Protestant priest, — to communicate and explain the Scriptures; and all the theological seminaries in the Protestant world for the education of clergymen are established chiefly for that function, — to teach the young man to communicate and explain the Scriptures to mankind; for belief in them is thought to be religion. Chillingworth, two hundred years ago, said, "The Bible is the religion of Protestants;" and meant, To believe the Bible is the religion of Protestants! And that is what is meant by salvation by faith.

The line of historical continuity is never broke. The Catholic priest, like the Hebrew and the Heathen, still claims to alter the mind of God by "intercession." The Protestant priest, like the Catholic, yet pretends to communicate salvation by the "sacraments," in the waters of baptism, or the bread and wine of communion; and to change the purposes of God, by prayer for rain in time of drought, for health in time of pestilence. However, the chief function of the Protestant priest is to communicate and explain the Scriptures; for he says, "Out of the range of belief in Scripture there is no salvation."

The Heathen and Hebrew priests say, "Offer the

sacrifice, and be saved." Says the Catholic priest, "Accept the sacrament, and be saved." Says the Protestant priest, "Believe the Scriptures, and be saved." That has been, or still is, the official function of these three classes of ministers in sacred things. They represent the three successive ideas of religion which have appeared in the Heathen and Hebrew church, in the Catholic church, and lastly in the Protestant church.

But at this day, in all the forms of religion which belong to the two leading races of mankind, the Caucasian and the Mongolian, — comprising the Hebrew, Zoroastrian, Buddhist, Christian, and Mahometan, — the priest has got an exceptional function. That has come upon him by accident, as it were, in the progress of man, — a human accident, for there are no divine ones; God lets nothing slip unawares from his pen: there are no accidents in his world. And that function is, to promote religion; to promote plain piety and plain morality — the love of God and the love of man.

This, I say, is exceptional. It is only a subsidiary part of the function, even of the Protestant minister. True, throughout all Christendom the priest demands righteousness. But mark this: He demands it as a Measure convenient for present expediency, not as a Principle necessary to eternal salvation. This exceptional function is more important with the Catholic than it was with the Heathen or Hebrew; more important with the Protestant than it is with the Catholic. Still, it is subsidiary; and it is thought that the sin of a whole life, however wicked, may be wiped out all at once, if, on his death-bed, a man repeats a few passages of Scripture, and declares his faith in the redemption of Christ, and a belief in the words of the Bible. A man so base as Aaron Burr — the most dreadful specimen of human depravity that America has yet produced, so far as I know — might have left an unblemished reputation for Christianity, if, a few weeks before he died, he had confessed his belief in every word between the lids of this Bible; had declared that he had no confidence in human virtue, hoped for salvation only through Christ; and if he had taken the communion at a priest's hand. That would have given him a better reputation in the churches than the noble career of Washington, and the long, philanthropic, and almost unspotted life of Franklin.

I say this is subsidiary. The Protestant priest does not rely on it as his main work; and, in proof of success, I have seldom known a minister point to the Morality of his parish, — not a drunkard in it, not a licentious man, not a dishonest man, in it. I have seldom known him refer even to the Comfort of his parish, — pauperism gone, all active, doing well, and well to do. He tells you of the number that he has admitted to the "Christian communion," of those that he has "sprinkled" with the waters of baptism; not the souls he has baptized with the Holy Ghost and its beauteous fire! Men wish to prove that the Americans are a "Christian people," a "religious people:" they tell the number of Bibles there are in the land; the number of churches that point their finger with such beauty to the sky; they never tell of the good deeds of the nation; of its institutions, of its ideas, its sentiments. And, when an outcry is made against the advance of "Infidelity," nobody quotes the three million slaves, the political corruption of the rulers, the venality of the courts, the disposition to plunder other nations; nobody speaks of intemperance and licentiousness, and dishonesty in trade: they only say that some man "denies total depravity, or the fall," or "the miracles," or "the existence of a devil," and thinks he is "wiser than the Bible." Anywhere in Christendom it would be deemed a heresy against all Christendom to say that human Nature was sufficient for human History, and had turned out on trial just as God meant it should turn out on trial; and that a man's salvation was his character, his heart, and his life.

If we start with the idea that God is infinitely perfect in power, in wisdom, in justice, and in love and holiness, — then the function of the minister is not to appease the wrath of God by sacrifice and intercession; not to communicate miraculous salvation;

not even to communicate and explain a miraculous revelation: it will be to promote Absolute Religion amongst mankind.

He will start with three facts: First, with the Infinite perfection of the dear God; next, with Human Nature, which God made as a perfect means to his perfect end, — human nature developed thus far in its history; and, as a third thing, with the Material Universe, — the ground under our feet and the heavens over our head; and he will take the universe, the world of matter and the world of man, as the Revelation of the Infinite God.

Then, I say, the function of the minister will be to teach and promote the Religion of Human Nature in all its parts. He will aim to teach, first, Natural Piety, the subjective service of God, the internal worship. I mean the love of God with mind and conscience, and heart and soul; in the intellectual form, the love of every truth and every beauty; in the moral form, the love of justice; in the affectional form, the love of God as love; and the love of God also as holiness: to say it in a word, love of the God of infinite wisdom, justice, love, and holiness, — the perfect God, the infinite Object, adequate to satisfy every spiritual desire of man.

Then he must aim to teach Natural Morality, the objective worship of God, which is the outward service. That is, the keeping of all the laws of the body and spirit of man; service by every limb of the body, every faculty of the spirit, and every power which we possess over matter or over men.

The minister is to show what this piety and morality demand, — in the form, first, of individual life; then in the form of domestic life; then of social, political, ecclesiastical, and general human life. He is to show how this religion will look in the person of a man, in a family, community, church, nation, and world. That is his function.

He is not to humanize God, but to humanize men; not to appease the wrath of God, — there is no such thing; not to communicate a mysterious salvation from an imaginary devil in another world; but, in this life, to help men get a real salvation from want, from ignorance, folly, impiety, immorality, oppression, and every form of evil. He is to teach man to save himself by his character and his life; not to lean on another arm. His function is not to communicate and explain a miraculous revelation. He knows revelation only by constant modes of operation; revelation by law, not against law; revelation in this universe of Matter and in this greater universe of Man, not revelation by miracle. What is the exceptional function of the Heathen, the Hebrew, the Catholic, and the Protestant priest, is the instantial and only function of the minister of the Infinite God, who would teach the Absolute Religion.

Well, this minister must have regard to man in his nature as Body and as Spirit. Natural religion,—why, it is for this life, as well as the life to come. It is but part of the function of religion to save me for the next world: I must be saved for this. He is to teach men to subordinate the body to the spirit, but to give the body its due; to subordinate the lower desires to the higher; all finite desires, duties, and rights, to the infinite desire, duty, and right; but to do this so that no one faculty shall tyrannize over any other, but that a man shall be the harmony which God meant him to be. He is to see to it that every one is faithful to his own individual character, and takes no man for master; everybody for teacher who can serve and teach; nobody for master barely to command. And, while he insists on individuality of life, he must also remember that the individual is for the family, that for the community, the community for the nation, and the nation for mankind; and that all of these must be harmoniously developed together. Thus the partiality of friendship, of connubial or parental love, the narrowness of the clan, neighborhood, or country, he is to correct by that universal philanthropy which takes in neighborhood, nation, and all mankind.

He is to remember, also, the immortal life of man, and to shed the light of eternity into man's consciousness, in the hour of passion, and in the more dangerous, long, cold, clear day of ambition. In the hour of distress and dreadful peril, he is to help men to that faith in God which gives stillness in every storm. He is to help them overcome this puerile fear of death, and to translate their fear of God into love for Him, — into perfect, blameless, absolute trust in the Father; and he is to bring the light of all this beneficence upon men in the season of peril, and in the dreadful hour of mortal bereavement, when father and mother and child and wife gather blackness in their countenance, and pass away. Over the gate of death he is to arch the rainbow of everlasting life, and bid men walk through unabashed, and not ashamed. He is to promote the sentiment of religion, as a feeling of dependence on God, obligation to God, trust in God, and love for God; of ultimate dependence on His providence, unalienable obligation to keep His law, absolute trust in his protection, and a perfect and complete faith in His infinite perfection.

Then he is to promote the practice of this religion, so that what at first is an instinctive feeling shall be next a conscious idea of this ultimate dependence, unalienable obligation, absolute trust, and perfect and complete love; he is to promote the application of this consciousness of religion to all the departments of human life, — individual, domestic, social, national, and universal. Of all doctrines he is to ask, Are they true? of all statutes, Are they just? of all conduct, Is it manly, loving, and kind? of all things,—institutions, thoughts, and persons, Are they conformable to the nature of mankind, and so to the will of God? So his aim must be to make all men perfect men; to do this first to his own little congregation, and next to all mankind.

Now, this cannot be done abstractly. Man is a body as well as a spirit. In a material world, by means of material things, must he work out his spiritual problems. The soul is a soul in the flesh, and the eternal duties of life, bear hard on the transient interests of to-day.

Man's character is always the result of two forces, —the immortal spirit within him, and the transient circumstances about him. The minister is to know, that nine persons out of ten have their character much influenced by the circumstances about them; and he is to see to it that those circumstances are good. Thus, the abstract work of promoting religion, and helping to form the character of the people, brings the minister into contact with the material forces of the world.

It is idle to say the minister must not meddle with practical things. If the sun is to shine in heaven, it must look into the street, and the shop, and the cellar; it must burnish with lovely light a filing of gold in the jeweller's shop, and it must illuminate the straggling straw in a farmer's yard. And just so religion, which communes with God with one hand, must lay the other on every human duty. So you see the relation which the minister must sustain to the great works of man, to political and commercial activity, to literature, and to society in general.

The State is a machine to work for the advantage of a special nation, for its material welfare alone, by means of certain restricted sentiments and ideas limited to that work, written in a Constitution, which is the norm of the statutes; by means of statute laws, which are the norm of domestic and social conduct. So the Legislature makes statutes for the material welfare of the majority of that nation; the Judiciary decides that the statutes conform to the Constitution; the Executive enforces the statutes, and the people obey. When the State has done this, it has done every thing which its idea demands of it at the present day.

Now, the minister is to represent, not America, not England, not France alone, but the Human Nature of all Mankind; and see that his nation harms no other nation; that the majority hinders no minority, however small; that it brings the weight of its foot upon no single man, never so little. He must see that the material comfort of to-day is not got at the cost of man's spiritual welfare for to-day, to-morrow, and eternity. So he is to try every statute of men by the Law of God; the Constitution of America by the Constitution of the Universe. National measures he must try by universal Principles; and if a measure does not square with the abstract true and the abstract right, does not conform to the will and the law of God, — then he must cry out, "Away with it!" Statesmen look at political economy; and they ask of each measure, "Will it pay, here and now?" The minister must look for Political Morality, and ask, "Is it right in the eyes of God?" So you see that at once the pulpit becomes a very near neighbor to the state-house; and the minister must have an eye to correct and guide the politicians. He must warn men to keep laws that are just, warn them to break laws that are wicked; and, as they reverence the dear God, never to bow before an idol of statesmen or the State.

Then he must have an eye to the Business of the nation; and, while the trader asks only, "What merchandise can we make?" the minister must also ask, "What men shall we become?" Both the politicians and the merchant are wont to use men as mere tools, for the purposes of politics and trade, heedless of what comes, by such conduct, to their human instruments. The minister is to see to it, that man is never subordinated to money, morality never put beneath expediency, nor eternity sacrificed to to-day. The slave-trade was once exceedingly profitable to Newport and Liverpool, and was most eminently "respectable." But the minister is to ask for its effects on men; the men that traffic, and the trafficked men. Once it was as disreputable in a certain church in this city to preach against slave-buying in Guinea and slave-selling in Cuba, as it is now to preach against slave-taking in Boston or New Orleans. The spirit of modern commerce is sometimes as hostile to the higher welfare of the people as the spirit of ancient war: both Old and New England have abundantly proved this in the present century.

The minister is to look also at the character of Literature; to warn men of the bad, and guide them to the good. At this day the power of the press is exceedingly great for good or for evil. In America, thank God, it is a free press; and no wicked censor lays his hand on any writer's page. See what a great expansion the press has got: what was a private thought one night in a senator's heart, is the next day a printed page, spread before the eyes of a million men. The press is an irresponsible power, and needs all the more to be looked after; and who is there to look after it, if not the minister that reverences the great God?

Then the minister is to study nicely the General Conduct of society, and seek to guide men from mere desire to the solemn counsels of duty; to check the redundance of appetite in the period of passion, and the redundance of ambition in the more dangerous period of calculation; to guard men against sudden gusts of popular frenzy.

The great concerns of Education come also beneath the minister's eye; and, while the press, business, and politics, keep the lower understanding intensely active and excessively developed, he is to guide men to the culture of reason, imagination, conscience, the affections, and the soul; is to show them a truth far above the Forum and the Market's din; is to lead them to justice and to love, and to enchant their eyes with the beauty of the infinite God. The minister of Absolute Religion must be the schoolmaster for the loftier intellect and the conscience; the teacher of a philanthropy that knows no distinction of color or of race; the teacher of a faith in God which never shrinks from obedience to his law.

In society, as yet, there is still a large mass of "Heathenism," — I mean of scorn for that which is spiritual in the body, and immortal in the soul; a contempt for the feeble, hatred against the unpopular transgressor, a contempt for justice, a truckling to expediency, and a cringing to men of large understanding and colossal wickedness. Hence, in the nation there is a Perishing Class three and thirty hundred thousand strong, held as slaves. In all our great cities, there is another perishing class, goaded by poverty, oppressed by crime. The minister is to be an especial guardian and benefactor of the neglected, the oppressed, the poor; eyes to the ignorant, and conscience and self-respect to the criminal. He is not to represent merely the gallows and the jail: he is to represent the spirit of the man who "came to save that which was lost," and the infinite goodness of God, who sends this sunlight on you and me, as well as on better men.

Then, in all our great cities, there is one deep, and dark, and ghastly pit of corruption, whereinto, from all New England's hills, there flows down what was once as fair and as pure and as virgin-fresh as the breath of maiden morn. It is the standing monument which shows the actual position of woman in modern society; that men regard her as the vehicle of their comfort and the instrument of their lust, — not a person, only a thing! The minister, remembering who it was that drew Moses out of the river Nile, and who washed the feet of one greater than Moses with her own tears, and wiped them with her hair, must not forget this crime, its consequences, which contaminate society, and its cause afar off, — contempt and scorn for woman: that is its cause.

In all this, you see how different is the position and function of the minister of Absolute Religion from that of the mere priest. In Russia, the few hold down the many, and the priest says nothing against it. He is there only to appease God, to administer Salvation, to communicate Scripture; not to teach Morality and Piety. In America, the many hold down the few, — the twenty millions chain the three; and the priest says nothing against it. What does he care? He goes on appeasing the Wrath of God, administering Salvation, explaining and communicating Scripture, and turns round and says: "This is all just as it should be, a part of the revelation, salvation, and sacraments too; come unto me, and believe, and be baptized with water." But the minister of Absolute Religion is to hold a different speech. He is to say: "My brethren, hold there! Stop your appeasing of God! — wait till God is angry. Stop your imputing of righteousness! There is no salvation in that. Stop your outcry of 'Believe, believe, believe!' Turn round and put an end to this hateful oppression, and tread it under your feet; and then come before your God with clean hands, and offer your gift. That is your sacrifice."

Warlike David plunders Uriah of the one lamb that lay all night in his bosom; then slays the injured man with the sword of the children of Ammon. The priest knows it all, and says against it not a single word; but he slays his bullocks, and offers his goats and his turtledoves, and makes his sacrifices, and spreads out his hands and says, "Save us, good

Lord! David is a man after the Lord's own heart." No word touches the conscience of the king under his royal robe. But there comes forth a plain man, not a priest, nay, a prophet: he points the finger, with his "Thou art the man!" and the penitent king lies prostrate and weeping in the dust.

A man of great intellect leads off the people: city by city they go over. All the priests of Commerce cry out, "Let us do as we list." "There is no Higher Law!" "I will send back my own brother." Then it is for the minister to speak, — words tender if he can, but at all events, words that are true, words that are just.

Just now the American Esau is hungry again. The Cuban pottage is savory. "Feed me," cries he; "for I am faint." "Eat, O Esau!" says the tempter, "rough and hairy, and tired with hunting gold in California, and negroes in New England. Eat of this, O American Esau! and be glad. There is no God!" But the minister is to say: "American Esau, wilt thou sell thy birthright of unalienable justice? Thou sell that! Dost not thou remember the Eye which never slumbers nor sleeps?"

This, my friends, is the Function of the minister. Well, has he Means adequate to his work? They are only his gifts by nature, and his subsequent attainments; his power of wisdom and justice, his power of love, and his power of religion; that is all.

nothing more than that, with his power of speech to bring it to the heart of men. But he has for ally the Human Nature which is in all men, which loves the true and the just, loves man and loves God. He has all the Forces of the Universe to help him just so far as he is on the side of truth and right; for all history is only a large showing, that "the way of the transgressor is hard;" and "the path of the righteous shineth more and more unto the perfect day." There are the august faces of noble men, who made the world loftier by their holiness, their philanthropy, and their faith in God. There are the prophets and apostles, — that Moses whom a woman drew out from the waters; this greater than Moses, whose feet a penitent sinner washed with her tears. There are the blessed words in this book, fragrant all over with beauty and with trust in God. There are the words in every wise book. And, if the minister is strong enough, the ground under his feet is his ally; and the heavens over his head, — they also are his help; they both shall mingle in his sermon as these various flowers at my side mingle their beauty in this cup.

There are living men and women about him already to help. Some of them will teach him new piety and new morality. There are great teachers thereof abroad in the world at this day; there are others equally far-sighted in the stillness of many a home. Helpers for a religious work — they are everywhere. Soon as the trumpet gives a not uncertain sound, they set themselves in order, and are ready for the battle. The noblest men of the times come round to the side of truth and right; and, when the hands of Moses hang heavy, men and women hold them up, till the sun goes down, and the sky flames with victory.

The minister has a most excellent position. It is so partly by old custom. Rest on Sunday, and the institution of preaching, are two habits exceedingly needful at this day, and of great advantage, if wisely used. But his position is great also by its nature; for the minister is to preach on themes most concerning to all, — on the conduct of life, its final destination; is to appeal to what is deepest, dearest, truest, and what is divinest too, in mortal or immortal man.

The most cultivated class care little for piety; but, with the mass of men, religion has always been a matter the most concerning of all their concerns. So no earnest man ever spoke in vain. John the Baptist, Jesus of Nazareth, peasant Luther, hardy Latimer, courtly Fenelon, and accomplished Bossuet, when they speak, draw crowds from earth, and the humblest sinner looks up and aspires towards God. Men in our day forget the power of the pulpit, they see so few examples thereof. They know that bodily force is power; that money, office, a place in the Senate, is power; they forget that the pulpit is power; that truth, justice, and love, are power; that knowledge of God and faith in Him are the most powerful of all powers.

The churches decline. All over New England they decline. They cannot draw the rich, nor drive the poor, as once they did of old. Why is it so? They have an idea which is behind the age; a theology that did very well for the seventeenth century, but is feeble in the nineteenth. Their science is not good science; you must take it on faith, not knowledge: it does not represent a fact. Their history is not good history: it does not represent man, but old dreams of miracles. They have an idea of God which is not adequate to the purposes of science or philanthropy, and yet more valueless for the purposes of piety. Hence men of science turn off with contempt from the God of the popular theology; the philanthropists can only loathe a Deity who dooms mankind to torture. And will you ask deeply pious men to love the popular idea of God? Here are in Boston a hundred ministers: you would hardly know it except by the calendar. Many of them are good, kind, well-conducted, well-mannered men, with rather less than the average of selfishness, and rather more than the average of charity. But how little do they bring to pass? Drunkenness reels through all the streets, and shakes their pulpit; the Bible rocks; but they have nothing to say, though it rock over. The kidnapper seizes his prey, and they have excuses for the stealer of men, but cannot put up a prayer for his victim; nay, would drive the fugitive from their own door. What is the reason? Blame them not. They are "ordained to appease the wrath of God," to "administer salvation" in wine or water, to "communicate and explain a miraculous revelation." They do not think that religion is Piety and Morality: it is belief in the Scriptures; compliance with the ritual. This is the cause which paralyzes the churches of New England and all the North. The clergy are better than their creed. But who can work well with a poor tool?

Well, my friends, it is to this pulpit that I have come. This is my function, such are my means. There was never such a time for preaching as this nineteenth century, — so full of vigor, enterprise, activity; so full of hardy-headed men. There was never such a time to speak in, such a people to speak to. In no country could I have so fair "a chance to be heard" as you have given me.

There is nothing between me and my God; only my folly, my prejudice, my pride, my passion, and my sin. I may get all of truth, of justice, of love, of faith in God, which the dear Father has treasured up for eternity, age after age. "Fear not, my son," says the Father: "thou shalt have whatsoever thou canst take." And there is nothing betwixt me and the twenty-three millions of America, or the two hundred and sixty millions of Christendom; nothing but my cowardice, my folly, my selfishness, and my sin; my poverty of spirit, and my poverty of speech. I am free to speak, you are free to hear; to gather the good into vessels, and cast the bad away. If old churches do not suit us, there is all the continent to build new ones on, all the firmament to build into. A good word flies swift and far. There is attraction for it in human hearts. Truth, justice, religion, and humanity, — how we all love them! Every day gives witness how dear they are to the hungry heart of man. Able men make a wicked statute, wicked judges violate the Constitution, and defile the great charter of human liberty with ungodly hoofs; but very seldom can they get the statute executed. "Keep it," says the priest: "there is no Higher Law!" The preaching comes to nothing; but a modest woman writes a little book — a great book: pardon me for calling it a little book — showing the wickedness of the law which men aim to enforce, and in thrice three months there are four hundred thousand copies of it in the bosom of the American and the British England; and it has become a flame in the heart of Christendom, which will not pass away.

Tell me of the "foolishness of preaching!" I have no confidence in "foolish preaching;" but I have an unbounded confidence in wise preaching, — in preaching truth, justice, holiness, and love; in preaching natural piety and natural morality. Only let the minister have a true Idea of God such as men need, and of Religion such as we want, and there was never such a time for preaching, for religious power. Let me pray the people's prayer of righteousness, of faith in man, in God; and I have no fear that the devil shall execute his "Lower Law."

There was never such a nation to preach to. Look at the vigor of America; only in her third century yet, and there are three and twenty millions of us in the family, and such a homestead as never lay out of doors before. Look at her riches, — her corn, cattle, houses, shops, factories, ships, towns; her freedom here at the North, — at the South it is not America: it is Turkey in Asia moved over. Look at the schools, colleges, libraries, lyceums. The world never saw such a population; so rich, vigorous, well-educated, so fearless, so free, and yet so young. I know America very well. I know her faults: I have never spared them, nor never will. I have great faith in America; in the American idea; in the ideal of our government, — a government of all the people, by all the people, for all the people; a government to serve the unalienable rights of man; government according to the Law of God, and His Constitution of the Universe. To the power of numbers, of money, of industry, and invention, I will ask the nation to add to the power of Justice, of Love, of Faith in God and in the Natural Law of

God. Then we might surpass the other nations, not only in vulgar numbers and vulgar gold, but in righteousness, which the good God asks of us.

I have confidence in America. I do not believe that American Democracy is always to be Satanic, and never celestial. I do not believe in the Democracy that swears and swaggers, that invades Mexico and Cuba, and mocks at every "Higher Law" which is above the passions of the mob. I know America better. The Democracy of the New Testament, of the Lord's Prayer, "Forgive as we forgive;" the Democracy of the Beatitudes,—that shall one day be a "Kingdom come." I have confidence in America, because I have confidence in man and confidence in God; for He knew what He did when He made the world, and made Human Nature sufficient for Human History and its own salvation.

I say I have great faith in preaching; faith that a religious sentiment, a religious idea will revolutionize the world to beauty, holiness, peace, and love. Pardon me, my friends, if I say I have faith in my own preaching; faith that even I shall not speak in vain. You have taught me that. You have taught me to have a good deal of faith in my own preaching; for it is your love of the idea which I have set before you, that has brought you together week after week, and now it has come to be year after year, in the midst of evil report — it was never good report. It was not your love for me: I am glad it was not.

It was your love for my Idea of Man, of God, and of Religion. I have faith in preaching, and you have given me reason to have that faith.

I well know the difficulty in the way of the religious development of America, of New England, of Boston. Look round, and see what blocks the wheels forward; how strong unrighteousness appears; how old it is, how ancient and honorable. But I am too old to be scared. I have seen too much ever to despair. The history of the world, — why, it is the story of the perpetual triumph of truth over error, of justice over wrong, of love against hate, of faith in God victorious over every thing which resists his Law. Is there no lesson in the life of that dear and crucified one? Eighteen hundred years ago, his voice began to cry to us; and now it has got the ear of the world. Each Christian sect has some truth the others have not: all have earnest and holy-hearted men, sectarian in their creed, but catholic in character, waiting for the consolation, and seeking to be men.

I may have an easy life, — I should like it very well: a good reputation, — it would be quite delightful; I love the praise of men, — perhaps no man better. But I may have a hard life, a bad name in society, in the State, and a hateful name in all the churches of Christendom. My brothers and sisters, that is a very small thing to me, compared with the glorious gladness of telling men the whole Truth, and the whole Justice, and the whole Love of Religion. Before me pass the whirlwind of society, the earthquake of the State, and the fire of the church; but through the storm, and the earthquake's crash, and the hiss of the fire, there comes the still small voice of Reason, of Conscience, of Love, and of Piety; and that is the Voice of God. Those things shall perish, but this shall endure when the heavens have faded, as these poor flowers shall vanish away.

I am astonished, my friends, that men come to hear me speak; not at all amazed at the evil name which attends me everywhere. I am much more astonished that you came, and still come, and will not believe such evil things. In the dark hall we left but a week ago, which has now become a brilliant spot in my memory, all the elements were against us: here they are in our favor. Here is clear air in our mouths; here is beauty about us on every side. The sacrament is administered to our eyes: O God, that I could administer such a sacrament of beauty also to your ear, and through it to your heart!

Bear with me and pardon me when I say that I fear that, of the many persons whom curiosity has brought hither to-day to behold the beauty of these walls, I cannot expect to gather more than a handful in my arms. Standing in this large expanse, with this crowd on every side, around and above me, and behind, I feel my weakness more than I have felt it ever before. If my word can reach a few earnest and holy hearts, and appear in their lives, then I thank my God that the word has come to me, and will try not to be faithless, but true.

I know my imperfections, my follies, my faults, my sins; how slenderly I am furnished for the functions I assume. You do not ask that I should preach to you of that; rather that I should preach thereof to myself, when there is no presence but the Unslumbering Eye which searches the heart of man.

If you lend me your ears, I shall doubtless take your hearts too. That I may not lead you into any wrong, let me warn you of this. Never violate the sacredness of your individual self-respect. Be true to your own mind and conscience, your heart and your soul. So only can you be true to God.

You and I may perish. Temptation, which has been too strong for thousands of stronger men, may be too great for me; I may prove false to my own idea of religion and of duty; the gold of commerce may buy me, as it has bought richer men; the love of the praise of men may seduce me; or the fear of men may deter my coward voice, and I may be swept off in the earthquake, in the storm, or in the fire, and prove false to that still small voice. If it shall ever be so, still the great Ideas which I have set forth, of Man, of God, of Religion, — they will endure, and one day will be "a flame in the heart of all mankind." To-day! why, my friends, eternity is all around to-day, and we can step but towards that. A Truth of the mind, of the conscience, of the heart, or the soul, — it is the will of God; and the omnipotence of God is pledged for the achievement of that will. Eternity is the lifetime of Truth. As the forces of matter, from necessity, obey the laws of gravitation; so the forces of man must, consciously and by our volition, obey the infinite will of God. Out of this Absolute Religion, which I so dimly see, — and it is only the dimness of the beginning of twilight which I behold, and whence I dimly preach, — there shall rise up one day men with the intellect of an Aristotle and the heart of a Jesus, and with the beauty of life which belongs to Human Nature; there shall rise up full-grown and manly men, womanly women, attaining the loveliness of their estate; there shall be families, communities, and nations; ay, and a great world also, wherein the will of God is the Law, and the children of God have come of age and taken possession. God's thought must be a human thing, and the religion of human nature get incarnated in men, families, communities, nations, and the world.

Can you and I do any thing for that? Each of us can take this great idea, and change it into daily life. That is the Religion which God asks, the Sacrament in which He communes, the Sacrifice which He accepts.

A

SERMON

OF THE

PUBLIC FUNCTION OF WOMAN.

PREACHED AT THE MUSIC HALL,

MARCH 27, 1853.

PREFACE.

THE following Sermon is part of a long course of Sermons on the Spiritual Development of the Human Race. One Chapter in that Series treated of WOMAN, and consisted of four Sermons: —

I. Of the historical Formation of the popular Idea of Woman, and of her consequent Position in the world past and present;

II. Of the peculiar Characteristics and the true Idea of Woman;

III. Of the Ideal Domestic Function of Woman;

IV. Of the Ideal Public Function of Woman.

These four make a whole by themselves, which I would gladly print, had I not already other matters in hand demanding more immediate attention. But I have been repeatedly asked to print the fourth of the series; and in such a manner that I cannot reasonably refuse. With a few additions, of things omitted for want of time at the delivery, I send it forth to the larger public.

THEODORE PARKER.

BOSTON, April 4, 1853.

SERMON.

"That our daughters may be as corner-stones." — PSALM CXLIV. 12.

LAST Sunday, I spoke of the Domestic Function of Woman — what she may do for the higher development of the human race at home. To-day, I ask your attention to a sermon of the Ideal Public Function of Woman, and the Economy thereof, in the higher development of the Human Race.

The domestic function of woman, as a housekeeper, wife, and mother, does not exhaust her powers. Woman's function, like charity, begins at home; then, like charity, goes everywhere. To make one half of the human race consume all their energies in the functions of housekeeper, wife, and mother, is a waste of the most precious material that God ever made.

I. In the present constitution of society, there are some unmarried women, to whom the domestic function is little, or is nothing; women who are not mothers, not wives, not housekeepers. I mean, those who are permanently unmarried. It is a great defect in the Christian civilization, that so many women and men are never married. There may be three women in a thousand to whom marriage would be disagreeable under any possible circumstances; perhaps thirty more to whom it would be disagreeable under the actual circumstances — in the present condition of the family and the community. But there is a large number of women who continue unmarried for no reason in their nature, from no conscious dislike of the present domestic and social condition of mankind, and from no disinclination to marriage under existing circumstances. This is a deplorable evil — alike a misfortune to man and to woman. The Catholic church has elevated celibacy to the rank of a theological virtue, consecrating an unnatural evil: on a small scale, the results thereof are writ in the obscene faces of many a priest, false to his human nature, while faithful to his priestly vow: and on a large scale, in the vice, the infamy, and degradation of woman in almost all Catholic lands.

The classic civilization of Greece and Rome had the same vice with the Christian civilization. Other forms of religion have sought to get rid of this evil by polygamy; and thereby they degraded woman still further. The Mormons are repeating the same experiment, based not on philanthropy, but on tyranny; and are thereby still further debasing woman under their feet. In Classic and in Christian civilization alone has there been a large class of women permanently unmarried — not united or even subordinated to man in the normal marriage of one to one, or in the abnormal conjunction of one to many. This class of unmarried women is increasing in all Christian countries, especially in those that are old and rich.

Practically speaking, to this class of women the domestic function is very little; to some of them it is nothing at all. I do not think that this condition is to last, — marriage is writ in the soul of man, as in his body, — but it indicates a transition, it is a step forward. Womankind is advancing from that period when every woman was a slave, and marriage of some sort was guaranteed to every woman, because she was dependent on man,; woman is advancing from that, to a state of independence, where she shall not be subordinated to him, but the two coördinated together. The evil is transient in its nature; and God grant it may soon pass away!

II. That is not all. For the housekeeper, the wife and the mother, the domestic is not the only function — it is not function enough for the mother, for the human being, more than it would be function enough for the father, for the man. After women have done all which pertains to housekeeping as a trade, to housekeeping as one of the fine arts, in their relation as wife and mother, — after they have done all for the order of the house, for the order of the husband, and the order of the children, they have still energies to spare — a reserved power for yet other work.

There are three classes of women: —

First, domestic Drudges, who are wholly taken up in the material details of their housekeeping, husband-keeping, child-keeping. Their housekeeping is a trade, and no more; and after they have done that, there is no more which they can do. In New England, it is a small class, getting less every year.

Next, there are domestic Dolls, wholly taken up with the vain show which delights the eye and the ear. They are ornaments of the estate. Similar toys, I suppose, will one day be more cheaply manufactured at Paris and Nürnberg, at Frankfort-on-the-Maine, and other toyshops of Europe, out of wax and papier-maché, and sold in Boston at the haberdasher's, by the dozen. These ask nothing beyond their function as dolls, and hate all attempts to elevate womankind.

But there are domestic Women, who order a house, and are not mere drudges, adorn it, and are not mere dolls, but Women. Some of these — yes, many of them — conjoin the useful of the drudge and the beautiful of the doll into one Womanhood, and have a great deal left besides. They are not wholly taken up with their function as housekeeper, wife, and mother.

In the progress of mankind, and the application of masculine science to what was once only feminine work, — whereby so much time is saved from the wheel and the loom, the oven and the spit, — with the consequent increase of riches, the saving of time, and the intellectual education which comes in consequence thereof, this class of women is continually enlarging. With us in New England, in all the North, it is already a large class.

Well, what shall these domestic women do with their spare energies and superfluous power? Once, a malicious proverb said — "The shoemaker must not go beyond his last." Every shoemaker looks on that proverb with appropriate contempt. He is a shoemaker; but he was a man first, a shoemaker next. Shoemaking is an accident of his manhood, not manhood an accident of his shoemaking. You know what haughty scorn the writer of the apochryphal book of Ecclesiasticus pours out on every farmer, "who glorieth in the goad" — every carpenter and blacksmith, every jeweller and potter. "They shall not be sought for," says this aristocrat, "in the public councils; they shall not sit high in the congregation; they shall not sit in the judges' seat, nor understand the sentence of judgment; they cannot declare justice." Aristotle and Cicero thought no better of the merchants; they were only busy in trading. Miserable people! quoth these great men, what have they to do with the affairs of state — merchants, mechanics, farmers? It is only for kings, nobles, and famous rich men, who do no business, but keep slaves! Still, a great many men at this day have just the same esteem for women that those haughty persons of whom I have spoken had for mechanics and for merchants. Many sour proverbs there are, which look the same way. But, just now, such is the intellectual education of women of the richer class in all our large towns, that these sour proverbs will not go down so well as of old. Even in Boston, spite of the attempts of the city government to prevent the higher public education of women — diligently persisted in for many years — the young women of wealthy families get a better education than the young men of wealthy families do; and that fact is going to report itself presently. The best educated young men are commonly poor men's sons; but the best educated young women are quite uniformly rich men's daughters.

A well-educated young woman, fond of Goethe, and Dante, and Shakspeare, and Cervantes, marrying an ill-educated young man, who cares for nothing but his horse, his cigar, and his bottle — who only knows how to sleep after dinner, a "great heap of husband," curled up on the sofa, and in the evening can only laugh at a play, and not understand the Italian words of the opera, which his wife knows by heart; — she, I say, marrying him, will not accept the idea that he is her natural lord and master; she cannot look up to him, but rather down. The domestic function does not consume all her time or talent. She knows how to perform much of her household work as a manufacturer weaves cotton, or spins hemp, or forges iron, — with other machinery, by other hands. She is the housekeeping head; and after she has kept house as wife and as mother, and has done all, she has still energies to spare.

That is a large class of women; it is a great deal larger than men commonly suppose. It is continually enlarging, and you see why. When all manufactures were domestic, — when every garment was made at home, every web woven at home, every thread spun at home, every fleece dyed at home; when the husband provided the wool or the sheepskin, and the wife made it a coat; when the husband brought home a sack of corn on a mule's back, and the wife pounded it in a mortar, or ground it between two stones, as in the Old Testament — then the domestic function might well consume all the time of a very able-headed woman. But now-a-days, when so much work is done abroad; when the flour mills of Rochester and Boston take the place of the pestle and mortar, and the hand mill of the Old Testament; when Lowell and Lawrence are two enormous Old Testament women, spinning and weaving year out and year in, day and night both; when so much of woman's work is done by the butcher and the baker, by the tailor and the cook and the gas-maker, and she is no longer obliged to dip or mould with her own hands every candle that "goeth not out by night," as in the Old Testament woman's housekeeping — you see how very much of woman's time is left for other functions. This will become yet oftener the case. Ere long, much lofty science will be applied to house keeping, and work be done by other than human hands, in the house, as out of it. And accordingly, you see that the class of women not wholly taken up by the domestic function will get larger and larger.

III. Then, there is a third class of women, who have no taste and no talent for the domestic function. Perhaps these are exceptional women; some of them exceptional by redundance — they have talents not needed in this function; others are exceptional by defect — with only a common talent, they have none for housekeeping. It is as cruel a lot to set these persons to such work, as it would be to take a born sailor and make him a farmer; or to take a man who is born to drive oxen, delights to give the kine fodder, and has a genius for it, and shut him up in the forecastle of a ship. Who would think of making Jenny Lind nothing but a housekeeper? or of devoting Madame de Stäel or Miss Dix or a dozen other women that any man can name, wholly to that function?

IV. Then there is another class of women — those who are not married yet, but are to be married. They, likewise, have spare time on their hands, which they know not what to do with. Women of this latter class have sometimes asked me what there was for them to do? I could not tell.

All these four put together, make up a large class of women, who need some other function beside the domestic. What shall it be? In the Middle Ages, when the Catholic Church held its iron hand over the world, these women went into the Church. The permanently unmarried, getting dissatisfied, became nuns, often calling that a virtue which was only a necessity, — making a religious principle out of an involuntary Measure. Others voluntarily went thither. The attempt is making anew in England, by some of the most pious people, to revive the scheme. It failed a thousand years ago, and the experiment brought a curse on man. It will always fail; and it ought to fail. Human nature cries out against it.

Let us look, and see what women may do here.

First, there are Intellectual Pursuits — devotion to science, art, literature, and the like.

In the first place, that is not popular. Learned women are met with ridicule; they are bid to mend their husband's garments, or their own; they are treated with scorn. Foolish young man number one, in a liquor shop, of a morning, knocks off the ashes from the end of his cigar, and says to foolish young man number two, who is taking soda to wash off the effect of last night's debauch, or preparing for a similar necessity to-morrow morning — in the presence of foolish young man number three, four, five, six, and so on indefinitely — "I do not like learned young women; they puzzle me." So they do; puzzle him very much. I once heard a silly young man, full of self-conceit and his father's claret, say, — "I had rather have a young woman ask me to waltz, than to explain an allusion in Dante." Very likely; he had studied waltzing, and not Dante. And his mother, full of conceit and her own hyson, said, — "I perfectly agree with you. My father said that women had nothing to do with learning." Accordingly, he gave her none, and that explained the counsel.

Then, too, foolish men no longer young, say the same thing, and seek to bring down their wives and daughters to their own poor mediocrity of wit and inferiority of culture.

I say, this intellectual calling is not popular. I

am sorry it is not; but even if it were, it is not wholly satisfactory — it suits but a few. In the present stage of human development, there are not many men who are satisfied with a merely intellectual calling; they want something practical, as well as speculative. There are a thousand practical shoemakers to every speculative botanist. It will be so for many years to come. There are ten thousand carpenters to a single poet or philosopher, who dignifies his nature with song or with science. See how dissatisfied our most eminent intellectual men become with science and literature. A Professor of Greek is sorry he was not a Surveyor or Engineer; the President of a College longs to be a Member of Congress; the most accomplished scholars, historians, romancers, — they wish to be Collectors at Boston, Consuls at Liverpool, and the like, — longing for some practical calling, where they can make their thought a thing. Of the intellectual men whom I know, I can count on the fingers of a single hand all that are satisfied with pure science, pure art, pure literature.

Woman, like man, wants to make her thought a thing; at least, wants things to work her pattern of thought upon. Still, as the world grows older, and wiser, and better, more persons will find an abiding satisfaction in these lofty pursuits. I am rejoiced to see women thus attracted thitherward. Some women there are already, who find an abiding satisfaction in literature; it fills up their leisure. I rejoice that it is so.

Then there are next, the various Philanthropies of the age. In these, the spare energies of woman have always found a congenial sphere. It is amazing to see how woman's charity, which "never faileth," palliates the injustice of man, which never has failed yet. Men fight battles; women heal the wounds of the sick:—

> "Forgot are hatred, wrongs, and fears,
> The plaintive voice alone she hears,
> Sees but the dying man,"—

and does not ask if foe or friend. Messrs. Pinchem & Peelem organize an establishment, wherein the sweat and tears and blood of the poor turn the wheels; every pivot and every shaft rolls on quivering human flesh. The wealthy capitalists,

> "Half ignorant,—they turn an easy wheel,
> Which sets sharp racks at work, to pinch and peel."

The wives and daughters of the wealthy house go out to "undo the heavy burdens, and let the oppressed go free;" to heal the sick and teach the ignorant, whom their fathers, their husbands, their lovers have made sick, oppressed, and ignorant. Ask Manchester, in Old England and in New, if this is not so; ask London, ask Boston.

The moral, affectional, and religious feelings of woman fit her for this work. Her patience, her gentleness, her power to conciliate, her sympathy with man, her trust in God, beautifully prepare her for this; and accordingly, she comes in the face of what man calls justice as an Angel of Mercy — before his hate as an Angel of Love — between his victim and his selfishness with the self-denial of Paul and the self-sacrifice of Jesus. Look at any village in New England and in Old England, at the Sacs and Foxes, at the Hottentots and the Esquimaux — it is the same thing; it is so in all ages, in all climes, in all stages of civilization; in all ranks of society, — the highest and the lowest; in all forms of religion, all sects of Christianity. It has been so, from Dorcas, in the Acts of the Apostles, who made coats and garments for the poor, down to Miss Dix, in our day, who visits jails and houses of correction, and coaxes President Fillmore to let Capt. Drayton out of jail, where he was placed for the noblest act of his life.

But these philanthropies are not enough for the employment of women; and if all the spare energies of womankind were set to this work, — to palliate the consequences of man's injustice, — it would not be exactly the work which woman wants. There are some women who take no special interest in this. For woman is not all philanthropy, though very much; she has other faculties which want to be developed besides the heart to feel. Still more, that is not the only thing which mankind wants of woman. We need the Justice which removes causes, as well as the Charity that palliates effects; and woman, standing continually between the victim and the sabre which would cleave him through, is not performing her only function, not her most important; high as that is, it is not her highest. If the feminine swallow drives away the flies from a poor fox struggling for life, another set of flies light upon him, and suck every remaining drop of blood out of his veins, as in the old fable. Besides, if the fox finds that a womanly swallow comes to drive off the flies, he depends on her wing and not on his own brush, and becomes less of a fox. If a miser, or any base man, sees that a woman constantly picks up the man whom he knocks down with the left hand of Usury, or the right hand of Rum, he will go on with his extortion or his grog, because, he says, "I should have done the man harm, but a woman picked him up, and money comes to my pocket, and no harm to the man!" The evils of society would become worse and worse, just as they are increased by indiscriminate almsgiving. That is not enough.

Then there are various Practical Works left by common consent to woman.

First, there is Domestic Service, — woman working as an appendage to some household; a hired hand, or a hired head, to help the housekeeper.

Then there is Mechanical Labor in a factory or a shop, — spinning, weaving, setting type, binding books, making shoes, coloring maps, and a hundred other things.

Next, there is Trade in a small way, from the basket-woman, with her apples at every street corner, up to the confectioner and haberdasher, with their well-filled shops. In a few retail shops which venture to brave popular opinion, woman is employed at the counter.

As a fourth thing, there is the business of Public and Private Teaching, in various departments.

All these are well; they are unavoidable, they are absolutely necessary; they furnish employment to many women, and are a blessed resource.

I rejoice that the Field-work of the farmer is not done by woman's hand in the free portions of America. It imbrutes women in Ireland, in France, and in Spain. I am glad that the complicated machinery of life furnishes so much more work for the light and delicate hand of woman. But I confess I mourn that where her work is as profitable as man's, her pay is not half so much. A woman who should teach a public school well, would be paid four or six dollars a week; while a man who should teach no better, would be paid two, three, four, or six times that sum. It is so in all departments of woman's work that I am acquainted with.

These employments are very well, but still they are not enough.

Rich women do not engage in these callings. For rich women, there is no profession left except marriage. After school-time, woman has nothing to do till she is married; I mean almost nothing; nothing that is adequate. Accordingly she must choose betwixt a husband and nothing,—and sometimes, that is choosing between two nothings. There are spare energies which seek employment before marriage, and after marriage.

These callings are not all that the race of woman needs and requires. She and man have the same human nature, and of course, the same natural human rights. Woman's natural right for its rightfulness does not depend on the bodily or mental power to assert and to maintain it,—on the great arm or the great head; it depends only on human nature itself, which God made the same in the frailest woman as in the biggest giant.

If woman is a human being, first, she has the Nature of a human being; next, she has the Right of a human being; third, she has the Duty of a human being. The Nature is the capacity to possess, to use, to develop, and to enjoy every human faculty; the Right is the right to enjoy, develop, and use every human faculty; and the Duty is to make use of the Right, and make her human Nature human history. She is here to develop her human nature, enjoy her human rights, perform her human duty. Womankind is to do this for herself, as much as mankind for himself. A woman has the same human nature that a man has, the same human rights, — to life, liberty, and the pursuit of happiness, — the same human duties; and they are as unalienable in a woman as in a man.

Each man has the natural right to the normal development of his nature, so far as it is general-human, neither man nor woman, but human. Each woman has the natural right to the normal development of her nature, so far as it is general-human, neither woman nor man. But each man has also a natural and unalienable right to the normal development of his peculiar nature as man, where he differs from woman. Each woman has just the same natural and unalienable right to the normal development of her peculiar nature as woman, and not man. All that is undeniable.

Now see what follows. Woman has the same individual right to determine her aim in life, and to follow it; has the same individual rights of body and of spirit, — of mind and conscience, and heart and soul; the same physical rights, the same intellectual, moral, affectional, and religious rights which man has. That is true of womankind as a whole; it is true of Jane, Ellen, and Sally, and each special woman who can be named.

Every person, man or woman, is an integer, an individual, a whole person, and also a portion of the race, and so a fraction of humankind. The rights of individualism are not to be possessed, developed, used, and enjoyed by a life in solitude, but by joint action. Accordingly, to complete and perfect the individual man or woman, and give each an opportunity to possess, use, develop, and enjoy these rights, there must be concerted and joint action: else individuality is only a possibility, not a reality. So the individual rights of woman carry with them the same domestic, social, ecclesiastical, and political rights as those of man.

The Family, Community, Church, and State, are four modes of action which have grown out of human nature in its historical development; they are all necessary for the development of mankind — machines which the human race has devised, in order to possess, use, develop, and enjoy their rights as human beings, their rights also as men.

These are just as necessary for the development of woman as of man, and as she has the same Nature, Right, and Duty as man, it follows that she has the same right to use, shape, and control these four institutions, for her general human purpose and for her special feminine purpose, that man has to control them for his general human purpose, and his special masculine purpose. All that is as undeniable as any thing in metaphysics or mathematics.

So, then, woman has the same natural rights as man. In Domestic Affairs, she is to determine her own sphere as much as man, and say where her function is to begin, when it shall begin, with whom it shall begin; where it shall end, when it shall end, and what it shall comprise.

Then she has the same right to Freedom of Industry that man has. I do not believe that the hard callings of life will ever suit woman. It is not little boys who go out as lumberers, but great men, with sinewy, brawny arms. I doubt that laborious callings, like navigation, engineering, lumbering, and the like, will ever be agreeable to woman. Her feminine body and feminine spirit naturally turn away from such occupations. I have seen women gathering the filth of the streets in Liverpool, sawing stone in a mason's yard in Paris, carrying earth in baskets on their heads for a railway embankment at Naples; but they were obviously out of place, and only consented to this drudgery when driven by Poverty's iron whip. But there are many employments in the departments of mechanical work, of trade, little and and extended, where woman could go, and properly go. Some women have a good deal of talent for trade—this in a small way, that on the largest scale. Why should not they exercise their commercial talents in competition with man? Is it right for woman to be a domestic manufacturer in the family of

Solomon or Priam, and of every thrifty husband; and wrong for her to be a public manufacturer on her own account? She might spin when the motive power was a wheel-pin of wood in her hand — may she not use the Merrimack and the Connecticut for her wheel-pin; or must she be only the manufacturing servant of man, never her own master?

Much of the business of Education already falls to the hands of woman. In the last twenty years, there has been a great progress in the education of women, in Massachusetts, in all New England. The High Schools for girls, — and still better, those for Girls and Boys, — have been of great service. Almost all the large towns of this Commonwealth have honored themselves with these blessed institutions; in Boston, only the daughters of the rich can possess such an education as hundreds of noble girls long to acquire. With this enhancement of culture, women have been continually rising higher and higher as teachers. The State Normal Schools have helped in this movement. It used to be thought that only an able-bodied man could manage the large boys of a country or a city school. Even he was sometimes thrust out at the door or the window of "his noisy mansion," by his rough pupils. An able-headed woman has commonly succeeded better than men merely able-bodied. She has tried conciliation rather than violence, and appealed to something a little deeper than aught which force could ever touch.

The women-teachers are now doing an important work for the elevation of their race and all human kind. But it is commonly thought woman must not engage in the higher departments thereof. I once knew a woman, wife, and mother, and housekeeper, who taught the severest disciplines of our highest college, and instructed young men while she rocked the cradle with her foot, and mended garments with her hands, — one of the most accomplished scholars of New England. Not long ago, the daughter of a poor widowed seamstress was seen reading the Koran in Arabic. There was but one man in the town who could do the same, and he was a "Learned Blacksmith." Another young woman also a mechanic's daughter, in a town adjoining this, the New England Ariadne, has threaded all the intricate windings of that mathematical labyrinth, La Place's Mécanique Céleste, for which few men have ever had the lengthy clue! The most accomplished philologist of Boston has also a feminine name. The God of Poetry likewise has bequeathed his most golden lyre to a woman's hand. Women not able to teach in these things! He must be rather a confident professor who thinks a woman cannot do what he can. I rejoice at the introduction of women into common schools, academies, and high schools; and I thank God that the man who has done so much for public education in Massachusetts, is presently to be the head of a college in Ohio, where women and men are to study together, and where a woman is to be professor of Latin and Natural History. These are good signs.

The business of public lecturing, also, is quite important in New England, and I am glad to see that woman presses into that, — not without success.

The work of conducting a journal, daily, weekly, or quarterly, woman proves that she can attend to quite as decently, and as strongly, too, as most men.

Then there are what are called the Professions, — Medicine, Law, and Theology.

The profession of Medicine seems to belong peculiarly to woman by nature; part of it, exclusively. She is a nurse, and half a doctor, by nature. It is quite encouraging that medical schools are beginning to instruct women, and special schools get founded for the use of women; that sagacious men are beginning to employ women as their physicians. Great good is to be expected from that.

As yet, I believe no woman acts as a Lawyer. But I see no reason why the profession of Law might not be followed by women as by men. He must be rather an uncommon lawyer who thinks no feminine head could compete with him. Most lawyers that I have known are rather mechanics at law, than attorneys or scholars at law; and in the mechanical part, woman could do as well as man — could be as good a conveyancer, could follow precedents as carefully, and copy forms as nicely. And in the higher departments of legal work, they who have read the plea which Lady Alice Lisle made in England, when she could not speak by attorney, must remember there is some eloquence in woman's tongue which courts find it rather hard to resist. I I think her presence would mend the manners of the court — of the bench, not less than of the bar.

In the business of Theology, I could never see why a woman, if she wished, should not preach, as well as men. It would be hard, in the present condition of the pulpit, to say she had not intellect enough for that! I am glad to find, now and then, women preachers, and rejoice at their success. A year ago, I introduced to you the Reverend Miss Brown, educated at an Orthodox Theological Seminary; — you smiled at the name of Reverend Miss. She has since been invited to settle by several congregations of unblemished orthodoxy, and has passed on, looking further.

It seems to me that woman, by her peculiar constitution, is better qualified to teach religion than any merely intellectual discipline. The Quakers have always recognized the natural right of woman to perform the same ecclesiastical function as man. At this day, the most distinguished preacher of that denomination is a woman, who adorns her domestic calling as housekeeper, wife, and mother, with the same womanly dignity and sweetness which mark her public deportment.

If woman had been consulted, it seems to me Theology would have been in a vastly better state than it is now. I do not think that any woman would ever have preached the damnation of babies new-born; and "hell, paved with the skulls of infants not a span long," would be a region yet to be discovered in Theology. A celibate monk — with God's curse writ on his face, which knew no child, no wife, no sister, and "blushed that he had a mother" — might well dream of such a thing: he had been through the preliminary studies. Consider the ghastly attributes which are commonly put upon God in the popular Theology, the idea of infinite wrath, of eternal damnation, and total depravity, and all that, — why, you could not get a woman who had intellect enough to open her mouth to preach these things anywhere. Women think they think that they believe them; but they do not. Celibate priests, who never knew marriage, or what paternity was, who thought woman was "a pollution," they invented these ghastly doctrines; and when I have heard the Athanasian Creed and the Dies Iræ chanted by monks, with the necks of bulls and the lips of donkeys, — why, I have understood where the doctrine came from, and have felt the appropriateness of their braying out the damnation hymns: woman could not do it. He shut her out of the choir, out of the priest's house, out of the pulpit, and then the priest, with unnatural vows, came in, and taught these "doctrines of devils." Could you find a woman who would read to a congregation, as words of truth, Jonathan Edwards's Sermons on a Future State — "Sinners in the hands of an Angry God," "the Justice of God in the damnation of Sinners," "Wrath upon the Wicked to the uttermost," "the Future Punishment of the Wicked," and other things of that sort? Nay, can you find a worthy woman, of any considerable culture, who will read the fourteenth chapter of Numbers, and declare that a true picture of the God she worships? Only a she-dragon could do it, in our day.

The popular Theology leaves us nothing feminine in the character of God. How could it be otherwise, when so much of the popular Theology is the work of men who thought woman was a "pollution," and barred her out of all the high places of the church? If women had had their place in ecclesiastical teaching, I doubt that the "Athanasian Creed" would ever have been thought a "Symbol" of Christianity. The pictures and hymns which describe the last Judgment are a protest against the exclusion of woman from teaching in the church. "I suffer not a woman to teach, but to be in silence," said a writer in the New Testament. The sentence has brought manifold evil in its train.

So much for the employments of women.

By nature, woman has the same Political Rights that man has, — to vote, to hold office, to make and administer laws. These she has as a matter of Right. The strong hand and the great head of man keep her down; nothing more. In America, in Christendom, woman has no political rights, is not a citizen in full; she has no voice in making or administering the laws, none in electing the rulers or administrators thereof. She can hold no office — cannot be committee of a primary school, overseer of the poor, or guardian to a public lamp-post. But any man, with conscience enough to keep out of jail, mind enough to escape the poor-house, and body enough to drop his ballot into the box, he is a voter. He may have no character, even no money, that is no matter — he is male. The noblest woman has no voice in the State. Men make laws disposing of her property, her person, her children; still she must bear it, "with a patient shrug."

Looking at it as a matter of pure Right and pure Science, I know no reason why woman should not be a voter, or hold office, or make and administer laws. I do not see how I can shut myself into political privileges and shut woman out, and do both in the name of unalienable right. Certainly, every woman has a natural right to have her property represented in the general representation of property, and her person represented in the general representation of persons.

Looking at it as a matter of Expediency, see some facts. Suppose woman had a share in the municipal regulation of Boston, and there were as many Alderwomen as Aldermen, as many Common Council women as Common Council men, — do you believe that, in defiance of the law of Massachusetts, the City Government, last Spring, would have licensed every two hundred and forty-fourth person of the city to sell intoxicating drink? would have made every thirty-fifth voter a rumseller? I do not.

Do you believe the women of Boston would spend ten thousand dollars in one year in a city frolic, or spend two or three thousand every year, on the Fourth of July, for sky-rockets and fire-crackers; would spend four or five thousand dollars to get their Canadian guests drunk in Boston harbor, and then pretend that Boston had not money enough to establish a High School for girls, to teach the daughters of mechanics and grocers to read French and Latin, and to understand the higher things which rich men's sons are driven to at college? I do not.

Do you believe that the women of Boston, in 1851, would have spent three or four thousand dollars to kidnap a poor man, and have taken all the chains which belonged to the city and put them round the Court House, and have drilled three hundred men, armed with bludgeons and cutlasses, to steal a man and carry him back to slavery? I do not. Do you think, if the women had had the control, "fifteen hundred men of property and standing" would have volunteered to take a poor man, kidnapped in Boston, and conduct him out of the State, with fire and sword? I believe no such thing.

Do you think the women of Boston would take the poorest and most unfortunate children in the town, put them all together into one school, making that the most miserable in the city, where they had not and could not have half the advantages of the other children in different schools, and all that because the unfortunates were dark colored? Do you think the women of Boston would shut a bright boy out of the High School or Latin School, because he was black in the face?

Women are said to be cowardly. When Thomas Sims, out of his dungeon, sent to the churches his petition for their prayers, had women been "the Christian clergy," do you believe they would not have dared to pray?

If women had a voice in the affairs of Massachusetts, do you think they would ever have made laws so that a lazy husband could devour all the substance of his active wife — spite of her wish; so that a drunken husband could command her bodily presence in his loathly house; and when an infamous man was divorced from his wife, that he could keep all the children? I confess I do not.

If the affairs of the Nation had been under woman's joint control, I doubt that we should have butchered the Indians with such exterminating savagery, that, in fifty years, we should have spent seven hundred million dollars for war, and now, in time of peace, send twenty annual millions more to the same waste. I doubt that we should have spread slavery into nine new States, and made it national. I think the Fugitive Slave Bill would never have been an Act. Woman has some respect for the Natural Law of God.

I know men say woman cannot manage the great affairs of a nation. Very well. Government is Political Economy — National Housekeeping. Does any respectable woman keep house so badly as the United States? with so much bribery, so much corruption, so much quarrelling in the domestic councils?

But government is also Political Morality, it is National Ethics. Is there any worthy woman who rules her household as wickedly as the nations are ruled? who hires bullies to fight for her? Is there any woman who treats one eighth part of her household as if they were cattle and not creatures of God, as if they were things and not persons? I know of none such. In government as housekeeping, or government as morality, I think man makes a very poor appearance, when he says woman could not do as well as he has done and is doing.

I doubt that women will ever, as a general thing, take the same interest as men in political affairs, or find therein an abiding satisfaction. But that is for women themselves to determine, not for men.

In order to attain the end, — the development of man in body and spirit, — human institutions must represent all parts of human nature, both the masculine and the feminine element. For the well-being of the human race, we need the joint action of man and woman, in the Family, the Community, the Church, and the State. A family without the presence of woman — with no mother, no wife, no sister, no womankind — is a sad thing. I think a Community without woman's equal social action, a Church without her equal ecclesiastical action, and a State without her equal political action, is almost as bad — is very much what a house would be without a mother, wife, sister, or friend.

You see what prevails in the Christian civilization of the Nineteenth Century: it is force — force of body, force of brain. There is little justice, little philanthropy, little piety. Selfishness preponderates everywhere in Christendom — individual, domestic, social, ecclesiastical, national selfishness. It is preached as gospel and enacted as law. It is thought good political conduct for a strong people to devour the weak nations — for "Christian" England and America to plunder the "Heathen" and annex their land; for a strong class to oppress and ruin the feeble class — for the capitalists of England to pauperize the poor white laborer, for the capitalists of America to enslave the poorer black laborer; for a strong man to oppress the weak men — for the sharper to buy labor too cheap, and sell its product too dear, and so grow rich by making many poor. Hence nation is arrayed against nation, class against class, man against man. Nay, it is commonly taught that mankind is arrayed against God, and God against man; that the world is a universal discord; that there is no solidarity of man with man, of man with God. I fear we shall never get far beyond this theory and this practice, until woman has her natural rights as the equal of man, and takes her natural place in regulating the affairs of the Family, the Community, the Church, and the State.

It seems to me God has treasured up a reserved power in the nature of woman to correct many of those evils which are Christendom's disgrace to-day.

Circumstances help or hinder our development, and are one of the two forces which determine the actual character of a nation, or of mankind, at any special period. Hitherto, amongst men, circumstances have favored the development of only intellectual power in all its forms — chiefly in its lower forms. At present, mankind, as a whole, has the superiority over womankind, as a whole, in all that pertains to intellect, the higher and the lower. Man has knowledge, has ideas, has administrative skill, — enacts the rules of conduct for the individual, the family, the community, the church, the State, and the world. He applies these rules of conduct to life, and so controls the great affairs of the human race. You see what a world he has made of it. There is male vigor in this civilization, miscalled "Christian;" and in its leading nations there are industry and enterprise which never fail. There is science, literature, legislation, agriculture, manufactures, mining, commerce, such as the world never saw. With the vigor of war, the Anglo-Saxon now works the works of peace. England abounds in wealth, — richest of lands; but look at her poor, her vast army of paupers, two million strong, the Irish whom she drives with the hand of famine across the sea. Martin Luther was right when he said, The richer the nation, the poorer the poor. America is "democratic" — "the freest and most enlightened people in the world." Look at her slaves: every eighth woman in the country sold as a beast; with no more legal respect paid to her marriage than the farmer pays to the conjunctions of his swine. America is well educated; there are four millions of children in the school-houses of the land: it is a States prison offence to teach a slave to read the three letters which spell God. The more "democratic" the country, the tighter is bondage ironed on the slave. Look at the cities of England and America. What riches, what refinement, what culture of man and woman too! Ay; but what poverty, what ignorance, what beastliness of man and woman too! The Christian civilization of the nineteenth century is well summed up in London and New York — the two foci of the Anglo-Saxon tribe, which control the shape of the world's commercial ellipse. Look at the riches — and the misery; at the "religious enterprise" — and the heathen darkness; at the virtue, the decorum, and the beauty of woman well-born and well-bred — and at the wild sea of prostitution, which swells and breaks and dashes against the bulwarks of society; every ripple was a woman once!

O, brother men, who make these things, is this a pleasant sight? Does your literature complain of it — of the waste of human life, the slaughter of human souls, the butchery of women? British literature begins to wail, in "Nicholas Nickleby," and "Jane Eyre," and "Mary Barton," and "Alton Locke," in many a "Song of the Shirt;" but the respectable literature of America is deaf as a cent to the outcry of humanity expiring in agonies. It is busy with California, or the Presidency, or extolling iniquity in high places, or flattering the vulgar vanity which buys its dross for gold. It cannot even imitate the philanthropy of English letters: it is "up" for California and a market. Does not the Church speak?—the English Church, with its millions of money, the American, with its millions of men—both wont to bay the moon of foreign heathenism? The Church is a dumb dog, that cannot bark, sleeping, lying down, loving to slumber. It is a Church without woman, believing in a male and jealous God, and rejoicing in a boundless, endless hell!

Hitherto, with woman, circumstances have hindered the development of intellectual power, in all its forms. She has not knowledge, has not ideas or practical skill to equal the force of man. But circumstances have favored the development of pure and lofty emotion in advance of man. She has moral feeling, affectional feeling, religious feeling, far in advance of man; her moral, affectional, and religious intuitions are deeper and more trustworthy than his. Here she is eminent, as he is in knowledge, in ideas, in administrative skill.

I think man will always lead in affairs of intellect—of reason, imagination, understanding—he has the bigger brain; but that woman will always lead in affairs of emotion—moral, affectional, religious—she has the better heart, the truer intuition of the right, the lovely, the holy. The literature of women in this century is juster, more philanthropic, more religious than that of men. Do you not hear the cry which, in New England, a woman is raising in the world's ears against the foul wrong which America is working in the world? Do you not hear the echo of that woman's voice come over the Atlantic — returned from European shores in many a tongue — French, German, Italian, Swedish, Danish, Russian, Dutch? How a woman touches the world's heart! — because she speaks justice, speaks piety, speaks love. What voice is strongest raised in continental Europe, pleading for the oppressed and down trodden? That also is a woman's voice!

Well, we want the excellence of man and woman both united; intellectual power, knowledge, great ideas — in literature, philosophy, theology, ethics — and practical skill; but we want something better — the moral, affectional, religious intuition, to put justice into ethics, love into theology, piety into science and letters. Everywhere in the family, the community, the church and the State, we want the masculine and feminine element coöperating and conjoined. Woman is to correct man's taste, mend his morals, excite his affections, inspire his religious faculties. Man is to quicken her intellect, to help her will, translate her sentiments to ideas, and enact them into righteous laws. Man's moral action, at best, is only a sort of general human providence, aiming at the welfare of a part, and satisfied with achieving the "greatest good of the greatest number." Woman's moral action is more like a special human providence, acting without general rules, but caring for each particular case. We need both of these, the general and the special, to make a universal human providence.

If man and woman are counted equivalent,—equal in right, though with diverse powers,—shall we not mend the literature of the world, its theology, its science, its laws, and its actions too? I cannot believe that wealth and want are to stand ever side by side as desperate foes; that culture must ride only on the back of ignorance; and feminine virtue be guarded by the degradation of whole classes of ill-starred men, as in the East, or the degradation of whole classes of ill-starred women, as in the West; but while we neglect the means of help God puts in our power, why, the present must be like the past— "property" must be theft; "law" the strength of selfish will; and "Christianity"—what we see it is, the apology for every powerful wrong.

To every woman let me say,—Respect your Nature as a human being, your nature as a woman; then respect your Rights; then remember your Duty to possess, to use, to develop, and to enjoy every faculty which God has given you, each in its normal way.

And to men let me say,—Respect, with the profoundest reverence respect the mother that bore you, the sisters who bless you, the woman that you love, the woman that you marry. As you seek to possess your own manly rights, seek also by that great arm, by that powerful brain, seek to vindicate her rights as woman, as your own as man. Then may we see better things in the church, better things in the State, in the community, in the home. Then the green shall show what buds it hid; the buds shall blossom; the flowers bear fruit, and the blessing of God be on us all.

A SERMON OF OLD AGE,

PREACHED AT THE MUSIC HALL,

ON

SUNDAY, JANUARY 29, 1854.

SERMON.

As the clear light is upon the holy candlestick; so is the beauty of the face in ripe age. — ECCLESIASTICUS xxvi. 17.

I HAVE often been asked to preach a Sermon of Old Age; and hitherto have declined, on the ground that I could not speak exactly from internal experience, but only from outward observation; and I hope to be able at some future time to speak on the theme: certainly, if I live, I may correct this present infirmity. To-day, I will try, — only asking all old persons to forgive the imperfections of this discourse; for they know what I only see. But as I was born into the arms of a father then one and fifty years old, who lived to add yet another quarter of a century thereunto; and as my cradle was rocked by a grandmother who had more than fourscore years at my birth, and nearly a hundred when she ceased to be mortal; and as my first "Christian ministry" was attending upon old age, — I think I know something about the character of men and women whom time makes venerable.

There is a period when the apple-tree blossoms with its fellows of the wood and field. How fair a time it is! All nature is woosome and winning; the material world celebrates its vegetable loves; and the flower-bells, touched by the winds of Spring, usher in the universal marriage of Nature. Beast, bird, insect, reptile, fish, plant, lichen, with their prophetic colors spread, all float forward on the tide of new life. Then comes the Summer. Many a blossom falls fruitless to the ground, littering the earth with beauty, never to be used. Thick leaves hide the process of creation, which first blushed public in the flowers, and now unseen goes on. For so life's most deep and fruitful hours are hid in mystery. Apples are growing on every tree; all Summer long they grow, and in early Autumn. At length the fruit is fully formed; the leaves begin to fall, letting the sun approach more near. The apple hangs there yet; not to grow, only to ripen. Weeks long it clings to the tree; it gains nothing in size and weight. Externally, there is increase of beauty. Having finished the form from within, Nature brings out the added grace of color. It is not a tricksy fashion painted on; but an expression which of itself comes out; — a fragrance and a loveliness of the apple's innermost. Within, at the same time, the component elements are changing. The apple grows mild and pleasant. It softens, sweetens; in one word, it mellows. Some night, the vital forces of the tree get drowsy, and the Autumn, with gentle breath, just shakes the bough; the expectant fruit lets go its hold, full-grown, full ripe, full colored too, and with plump and happy sound the apple falls into the Autumn's lap; and the Spring's marriage promise is complete.

Such is the natural process which each fruit goes through, blooming, growing, ripening.

The same divine law is appropriate for every kind of animal, from the lowest reptile up to imperial man. It is very beautiful. The parts of the process are perfect; the whole is complete. Birth is human blossom; youth, manhood, they are our summer growth; old age is ripeness. The hands let go the mortal bough; that is natural death. It is a dear, good God who orders all for the apple-tree, and for mankind. Yea, his ark shelters the spider and the toad, the wolf and the lizard and the snake; — for He is Father and Mother to all the world.

I cannot tell where childhood ends, and manhood begins; nor where manhood ends, and old age begins. It is a wavering and uncertain line, not straight and definite, which borders betwixt the two. But the outward characteristics of old age are obvious enough. The weight diminishes. Man is commonly heaviest at forty, woman at fifty. After that, the body shrinks a little; the height shortens as the cartilages become thin and dry. The hair whitens and falls away. The frame stoops, the bones become smaller, feebler, have less animal and more mere earthy matter. The senses decay, slowly and handsomely. The eye is not so sharp, and while it penetrates further into space, it has less power clearly to define the outline of what it sees. The ear is dull; the appetite less. Bodily heat is lower; the breath produces less carbonic acid than before. The old man consumes less food, water, air. The hands grasp less strongly; the feet less firmly tread. The lungs suck the breast of heaven with less powerful collapse. The eye and ear take not so strong a hold upon the world;

> "And the big manly voice,
> Turning again to childish treble, pipes
> And whistles in his sound."

The animal life is making ready to go out. The very old man loves the sunshine and the fire, the arm-chair and the shady nook. A rude wind would jostle the full-grown apple from its bough, full ripe, full colored too. The internal characteristics correspond. General activity is less. Salient love of new things and of new persons, which bit the young man's heart, fades away. He thinks the old is better. He is not venturesome; he keeps at home. Passion once stung him into quickened life; now that gad-fly is no more buzzing in his ears. Madame de Stael finds compensation in Science for the decay of the passion that once fired her blood; but Heathen Socrates, seventy years old, thanks the gods that he is now free from that "ravenous beast," which had disturbed his philosophic meditations for many a year. Romance is the child of Passion and Imagination; — the sudden father that, the long-protracting mother this. Old age has little romance. Only some rare man, like Wilhelm Von Humboldt, keeps it still fresh in his bosom.

In intellectual matters, the venerable man loves to recall the old times, to revive his favorite old men, — no new ones half so fair. So in Homer, Nestor, who is the oldest of the Greeks, is always talking of the old times, before the grandfathers of men then living had come into being; "not such as live in these degenerate days." Verse-loving John Quincy Adams turns off from Byron and Shelley and Wieland and Goethe, and returns to Pope,

> "Who pleased his childhood and informed his youth."

The pleasure of hope is smaller; that of memory greater. It is exceeding beautiful that it is so. The venerable man loves to set recollection to beat the roll-call, and summon up from the grave the old time, "the good old time," — the old places, old friends, old games, old talk; nay, to his ear the old familiar tunes are sweeter than any thing that Mendelssohn, or Strauss, or Rossini can bring to pass. Elder

Brewster expects to hear St. Martins and Old Hundred chanted in Heaven. Why not? To him Heaven comes in the long-used musical tradition, not in the neologies of sweet sound.

He loves the old doctrines. The Christian of the fourth century, who in manhood went through fire for Christianity's sake, and confessed Jesus in the jail and on the rack, in his old age goes back to the castle of Dame Venus, whom in his heady youth he had forsworn. He loves the temples and statues of his father's religion, and rebuilds the faith which once he destroyed. The Protestant who stood by Luther's doctrine in all his manly days, now that he is old thinks of the Madonna of his childhood, and dies with the once hated wafer in his lips. The Unitarian woman at her Thursday lecture, who in her prime, with Ware and Channing, endured the reproach of thinking for herself, and bore the common Church's scoff and scorn, now fans her faded cheek with denunciations of all who doubt a miracle; deals "damnation round the land;" getting old and cold-blooded, she goes back to Orthodoxy, and wants a chance to warm her shrivelled limbs and poor thin blood at the fire of eternal torment. An old Poem of the North tells of a brave boy, who in his earlier days found his mother's cottage too narrow, mourned at tending the goats on the mountain side, and felt his heart swell in him like a brook from the melting of the snow, when he saw a ship shoot like an arrow into the bay. He ran from his mother and the goats. The Viking took him on board. The wind swelled the sails. He saw the hill-top sink in the blue deep, and was riotously glad. He took his father's sword in hand and swore to conquer him "houses and land by the sea." He also is a Viking. He has been all over the Mediterranean coast, and conquered him "houses and lands by the sea;" now, in his old age, his palace in Byzantium is a weariness to him, and he longs for the little cottage of his mother. He dreams of the goats; all day the kids bleat for him. He enters a little barque; he sails for the Scandinavian coast, and goes to the very cottage too narrow for his childhood, and eats again the barken bread of Sweden, and drinks its bitter beer; bares his forehead to the storm; sits on the rocks, and there he dies. "Bury me not I pray thee in Egypt," said old Jacob, "but I will lie with my fathers: bury me in their burying-place."

Then the scholar becomes an antiquary; he likes not young men unless he knew their grandfathers before. The young woman looks in the newspaper for the marriages, the old man for the deaths. The young man's eye looks forward; the world is "all before him, where to choose." It is a hard world; he does not know it: he works little, and hopes much. The middle-aged man looks around at the present; he has found out that it is a hard world: he hopes less, and works more. The old man looks back on the fields he has trod; "this is the tree I planted; this is my footprint," and he loves his old house, his old carriage, cat, dog, staff, and friend. In lands where the vine grows, I have seen an old man sit all day long, a sunny autumn day, before his cottage door, in a great arm-chair, his old dog couched at his feet, in the genial sun. The autumn wind played with the old man's venerable hairs; above him on the wall, purpling in the sunlight, hung the full clusters of the grape, ripening and maturing yet more. The two were just alike; the wind stirred the vine leaves, and they fell; stirred the old man's hair, and it whitened yet more. Both were waiting for the spirit in them to be fully ripe. The young man looks forward; the old man looks back. How far-extended the shadows lie in the setting sun; the steeple a mile long reaching across the plain, as the sun stretches out the hills in grotesque dimensions. So are the events of life in the old man's consciousness.

I spoke the other day of the Dangers of early Manhood; and again of those of later Manhood; of the period of passion, and the period of calculation. This, I take it, — I say it with reverence, and under correction, — is the danger of old age: — that the man should be querulous; should slight the needful and appropriate joys of youth and manhood; that he should be timid of all things which are new, consult with his fear, and not his hope, and look backwards and not forth. These, it seems to me, are the special dangers of the old man. Pardon me, venerable persons, if I mistake! I read from only without; you can answer from within. It is said that men seldom get a new idea after five and forty. It is perhaps true; but it has also been my fortune to know men and women who in their old age had a long Indian Summer, in which the grass grew fresh again, and the landscape had a richness, a mellowness of outline and of tint; yea! and a beauty, too, which it had lacked in earlier years. What has been exceptional in my observation, may perhaps be instantial, and belong to the nature of old men.

Divers diseases invade the flesh in old age, which, most of them, it seems to me, come from our general ignorance, or the violation of Nature's laws. Childhood is unnatural. Half the human race is cradled in the arms of death. The pains we cause at birth, the pains we bear, are alike unnatural. So are many of the pains of old age. The old lion, buffalo, eagle, elephant, dies as the apple falls from the tree, with little pain. So have I seen a pine-tree in the woods, old, dry at its root, weak in its limbs, capped with age-resembling snow; it stood there, and seemed like to stand; but a little touch of wind drove it headlong, and it fell with long-resounding crash. The next morning the woodsman is astonished that the old tree lies prostrate on the ground. This is a natural death, for the old tree, and the venerable man. But our cradle and couch are haunted now with disease, which I doubt not wisdom, knowledge of Nature's laws, and the true religion of the flesh, will one day enable us to avoid. Now sickness attends our rising up and our lying down. These infirmities I pass by.

The man reaps in his old age as he sowed in his youth and his manhood. He ripens what he grew. The quantity and the quality of his life are the result of all his time. If he has been faithful to his better nature, true to his conscience and his heart and his soul,—in his old age he often reaps a most abundant reward in the richest delight of his own quiet consciousness. Private selfishness is less now than ever before. He loves the Eternal Justice of God, the great Higher Law. Once his hot blood tempted him, and he broke perhaps that law; now he thinks thereof with grief at the wrong he made others suffer: though he clasps his hands and thanks God for the lesson he has learned even from his sin. He heeds now the great attraction whereby all things gravitate towards God. He knows there is a swift Justice for nations and for men, and he says to the youth: "Rejoice, O young man, in thy youth! Let thy heart cheer thee! But know thou that for all these things God will bring thee into account. Hear the sum of the whole matter: Love God and keep His commandments, for this is the whole of man."

In the old saint, perhaps instinctive conscience, like his natural eye and ear, has grown more feeble. But yet the well developed moral sense, strengthened by inward and outward observation, and enforced by the momentum which long habit gives, endows him with greater moral power than he ever had before;

> "And old experience doth attain
> To something like prophetic strain."

You cannot swerve him from the right. What bribe could make old Washington unjust, or Franklin false to his love for the Slave, the sick, the poor, for all men? In long time, our good old man has got a great estate of righteousness, which no genius could have accumulated in a short period.

His affections now are greater than before; yet it is not the mere power of instinctive affection — the connubial instinct which loves a mate, or the parental instinct which loves a child; but a general human, reflective, volitional love, not sharpened by animal desire, not narrowed by affiliated bounds, but coming of his freedom, not his bondage. Of mere instinctive affection he has perhaps less than before. That fades with the age which needs it, as the blossom falls when the fruit is set, and the leaves when it has grown. With this pure human affection, he loves his venerable wife better than before; she him: they have been rising in love these sixty or seventy summers. Once, in their spring of life, their connubial love bloomed passion-red; then it grew to summer beauty; now it is autumn ripe, it is all affection; there is no romance; passion is gone. It is affection ripened by half a hundred years of use and wont; a gradual marriage sloping up to a complete wedlock of the man and woman. Now the two are one; dualism is unified in a long life. This unity and its joy — that is God's benediction on a true marriage, fifty years a-making. All the wife's spiritual womanhood is his; all the spiritual manhood of the husband is hers. Neither has lost; both have won; each has gained the whole value of what was exchanged in this matrimonial barter.

The old grandfather loves his grandchild better than once he loved his new-born boy or girl; with less instinctive fire of paternity, but with more general human love; for his character has grown more and more. Once his love was the fiery particle drawn from a voltaic pile of only five and twenty years; now it gathers power from the combination of eighty several summers and winters. He loves with all that added force. He no longer limits his love to his family; it has not the intensity of instinct, nor its narrow bound. His heart went to school in his early passionate love. Marriage, paternity, brought new education to his affections. His babies taught him. Early his affection rode on the shoulders of his wife; then on the backs of his boy and girl; now it overtakes all men — friends, countrymen; yea, all whom God's love broods over in the world's wide nest.

Once, when hot blood was in him, he said, Aha! among the trumpets, smelling the battle afar off, and he loved war; now he hates strife, loves peace. And so he honors the gentle deeds of charity, benevolence, and piety. General Jacksons, and Nelsons, and Napoleons, and Wellingtons, are not heroes of his: the good Samaritans are his beloved; not the great soldiers, with their innumerable trains of artillery and baggage-wagons, and their famous "great victories;" it is the good maiden, the angel of mercy in the neighboring street; it is the kind man, whose wise heart goes out as medicine to the sick, the old, the feeble, the poor, — these are his heroes. The heroism of hate he has trod underfoot; the heroism of love — he looks up and thanks God for that.

His religion is deeper, more inward than before. It is not doctrine alone, nor mere form. There is little rapture; he is still, and knows that God is Father and Mother of the world. His religion is love of God; faith and trust in Him; rest, tranquillity, peace for his soul. From the wide field of time, deeply labored for eighty years, he reaps a great harvest of life, and now his sheaves are with him; the eternal riches of heaven are poured into his lap. He fears nothing; he loves. His hope for this world is something small; for his immortal future he knows no bounds. The farmer tills his ground for the annual harvest, but his good tillage fertilizes the soil; and without his thinking of it, his farm grows richer and his estate larger. And just so it is with the true, good man: as the years go by him, his estate of religion greatens, and becomes more and more. The little flowers of humanity — a warm spring day calls them out, where there is no deepness of earth: but to raise the great oak-trees of human righteousness, you want a deep, rich soil, and threescore, fourscore, fivescore summers and winters, for the tree to grow in, broadly buttressed below, broad-branched above, to wrestle with the winds, and take the sunshine of God's heaven on its top. And that is the value of long life — it is an opportunity to grow great and ripen through. It is out of Time and Nature that man makes life; long time is needed, as well as noble nature, for a great life.

Alas for the man who has lived meanly! his old age is a sad and wintry day, whereunto the spring offers no promise. He sowed the wind: it is the storm he reaps.

Here is an old sensualist. In his youth, he threw the reins on the neck of every lust which wars against the soul, and so went through the period of instinctive Passion. In his graver years, his Calculation was only for the appetites of the flesh, ambition for sensual delight. Now he is old, his desire has become habit; but the instruments of his appetite are dull, broken, worn out. He recollects the wine and the debauch once rejoiced in; now they have lost their relish; his costly meat turns to gall in him. He remembers nothing but his feasting, and his riot, and his debauch. He has had his skin-full of animal gluttony, nothing more. He thinks of the time when the flesh was strong about him. So the Hebrews, whom Moses led out of thraldom, remembered the leeks and the onions and the garlic which they did eat in Egypt freely, and said, "Carry us back to Egypt, that we may serve false gods, and be full." He dreams of his old life: some night of sickness, when opium has drugged him to sleep, it comes up once more. His old fellow sinners have risen from the dead; they prepare the feast; they pour the wine; they sing the filthy, ribald song; the lewd woman comes in his dream; — alas! it is only a dream; he wakes with his gout and his chagrin. Let us leave him with his bottle and his bloat, his recollection and his gout. Poor old man! — his gray hairs not venerable, but stained with drunkenness and lust. So have I seen, in other lands, the snows of winter fall on what was once a mountain that spouted cataracts of fire. Now all is cold, and the volcano's crater is but a bowl of ice, which no mortal summer can melt; and underneath it there are the scoriæ and the lava which the volcano threw up in its heat — cold, barren, ugly to look on. O, young man! young maid! would you be buried alive, to die of rot, in such a grave as that?

Here is an old man who loved nothing but money. Instead of a conscience, heart, and soul, he had only a three-headed greedy-worm, which longed for money — copper, silver, gold. In youth, he minted his passion into current coin, courting an estate; in manhood, he was ambitious only for gold; in old age, he has his money, the passion and ambition therefor, the triple greedy-worm, three times more covetous than before. As the powers of the body fail, his lust for gold grows fiercer in that decay:

> "—— the interest table is his creed,
> His paternoster and his decalogue."

How afraid he is of the assessor! In youth, avarice was a passion; in manhood, calculation; but now, the passion is stronger, the calculation more intense, and there is the habit of covetousness, eighty years old. The accumulated fall of eighty winters gives his covetousness such a momentum as carries him with swiftly accelerated speed down into the bottomless pit of hunkerism. He has no care for right and justice: no love for mankind; none for God. Mammon is his sole divinity, that Godhead a trinity of coin. What an end of what a life! His gray hairs cover only an estate; he is worth nothing.

Did you ever see the old age of a covetous man who for eighty years had gathered gold, and nothing more? I have seen more than one such. It is the sin of New England. I spoke of poverty the other day; of want which I saw in the cellars of Broad Street and Burgess Alley, in the attics of the North End Block. There is no want so squalid, no misery of poverty so desperate as the consciousness of an old miser, in his old age of covetousness. Pass him by.

Here is an old man who in his long time has sought only power and place, and thence-accruing fame. His passion was all ambition, his calculation only for place and name. With strange fire he sacrificed youth and manhood on this unholy altar. He has not yet won the place he longs for; nor never will. He sets his hungry eye on it, and grows more reckless in the means that seem to lead thereto, "for he knoweth that his time is short." Nothing stands between him and what he aims at. Friendship is nothing; his plighted word is only the oath of a dicer who throws for place. His past life is nothing; he will eat his own words, though hard as cannon-shot. His conscience is nothing; his affections nothing; his soul nothing; and his God — that is a word to swear by, and beguile the people with. He knows no Higher Law — only the passion of the many, the ambition of the few.

I have seen the old age of such; I remember their faces — the face of a volcano, rent with hidden fires, scarred and streaked with the ruin they had thrown out from their own ambition! God save you from such an end, and me!

Look around you and see men conspicuous in American politics to-day — men whose passions of the flesh time has cooled, and tamed, and chilled, and frozen through; but the passion for place wars still in their members, and yet more against the soul. Old men, they mock at conscience; they pimp and pander to every vice of America. "Give us place," say they, "and you shall have Cuba and Mexico for your Slavery; yea, the bloodhounds of America shall bark from the Mexique Bay to the British line, and the tide of Slavery shall break over the Rocky Mountains' top!"

Would you wish such an old age? Look at the Senate of the United States to-day; at the aspirants for the presidency, I know not how many of them. Nay, look in less eminent places, for the ambition of obscurer men, and see how it eats out the heart of such as time has spared.

The old age of the sensualist, the miser, of him who worships only place, and fame, and power — what a judgment it is against the sin! I have no eloquence, nor nature's simple power of speech, to paint in words the ghastly fact.

There was once a man in America, of large talent and extraordinary culture, born also of a family venerable for the great men it had cradled in its bosom. In him, the discordant vices of passion and calculation seemed both to culminate. He was the favorite of a powerful party: thirty-five times did the Federalist delegates in Congress give their voice for him. They made him Vice-President of the nation. He was possessed of almost every loathly sin that human nature could hold, and yet hold together. He was more than eighty years old when he died. But the old age of Aaron Burr — would you wish worse punishment for the worst man that ever lived? The nation hated him, not without cause; for he turned a traitor to America. Within him, all was rotten: he was a faithless friend; a subtle and merciless enemy; a deceitful father, who sought to sell the honor of his only daughter, and she a wife and mother too! Some night in his last days, when pain, most ignominiously got, kept him from sleep, perhaps conscience came and beat the reveillez in his heart, and his memory gave up its dead; the buried victims of his deceit rose before him, of his treason, his lust, his malice, his covetousness, and his revenge! Pass him by, only fit "to point a moral and adorn a tale," — perhaps the worst great man Young America ever gendered in her bosom.

Here is a woman who has sought chiefly the admiration of the world, the praise of men. Her life is vanity long drawn out, the only frailty which joins her to mankind. Now she is an old woman of fashion — wearing still the garments of her earlier prime, which, short and scanty as they were, are yet a world too wide for shrunken age to fill. How ill those gaudy ruffles become the withered dew-lap that hangs beneath her chin! Her life has been a long cheat; she has had no calculation but for vanity, setting a trap to catch a compliment: it is fit her age should be a deceit. That color — the painter did it; the plumpness — it is artificial; the hair — false; the teeth — are purchased at a shop; the hands — all glove and bone, and great big veins; the tongue — it was always artificial and false; it needs no other change. Yet she apes the tread of youth. Alas! poor fly! For this you have lived; nay, flirted! — it is not life. This, then, is the end of the waltzes, and polkas, and cracoviennes; this is the pay for the morning study over dress, the afternoon prattle about it, the evening spent in putting on this gaudy attire! Poor creature! in youth, a worm; in womanhood, a butterfly; in old age, your wings all tattered, your plumage rent, a "fingered moth," — old, shrivelled, sick, perching on nothing, and perishing into dust; the laughter of the witty; the scorn of the thoughtless; only the pity of the wise and good! What a three-act drama is her life — youth, womanhood, age! Vanity sits there in front of the stage, known but not seen, and prompts the play — the words, the grimace. What music it is! from the opera, the lewdest and the wildest, and from the Catholic Judgment-Hymn, mingled together in the same confusion which behind the scenes her toilet table brings to view, where you also find "puffs, powders, patches, Bibles, billet-doux." Now the audience is tired of her, and laughs at the hollow voice, the bleary eye, the spindle limbs. The curtain falls; the farce is at an end. Poor old butterfly! Death and Vanity carry her between them to fitting burial and the Mercy-Seat of the Infinite God.

What a beautiful thing is the old age which crowns a noble life, of rich or poor! How fair are the latter days of many a woman — wife, mother, sister, aunt, friend — whom you and I have known! How proud were the last years of Washington; the old age of Franklin! How beautiful in his late autumn is Alexander Von Humboldt! The momentum of manliness bears on the venerable man beyond his four and eightieth year. There you see the value of time. It takes much to make a great life, as to make a great estate. No amount of genius that God ever gives a man could enable one to achieve at forty what Von Humboldt has only done at more than eighty. It was so with Socrates, Plato,

Aristotle, Leibnitz, every great man who has awed the world by the action of a mighty intellect, with corresponding culture.

These are men of high talent, station, genius perhaps. But the old age of a Quaker tailor in Philadelphia and New York was not a whit less fair. The philanthropy of Isaac Hopper blessed the land; in his manhood, it enriched the world; in his old age, it beautified his own life, giving an added glory to his soul.

How many farmers, mechanics, traders, servants, how many mothers, wives, and aunts have you and I known, whose last days were a handsome finish to a handsome life; the Christian ornament on the tall column of time! Their old age was the slow setting of the sun, which left

> "The smile of his departure spread,
> O'er the warm-colored heaven and ruddy mountain head."

Miss Kindly is aunt to everybody, and has been so long that none remember to the contrary. The little children love her; she helped their grandmothers to bridal ornaments, threescore years ago. Nay, this boy's grandfather found the way to college lay through her pocket. Generations not her own rise up and call her blessed. To this man's father, her patient toil gave the first start in life. That great fortune — when it was a seed, she carried it in her hand. That wide river of reputation ran out of the cup her bounty filled. Now she is old; very old. The little children, who cling about her, with open mouth, and great round eyes, wonder that anybody should ever be so old; or that Aunt Kindly ever had a mother to kiss her mouth. To them she is coeval with the sun, and like that, an institution of the country. At Christmas, they think she is the wife of Saint Nicholas himself, such an advent is there of blessings from her hand. She has helped lay a Messiah in many a poor man's crib.

Her hands are thin; her voice feeble; her back is bent; she walks with a staff—the best limb of the three. She wears a cap of antique pattern, yet of her own nice make. She has great round spectacles, and holds her book away off the other side of the candle when she reads. For more than sixty years she has been a special providence to the family. How she used to go forth — the very charity of God — to soothe, and heal, and bless! How industrious are her hands! how thoughtful and witty that fertile mind! Her heart has gathered power to love in all the eighty-six years of her toilsome life. When the birth-angel came to a related house, she was there to be the mother's mother; ay, mother also to the new-born baby's soul. And when the wings of death flapped in the street, and shook a neighbor's door, she smoothed down the pillow for the fainting head; she soothed and cheered the spirit of the waiting man, opening the curtains of heaven that he might look through and see the welcoming face of the dear Infinite Mother: nay, she put the wings of her own strong, experienced piety under him, and sought to bear him up.

Now, these things are passed by. No, they are not passed by; they are recollected in the memory of the dear God, and every good deed she has done is treasured in her own heart. The bulb shuts up the summer in its breast which in winter will come out a fragrant hyacinth. Stratum after stratum, her good works are laid up, imperishable, in the geology of her character.

It is near noon, now. She is alone. She has been thoughtful all day, talking inwardly to herself. The family notice it, and say nothing. In her chamber, from a private drawer, she takes a little casket; and from thence a book, gilt-edged and clasped; but the clasp is worn, the gilding is old, the binding faded by long use. Her hands tremble as she opens it. First she reads her own name, on the fly leaf; only her Christian name, "Agnes," and the date. Sixty-eight years ago this day it was written there, in a clear, youthful, clerkly hand — with a little tremble in it, as if the heart beat over quick. It is very well worn, the dear old Bible. It opens of its own accord, at the fourteenth chapter of St. John. There is a little folded piece of paper there: it touches the first verse and the twenty-seventh. She sees neither: she reads both out of her soul: — "Let not your heart be troubled; ye believe in God; believe also in me:" "Peace I leave with you. My peace give I unto you. Not as the world giveth, give I unto you." She opens the paper. There is a little brown dust in it; perhaps the remnant of a flower. She takes the precious relic in her hand, made cold by emotion. She drops a tear on it, and the dust is transfigured before her eyes: it is a red rose of the spring, not quite half blown, dewy fresh. She is old no longer. It is not Aunt Kindly, now; it is sweet Agnes, as the maiden of eighteen was, eight and sixty years ago, one day in May, when all nature was woosome and winning, and every flower-bell rung in the marriage of the year. Her lover had just put that red rose of the spring into her hand, and the good God another in her cheek, not quite half-blown, dewy fresh.* The young man's arm is round her; her brown curls fall on his shoulder; she feels his breath on her face, his cheek on hers; their lips join, and like two morning dew-drops in that rose, their two loves rush into one. But the youth must wander to a far land. They will think of each other as they look at the North Star. She bids him take her Bible. He saw the North Star hang over the turrets of many a foreign town. His soul went to God — there is as straight a road from India as from any

* This image is borrowed from a popular story by Hans Christian Anderson.

other spot — and his Bible came back to her — the Divine love in it, without the human lover, the leaf turned down at the blessed words of St. John, first and twenty-seventh of the fourteenth chapter. She put the rose there to note the spot; what marks the thought holds now the symbol of their youthful love. To-day, her soul is with him, her maiden soul with his angel soul; and one day the two, like two dew-drops, will rush into one immortal wedlock, and the old age of earth shall become eternal youth in the Kingdom of Heaven.

Grandfather is old. His back also is bent. In the street, he sees crowds of men looking dreadfully young, and walking fearfully swift. He wonders where all the old folks are. Once, when a boy, he could not find people young enough for him, and sidled up to any young stranger he met on Sundays, wondering why God made the world so old. Now he goes to Commencement to see his grandsons take their degree, and is astonished at the youth of the audience. "This is new," he says; "it did not use to be so fifty years before." At meeting, the minister seems surprisingly young, the audience young; and he looks round and is astonished that there are so few venerable heads. The audience seems not decorous; they come in late, and hurry off early, clapping the doors too after them with irreverent bang. But Grandfather is decorous, well-mannered, early in his seat: jostled, he jostles not again; elbowed, he returns it not; crowded, he thinks no evil. He is gentlemanly to the rude, obliging to the insolent and vulgar; — for Grandfather is a gentleman, not puffed up with mere money, but edified with well-grown manliness. Time has dignified his good-manners.

Now it is night. Grandfather sits by his old-fashioned fire. The family are all a-bed. He draws his old-fashioned chair nearer to the hearth. On the stand which his mother gave him are the candlesticks, also of old time. The candles are three quarters burnt down; the fire on the hearth also is low. He has been thoughtful all day, talking half to himself, chanting a bit of verse, humming a snatch of an old tune. He kissed more tenderly than common his youngest granddaughter, — the family pet, — before she went to bed. He takes out of his bosom a little locket: nobody ever sees it. Therein are two little twists of hair; common hair: it might be yours or mine. But as Grandfather looks at them, the outer twist of hair becomes a whole head of most ambrosial curls. He remembers the stolen interviews, the meetings by moonlight, and how sweet the evening star looked, and how he laid his hand on another's shoulder. "You are my evening star," quoth he. He remembers

> "The fountain heads, and pathless groves,
> Places that pale Passion loves."

He thinks of his bridal hour.

In the stillness of the great slumbering town, while life breaks only in a quiet ripple on all those hundred thousand lips, he hears no noise; but with wintry hands solemnly the church clock strikes the midnight hour. In his locket he looks again. This other twist is the hair of his first-born son. At this same hour of midnight, once, — it is now many years ago — when the long agony was over he knelt and prayed — "My God, I thank thee that I, though father, am still a husband too! O, what have I done! what am I, that unto me thus a life should be given, and another spared!" Now he has children, and children's children — the joy of his old age. But for many a year his wife has looked to him from beyond the Evening Star; yea, still she is herself the Evening Star, yet more beautiful; a star that never sets; not mortal wife, now, but angel; and he says, "How long, O Lord? when lettest thou thy servant depart in peace, that mine eyes may see thy salvation?"

The last stick on his andirons snaps asunder, and falls outward. Two faintly smoking brands stand there. Grandfather lays them together, and they flame up; the two smokes are one united flame. "Even so let it be in heaven," says Grandfather.

Dr. Priestly, when he was young, preached that old age was the happiest time of life; and when he was himself eighty, he wrote, "I have found it so." But the old age of the glutton, the fop, the miser, the hunter after place, the bigot, the shrew, what would that be? Think of the old age of a Boston Kidnapper! It is only a noble, manly life, full of piety, which makes old age beautiful. Then we ripen for Eternity, and the dear God looks down from heaven, and lays his hand on the venerable head. "Come, thou beloved, inherit the Kingdom prepared for thee."

APPENDIX.

BILL OF SALE OF AN AMERICAN CLERGYMAN.

REV. DR. PENNINGTON.

It may be interesting to many persons to see a copy of the documents which enable a "chattel personal" to become a man. A friend at Hartford has kindly procured them for me.

[COPY.]

Know all men by these presents: That I, William B. Clarke of Washington County in the State of Maryland, Administrator of Frisbie Tilghman, deceased, late of said County and State, in pursuance of my power as said Administrator, and in obedience to an order of the *Orphan's Court* (!) of said County, passed on the twentieth day of May, 1851, and also for and in consideration of the sum of one hundred and fifty dollars current money to me in hand paid by John Hooker of Hartford, Hartford County, in the State of Connecticut, at or before the sealing and delivery and of these presents, the receipt whereof I, the said William B. Clarke do hereby acknowledge, have bargained and sold, transferred and assigned, and by these presents do bargain and sell, transfer and assign unto the said John Hooker, his executors, administrators, and assigns, a negro man, Slave for life, called and known by the name of James Pembroke, now about forty years of age, of middling height, pretty stoutly built, and a full-blooded negro, together with all my right, title, interest, claim, and demand as Administrator as aforesaid, of, in, and to the said negro man, Slave for life, to have and to hold the said negro Slave above bargained and sold, or intended so to be, to the said John Hooker, his executors, administrators, and assigns forever.

In witness whereof, the said William B. Clarke, Administrator as aforesaid, hath hereunto set his hand and seal on this twentieth day of May, 1851.

W. B. CLARKE, (L. S.)
Administrator of Frisby Tilghman, deceased.

Signed, sealed, and delivered in presence of
C. SHEPPARD.

State of Maryland, Washington County, sct.

Be it remembered, and it is hereby certified, that on the day and year above written, before the subscriber, a Justice of the Peace of the State of Maryland, in and for Washington County aforesaid, personally appears the within named William B. Clarke, he being known to me, of my own knowledge, to be the person who is named and described as and professing to be a party to the foregoing bill of sale, and doth acknowledge the said instrument of writing to be his free act and deed.

In testimony whereof, I hereunto subscribed my name on the day and year aforesaid.

C. SHEPPARD, J. P.

Recorded in Liber I. N., No. 5, folios 720, 721, Land Records of Washington County, Maryland.

[COPY.]

Know all men by these presents: That I, John Hooker, of Hartford, in the County of Hartford and State of Connecticut, in consideration of one dollar received to my full satisfaction of James Pembroke, formerly the Slave of Frisbie Tilghman, of Hagerstown, in the State of Maryland, more commonly known as the

REV. DR. JAMES W. C. PENNINGTON,

of the city and State of New York, — the said James Pembroke having been recently purchased by me of the Administrator of the estate of said Frisbie Tilghman, and by said Administrator transferred to me, as appears by bill of sale recorded in the Land Records of Washington County in said State of Maryland, Liber I. N., No. 5, folios 720, 621, which purchase was made at the instance of said James Pembroke, and for the purpose of manumitting him, — and in further consideration of the inherent and indefeasible *right* of the said James to his freedom, have manumitted, and do hereby manumit and set

FOREVER FREE FROM SLAVERY

the said James Pembroke, and do hereby release all right, title, and claim, in and to the person, labor, and service of him the said James, and him the said James do give, grant, and transfer to himself as his own forever.

In witness whereof, I have hereunto set my hand and seal this third day of June, in the year of our Lord one thousand eight hundred and fifty-one.

JOHN HOOKER. (L. S.)

Signed, sealed, and delivered in presence of

JOSEPH R. HAWLEY.
HENRY FRANCIS.

State of Connecticut, } ss. HARTFORD, June 3d, A. D. 1851.
County of Hartford, }

Personally appeared John Hooker, signer and sealer of the foregoing instrument, and acknowledged the same to be his free act and deed, before me.

JOSEPH R. HAWLEY, Justice of the Peace.

Received for Record, June 3d, 1851, and entered on Hartford Town Records, Vol. 76, Page 356, by

HENRY FRANCIS, Town Clerk.

I have carefully compared the foregoing copies with the originals, and find them correct.

J. R. HAWLEY.

The following works of Mr. Parker may be had of Messrs. Little, Brown & Co.:—

A Discourse of Matters pertaining to Religion. 3d Ed. 1847. 1 vol. 12mo. $1.25.

An Introduction to the Old Testament, from the German of De Wette. 2d Ed. 1850. 2 vols. 8vo. $3.75.

Critical and Miscellaneous Writings. 1843, 1 vol. 12mo. $1.25.

Addresses and Occasional Sermons. 1852. 2 vols. 12mo $2,50.

Ten Sermons of Religion. 1852. 1 vol. 12mo. $1.

Sermons of Theism, Atheism, and the Popular Theology. 1853. 1 vol. 12mo. $1.25.

Additional Speeches, Addresses, and Occasional Sermons. 1855. 2 vols. 12mo. $2.50.

Pamphlets.—*Sermons on the following Subjects:—*

Of Old Age. 1854. 15 cents.

Of the New Crime against Humanity. 1854. 20 cents.

Of the Laws of God and the Statutes of Men. 1854. 15 cents.

Of the Dangers which threaten the Rights of Man in America. 1854. 20 cents.

Of the Moral Dangers incident to Prosperity. 1855. 15 cents.

Of the Consequences of an Immoral Principle. 1855. 15 cents.